CALIFORNIA
TWILIGHT

ESSAYS AND MEMORIES OF THE END OF THE GOLDEN STATE

MARK RAY CROMER

WILDBLUE
PRESS

WildBluePress.com

CALIFORNIA
TWILIGHT

For Julianne
and for my family

CONTENTS

Act One

Act Three

FOREWORD

When I think of immigration today, I am reminded of the climactic scene from *The Devil's Advocate,* as Al Pacino masterfully reveals that he's a little more than just a successful Manhattan lawyer named John Milton, senior partner at the rather diabolical firm of Milton, Chadwick & Waters.

A still reeling Keanu Reeve asks, "Why lawyers? Why the law?"

Pacino's Satan lays it out for him in plain English, giddily getting right down to brass tacks. "Because the law, my boy, puts us into everything. It's the ultimate backstage pass. It's the new priesthood, baby! Did you know that there are more students in law school than there are lawyers walking the earth? We're coming out, guns blazing!" he declares in his wind-up to a jubilant crescendo. "Acquittal after acquittal after acquittal, until the stench of it reaches so high and far into heaven it chokes the whole fuckin' lot of them!"

I am reminded of that epic scene from the classic 1997 film because in 2024, one can't legitimately discuss any significant issue, be it political, cultural, economic, or environmental, without talking about immigration—the elephant that has been in the American living room for nearly a half-century.

Facing an unrelenting thunderous stampede of mass migration across America's southern frontier as tens of millions of migrants from all corners of the globe converge on the United States even as mass human waves crash across European shores, the gleeful declaration of Pacino's Satan reverberates even more loudly today. Immigration is infused into *every issue*: law enforcement, environmental impacts, education standards and curriculum, housing availability and affordability, labor markets, hiring practices, wage competition, employment sectors, STEM-focused industries, election integrity, unskilled labor prospects, social benefits, taxation, university admissions, public service, and the arts.

And virtually everything else in between. Everything.

Immigration is threaded through all of it, transcending the utterly vacant platitudes and simplistic slogans declaring, "We are a nation of immigrants" or "Immigration is our strength," meaningless mantras applied as a salve and a concealer for Americans who are watching their country disappear under a human tsunami.

As a second-generation native of Southern California who was born in the 1960s and grew up and came of age in the 1970s and early 1980s, I had a front-row seat to the sweeping impacts that mass immigration wrought upon the state. It was a demographic relandscaping of staggering proportions whose roots can be traced back to 1965's Immigration and Nationality Act, but one that was dramatically accelerated by the Simpson-Mazzoli Act in 1986, which was sold to the American people essentially as a small matter of immigration housekeeping that was necessary to legalize the status of approximately 800,000 immigrants who had been living and working illegally in the country for decades.

Once the bill was passed and signed into law by President Ronald Reagan, three million illegal immigrants—more than triple the figure that Washington used to market the bill—would go on to receive legal status through the fraud-riddled process. Perhaps even more profound, however, was that the much-touted tough enforcement measures promised to the American people in exchange for granting such a massive amnesty never materialized. Not at the border and not in the interior of the nation. Nada. Nothing.

That fact became an increasingly bitter pill for Americans to swallow as millions more migrants began what has proven to be an endless tide of humanity crossing into the country illegally, all supplementing the million-plus legal immigrants admitted annually through the most generous legal immigration system among all nation-states.

By 2005, an exhaustive study conducted by investment bank Bear Stearns concluded that less than two decades after the 1986 "amnesty-for-enforcement" scheme peddled by a bipartisan cadre inside the Beltway, the number of migrants living and working illegally in the country had risen to as many as 25 million people.

As I watched the public schools and hospitals buckle and, in some cases, collapse under the sheer weight of the mass migration flow, and as worksites across entire industries such as construction, hospitality, landscaping, and manufacturing were denuded of Americans who were replaced by migrants working illegally, I began to increasingly understand that such a tectonic shift represented not just the end of an era in California, but indeed the end of California itself and all that the Golden State once promised and delivered.

I was the first registered Democrat in my family since FDR and the Great Depression. As an activist liberal, I was a campaign volunteer for Sen. Alan Cranston in his tight 1986 race against GOP Congressman Ed Zschau and on election night I got to ride the elevator down with Cranston to the hotel ballroom in the wee hours of the morning to watch him announce that he had won and the Democrats had retaken the Senate.

Twenty years later, I finally left the party as a result of its support of mass immigration, re-registering as "Decline to State," since I could never bring myself to register as a Republican. I fired off a "Nice Knowing Ya!" letter to Senators Ted Kennedy, Hillary Clinton, and Dianne Feinstein, but only heard back from Feinstein months later when her campaign wrote to ask me for money. I had interviewed Feinstein during her first run for the Senate in 1992 and back then she appeared to be my kind of Democrat, sporting traditional liberal credentials but supporting the death penalty and seemingly committed to doing something about the southern border. But those days were not to last.

I started writing what would become *California Twilight* more than a quarter-century ago, ultimately watching it take shape as part personal journal, part reporter's notebook, over my years as a journalist writing for a wide array of newspapers and magazines across Southern California and as a senior writing fellow at a California think tank.

I spoke to many college and university audiences during my years as a senior writing fellow at Californians for Population Stabilization (CAPS) in Santa Barbara, sometimes appearing as part of a panel of speakers featuring a spectrum of viewpoints on mass migration and illegal immigration, and other times simply as a featured speaker addressing the subject and taking a host of questions from college students. On campuses that stretched from USC to Claremont Graduate University and Occidental College to UC Irvine and others throughout California, I encountered students who were very concerned about the holistic impacts of mass migration; these were college kids who were very engaged on the issue and what it meant for their future.

I also encountered the now ubiquitous ethnic studies professors who were quite experienced in deploying transparent deflections that are now standard issue for those who can't adequately debate the issue or successfully advocate for an alternative policy position, choosing instead to seek shelter amid hysterical efforts to smear their ideological adversaries and philosophical opponents with volleys of toxic labels.

Over the years I would come to meet and often socialize with many of the marquee players not just in the immigration restrictionist movement, but also a variety of well-heeled and well-meaning (if out of their minds) supporters for expanded and accelerated immigration. Among the A-Team for closing the borders was Pat Buchanan, a gifted scribe who had written his way from the newspapers into the Nixon and Reagan Administrations. I had first met Pat on the campaign trail as a reporter covering his 1992 primary challenge to George H. W. Bush when it rolled into Southern California, then again at Nixon's funeral. We met again at various immigration-related conferences in Washington, DC over the years, where we spoke of what was happening to America. I got an impish laugh from Pat when I noted that we had both written for *The Nation*, one of the premier Leftist publications in the country.

Senator Jeff Sessions, who would go on to become, perhaps ill-advisedly in hindsight, the U.S. Attorney General during the opening of Trump's convulsion-riddled presidency, was an insightful inspiration over a lunch I had with him while he was still one of the most influential voices on immigration in the Senate and forecast with deadly accuracy what awaited the nation if mass immigration was not soon checked. They were among many fellow travelers I encountered on the immigration trail, including former Colorado Governor Dick Lamm and former Georgia Governor Nathan Deal, along with the mayor of Hazelton Pennsylvania, Lou Barletta, who created national headlines through his early efforts to resist the overrunning of small northeastern city.

I spoke repeatedly with legendary Los Angeles homeless and civil rights activist Ted Hayes, who founded Dome Village in downtown LA during the early 1990s as a prototype of how to effectively use temporary housing to get people off the streets. Hayes had gone after City Hall for policies that were incentivizing illegal immigration and prioritizing migrants over struggling Americans and to devastating effect with the available affordable housing stocks. I also spent time with and interviewed the late Terry Anderson, a popular radio show host and lifelong resident of South-Central LA and who, like Hayes, was a frontline voice for Black Americans who were getting pummeled by the impacts of mass migration. A firebrand who had had it with City Hall and pro-mass immigration activists, Anderson was fond of reminding his listeners with what became the slogan of his show: "If you ain't mad, you ain't payin' attention."

On the other side of the aisle, I found friends and frenemies-over-drinks as I kicked around the high-voltage issue with the likes of Tom Hayden, Jane Fonda's original leading man who co-founded Students for a Democratic Society and co-authored its seminal Port Huron Statement. Hayden offered a cleareyed perspective of the issue, at least conversationally, that acknowledged the dangers of mass migration. As did Ralph Nader, the legendary consumer activist and presidential contender—I cast my ballot for him in 2000, 2004, and 2008—who spoke at length on the dislocations and resultant suffering that accompanies unchecked expansion of the labor pool. And my old brother and comrade in journalistic arms Charles Rappleye, author of the critically acclaimed *Sons of Providence: The Brown Brothers, the Slave Trade and the American Revolution,* who also provided me with a rollicking ideological and policy proving ground during our many soirees-turned-boozy-all-nighters as we alternately hectored and hailed each other's positions on immigration but always stayed within our friendship/brotherhood that spanned a quarter-century until he passed away in 2018. A New England Yankee by birth, Charlie used my perspective on immigration and my life experience in California for some necessary ballast and counterpoint in his essay "Mexico, America and the Continental Divide," which was published in the prestigious *Virginia Quarterly Review* in Spring 2007. Years later, Charlie asked me one day, "What do you think California would look like if it was still part of Mexico?" I remember he had asked that rather odd question with a wistful tone and a gleam in his eye that suggested he was daydreaming of some mythical Aztlán paradise right at that very moment, so I couldn't resist a little levity to snap him out of it. "Dude, what are you talking about? Take a look around. *It's becoming part of Mexico even as we speak and more so every day.*" He smirked and then chuckled as I laughed and we ordered another round. I resisted suggesting to him that we hit a dog fight or two and then find our way into a donkey show.

And perhaps Charlie offered me a subtle nod or a friendly flip-of-the-bird from the cosmic other side as the Los Angeles Press Club endowed a Charles M. Rappleye Investigative Journalism Award for writers who wish to explore, among other things, "...the history of *Alta California.*" Ha! Well, Charlie had brought me into venerable press organization during the late 1990s to reinvigorate its anemic journalistic trade publication *The 8-Ball*, which itself became an inside joke between us and our crew of LA writers, and whenever we were asked about our dusk-till-dawn habits we would reply, semi-truthfully, that we had been up all night "working on the 8-ball," so I appreciate his commitment to *La Causa* that continued on post-mortem, and I surely miss my good pal and our long and occasionally notorious run in LA.

My years as a senior writing fellow for CAPS also afforded me the opportunity to write about the experiences of so many of my fellow Californians and Americans who were struggling under the impacts of mass migration and illegal immigration. People like Dr. Gene Rogers, a Vietnam vet and MASH surgeon who became the medical director for the Indigent Health Services program in Sacramento

County until he was fired from that job for objecting to and then exposing Sacramento County's policy of providing medical services—including elective medical procedures—to illegal immigrants at the expense of impoverished American citizens.

Then there was John Ward, a history teacher at Tucson Unified School District who had been forced out of the district after objecting to a scheme that demanded credentialed educators like him merely assign grades while racial activists delivered a radicalized curriculum in class to students each week. Ward and teachers like him across the district found their presence in the classroom was needed to comply with state and federal laws, but mass migration and Critical Race Theory activists would be the ones who were actually running the classrooms.

I met with business owners large and small who struggled to hire Americans at a livable wage in markets awash with the profit margins provided by illegal immigrant labor, with some succumbing and closing their doors as a result of pervasive unfair business practices. And I spoke with many Americans across the professional spectrum who were struggling to either find work or hold onto it in the face of the massive inflows of migrant labor that extended everywhere in California, not just confined to the verdant farmland and orchards of the Central Valley where the toil of migrant labor has long been ruthlessly exploited. I will never forget speaking with the predominantly Black members of a carpenters' union as they stood in front of the Cathedral of Our Lady of the Angels at Grand Avenue and Temple Street in downtown Los Angeles, desperately protesting the diocese using contractors that cut Black Americans off their rosters in favor of migrants willing to work for much less.

I sat down for a long discussion about the impacts of mass migration with Los Angeles County Supervisor Mike Antonovich, who spent 36 years in his board seat, and was amazed at the casual nature in which he related that some estimates put the population of illegal immigrants in Los Angeles County at as many as two million people. Which, if true, meant that one out of every five people in the county were in the country illegally. I had interviewed Antonovich several times over the years covering a variety of issues and he always came across as a sincere politico who wasn't prone to dramatic or hysteric statements, but even if his mild-mannered assessment was only half-right, the prospect of a million immigrants living illegally within the 4,000-square-mile county was pretty stunning.

And I will never forget the families of people who were murdered by illegal immigrants with long criminal rap sheets who had avoided deportation as a result of so-called "sanctuary" mechanisms that spider-web the state in local, county, and statewide through policy and legal requirements. I sat in the home of the parents of Jamiel Shaw II and interviewed them about the details of their son's killing at the hands of Pedro Espinoza, a member of LA's 18th Street gang who had been in the country illegally for years and had notched arrests that ranged from felony gun possession to assault on police officers—none of which qualified him for deportation in California's safe haven environment for illegal immigrants. Shaw was only three blocks from his family's home when Espinoza spotted him and, pursuant to the street gang's visceral racial animus toward Blacks, walked up to him and summarily executed him on the street, shooting him in the face. I spent time with the family years before Donald Trump invited them out on the campaign trail in 2016, and the horrific pain and suffering of their loss is difficult to truly grasp. Shaw's father had just spoken with his son, heard the gunshots ring out from the living room of their home, and ran to his dying son on the sidewalk. A jury convicted Espinoza and sentenced him to death in 2012, but Espinoza will not be executed in California— despite continued widespread majority support for the death penalty among voters who recently again rejected calls to repeal it—because Governor Gavin Newsom has declared he will not allow any executions to move forward on his watch. There is some chance that Espinoza will one day be released from prison and the Shaws must now live out their days wondering whether their son's killer will be allowed to return to the streets of the country he had no legal right to be in when he gunned down their son for bragging rights and the gang "credibility" that came with the heinous killing.

Those professional vantage points from which I observed California's long walk into the sunset were enhanced by my years as an investigator in the field of business intelligence, where I worked for firms as large as Kroll and as boutique as Sapient Investigations, Inc., where I was a senior staff investigator for more than a decade. As a corporate gumshoe who burned a lot of shoe leather working cases that carried me all over the state, my experiences with the true scope of mass immigration's impact were deepened even further through investigations that took me into teeming multifamily housing tracts across Southern California, where migrants often lived as many as a dozen or more in two-bedroom apartments and cast further light on the parallel universe that has been created in order to accommodate them at scale; from enforcement of occupancy laws and health codes to work requirements and employment restrictions to truancy laws and pet restrictions (think roosters, spaying/neutering, licensing and leash laws, for starters).

During my tenure in the shadowy world of business intelligence and investigations I also was part of investigative teams that looked into allegations surrounding two United States Senators, both Republicans, who are among the most prominent advocates for mass immigration in Washington, relentlessly championing mass amnesty and expanded immigration. Suffice it to say their cultish support for drowning America and its way of life in a sea of migrants is hardly the most objectionable item hanging in their closets.

All of it coalesced and informed my sense that as I watched the California that was slip over the horizon, irretrievably lost to oblivion, I was watching a friend and family suffer a slow death by a terminal illness that was partly inflicted upon it by a coalition of government, corporate, and radical activist interests and partly self-inflicted by a larger populace across the state that failed time and again to politically punish the responsible elected officials and the offending business interests.

It has been three decades since Californians overwhelming passed Proposition 187 in a desperate effort to stem the tide. The wildly popular referendum, which barred illegal migrants from a wide array of public services and benefits that serve as "pull factors" or enticements to illegal immigrants, subsequently suffered a death by subterfuge in Sacramento and a highly financed smear campaign across the national media.

And what was done about that by California voters? What vengeance did they seek at the polls across the following election cycles?

In a word: *nothing*.

Like boiling frogs, many Californians have attempted to acclimate themselves to having their once spacious jacuzzi turned into a Crock-Pot that's stewing with Third World ingredients, often hunkering down and trying to hold on in communities and neighborhoods that still offer some semblance of the California of yore.

Many others have simply pulled up stakes and gotten the hell out of Dodge while the getting is still at least feasible if not exactly good.

As the summer of 2024 slipped onto the calendar amid the volatile mix of rising temperatures and rising sociopolitical tempers across the country, I took a late morning one weekend to drive my mother out to Draper

Mortuary & Funeral Home in Ontario, where we paid our respects to several members of our family who are interred there, most of whom were born at the dawn of the 20th century and had lived through California's ascent to its golden age and all that it offered but had perished before the state was scuttled.

My mother has spent the better part of a century living within a few square miles in neighboring Pomona, California, a lifespan that has stretched from when the hitching posts on historic streets were still in use and through the apex of the Eisenhower and Kennedy era, those happy days of suburban bliss that allowed my father and her to buy their first three-bedroom single family home in a neighborhood of neatly trimmed yards for $18,000.

On the way home from the cemetery I drove my mom by that house on Palmgrove Avenue, the home I was born into, and as we made our way slowly down the street to linger in front of what remains of it the sense of being in a graveyard of a different sort was palpable. A few residents have managed to maintain the public face of their homes to the standards that were common in the mid-20th century, but most others appear to have fallen into disrepair and stayed there amid crowded driveways and streets.

The era known for its nuclear family of four, their home and two functioning cars parked in the driveway has been replaced by two or more families to a home and half-dozen or more cars jammed in the drives and on the streets with perhaps only half of them operable.

As we gazed at the ghostly remains of the old family home, completely denuded of its once handsome landscaping and the big fruitless mulberry tree that had dominated the front yard and the silver maple that had stood tall in the back had been cut down as well, replaced by nothing, a fate my mother and I noted had befallen many of the trees that once punctuated the neighborhood.

Before we pulled away, I noticed that the patch of sidewalk that my father had surreptitiously engraved with the names of my brother and me back in the late 1960s was gone too, a sad but perhaps fitting disappearance since we had remained stubbornly in name only, like so much else of the state we once savored.

Part personal journal, part reporter's notebook and part eulogy, the collection of columns and essays that comprise *California Twilight* also serves as a red-light warning to the rest of the nation and particularly to those states, both "red" and "blue," that still possess the heritage and legacy they inherited from the Greatest Generation and perhaps still have time to preserve it.

I recently learned that Californians for Population Stabilization had shut its doors in December 2023, following 34 years of carrying the torch across the state and nation to raise awareness of population impacts and particularly highlight the blast radius mass immigration. Its final newsletter heralded a mission accomplished-style declaration: "California's Population Has Stabilized."

While it was a real pleasure to work with CAPS throughout those years and alongside the many fine and talented people who made the organization hum, the declaration "For those who championed the idea of California population stabilization, our goal has finally come" would surely fall a little flat among the state's approximately 40 million residents. If the population statistic of 40 million people remains relatively static for a few years it may arguably be a glass half-full moment, but ask residents across the state if they feel *anything* has really stabilized in California.

I suspect the overwhelming number of people who live in the Golden State today, from San Ysidro to Yreka, don't really share in any sense of relief, but rather harbor the nagging suspicion that the sun is finally setting on California and is unlikely to ever shine on her so luminously again.

I have been writing about the impacts of mass immigration for more than three decades and much of my work on the subject, including some of the columns and essays selected for *California Twilight*, have been previously published in newspapers and on media sites across the nation and internationally, including the *Los Angeles Times, Los Angeles Daily News, Orange County Register, San Francisco Chronicle, San Diego Union Tribune, Santa Monica Daily News, Houston Chronicle, Austin American-Statesmen, Fort Worth Star-Telegram, Charlotte Observer, Contra Costa Times, Las Vegas Review Journal, Youngstown Vindicator, Pittsburg Times-Review, Washington Times, Arizona Daily Sun, Santa Barbara News-Press* and *The Gulf Times*, among many other publications. My work on immigration has also been featured on the sites of think tanks and public policy groups such as Californians for Population Stabilization, Progressives for Immigration Reform, Federation for American Immigration Reform, Negative Population Growth Inc., and other advocacy organizations and groups which favor immigration restrictions and some of that previously published work appears here as well.

Trigger Warning Disclaimer: Just kidding. I don't believe any of the language used in this book is "potentially triggering" and certainly couldn't possibly be any more inflammatory than watching your neighborhood, town, and state along with much of the nation swallowed whole under a relentless tide of mass migration. If you are reading this book, it seems a good bet that you understand this, and if you don't, keep reading anyway and see how you feel at the end of it. If you feel "triggered," hopefully it will be to do what you can to save what's left.

"All I can say is that we're not in the business of printing things we don't know to be true."

— Craig Turner, front-page story editor for the *Los Angeles Times*

"I have no idea. I have no idea if it is."

— Anna Gorman, *Los Angeles Times* immigration reporter, on whether the figure of 12 million illegal immigrants present in the U.S. that has remained static in the newspaper's stories for more than a decade is accurate.

CALIFORNIA TWILIGHT

A native bears witness to the end of the Golden State

*"This is a story about love and death in the
golden land, and begins with the country."*

Joan Didion, from *Some Dreamers of the Golden Dream*

First published in 2010

California, the adage once held, is a place where seemingly everyone comes from somewhere else.

The Pacific borderland of America's epic push westward that was transformed from a dusty western outpost where speculators risked all to pull gold from the ground into a mythical Mecca where those desperate dreamers that Didion so famously detailed came seeking the quintessential *good life*.

And the word was that California was indeed a place where the good life was as ripe, sweet, and accessible as the low-hanging fruit in the ubiquitous orchards that sprang from its fertile earth.

The cynics would come to deride the state as little more than a vast tidal pool brimming with eccentrics, outlaws, riffraff, and professional loafers posing as gurus with "The Answer," but those who lived here knew the pleasant truth: while perhaps not a divine Holy Land, California was a beautiful, promising place to live.

In the summer of 1985, that promise was as indisputably real to me as the waves that I watched roll in off Ventura, where my friends and I had rallied our VW minibus to catch the Grateful Dead as the quintessential California band enjoyed its second act in American rock n' roll. Jerry and Bob grooved out "Sugar Magnolia" as thousands of us young Californians danced on the beach and in the fairgrounds like young Romans gleeful of our inheritance. Our tribal fires burned bright at night as braless hippie girls served electric strawberries and free love seemed somehow not only hip again, but wonderfully true. Valid. Just weeks earlier I had got to hang out with California's counterculture ombudsman, Timothy Leary, and his intrinsic Zen had partially rubbed off on me and my friends, so we said "yes" a lot and considered it a personal revolutionary act.

Looking back now, a Doors song we sang that summer was a portent of things to come.

"Morning found us
calmly unaware
noon
burned gold into our hair
at night we swam the laughing sea
when summer's gone
where will we be?"

A second-generation Southern California native, I was born in 1965, when the real-world manifestations of the California Dream were arguably at their zenith. Governor Edmund G. "Pat" Brown was overseeing a massive investment into the state's infrastructure, seeking to ensure a quality of life for most Californians as comfortable as the state's legendary warm weather.

In 1965, there were just over 18 million people living in California, a sustainable population that could accommodate reasonable growth while continuing to expand opportunity and comfort for its citizens. It was a time when the state's great coastal cities, Los Angeles and San Francisco, were giving birth to the fabled youth culture that would be instrumental in shaping the world's perception of America, and of California as an oasis where one could "take it easy."

Indeed, the hippie esthetic that emerged full bloom in California during the 1960s was imbued with a variety of traditional agrarian qualities that were melded with the more progressive sensibilities that were reshaping the cities. It was a time when coastline communities from Laguna to Big Sur were still real bohemian enclaves of artists and writers mingling with academics and old money; distinct places separated by undeveloped coast that were connected by the veins of open asphalt.

In the vernacular of the era, California was *peaking*.

Even in Sacramento, the prospect of some endless summer seemed to waft in the legislative air. Development and the notion of "progress" were a means to a desirable end; not yet having mutated into runaway growth with no end in sight.

"My son asked me what I hoped to accomplish as governor," Brown remarked. "I told him: essentially to make life more comfortable for people, as far as government can. I think that embraces everything from developing the water resources vital to California's growth, to getting a man to work and back fifteen minutes earlier if it can be done through a state highway program."

Those were the days.

By 1975, the nation's hangover from the Vietnam War and the battle for civil rights settled into the malaise of the Ford and Carter era. While California's luster still glimmered like so many Chinese lanterns on a summer's night, the scent of decay was slowly rising about the sweetness of the night-blooming jasmine that hung in the air. Across the dusty stretch of Southern California, open space and architecture rich with history still allowed cities and towns a sense of distinct identity, a place and time where the phrase "city limits" implied an undeveloped landscape beyond.

In the Pomona Valley, reminders of the region's citrus-growing past could still be easily glimpsed, with old orange groves dotted with smudge pots on virtually every other block. To the west lay the rolling hillsides of Walnut and Diamond Bar and to the south, the great dairies and farms of Chino, Ontario, Norco, and Corona with thousands of heads of cattle. Lush vineyards and eucalyptus groves broke up the scattered homes in Upland, Alta Loma, and Cucamonga along the foothills that ran into the eastern reaches of the Pomona Valley at the base of the Cajon Pass. The belching smoke stacks of Kaiser Steel in Fontana served as a reminder of the industrial might of the blue-collar, skilled labor jobs that anchored the region's post-war prosperity, along with military-industrial complex giants like General Dynamics, Lockheed Martin, Xerox, and PerkinElmer.

While it was growing a little rougher around the edges, the inherent balance of the community was still evident throughout everyday life.

Those days are long, long gone—much like the open fields that once defined them.

The industrial giants that had anchored either end of the Pomona Valley closed down years ago, taking tens of thousands of skilled labor jobs and wages with them, an economic bleed-out that sapped the region, leaving it staggering like an anemic man promised a transfusion even as Washington winked and read the Last Rites.

Following the Reagan boom years and the bust of George H. W. Bush's administration, the population of the valley, like much of the rest of Southern California, began to grow dramatically, with new tracts of homes and multi-family apartments being erected in the old groves and fields. Even as the region was shedding large numbers of jobs, it was conversely adding large numbers of people. And for the first time in memory, by the mid-1990s, increasingly large numbers of those people coming to the valley were Spanish-speaking immigrants, most of them from Mexico and many of them in the country illegally.

In Pomona proper, the impact could be seen clearly, from the increasingly crowded emergency rooms to the portable classrooms that began to fill the blacktops of playgrounds and the grassy fields where students once played sports or enjoyed leisure time with their families.

Apartment complexes first, and then single-family homes, began to overfill with two, three, and four families at a time living in space designed for one. Garages across the city began to double as additional homes for even more immigrant families. As traditional mom-and-pop American businesses closed their doors, victims of an eroding middle-class base, small shops catering specifically to Mexican immigrants began to spring up along the old commercial loops of Holt Avenue and Mission Boulevard.

Like a domino effect, as Pomona's immigrant population surged, more school space was needed than could be built, so the school district began taking over failed retail and commercial space and converting them into classrooms.

By the dawn of the millennium, Pomona's transformation was complete. In less than two decades, an immigrant tsunami swept through the city and irrevocably reshaped its demographics. By 2004, the city's officially projected population of just under 150,000 people was nearly 65 percent Latino; but that figure is almost certainly an undercount considering the thousands—possibly tens of thousands—of illegal immigrants living in converted garages, transient motel rooms, and apartments, who are unlikely to participate in a government census canvass.

The ethnic shift in the city's public schools has been even more staggering and the true diversity that once was a hallmark of the Pomona Unified School District has been virtually eliminated altogether. With mostly immigrant Latinos now cresting to nearly 90-percent majorities on many of the campuses, Pomona today is nowhere near as diverse a city as it was when I was growing up on its streets 30 years ago, an era when Anglos, Blacks, and Chicanos mingled together in relative balance, all connected by economic and common cultural threads. Today, the elementary school I first enrolled in 1970 is now 90 percent Latino, with nearly that same amount on the subsidized lunch and breakfast programs. My old junior high is now 89 percent Latino, with 92 percent getting a "free" breakfast and lunch. The high school I attended, like my parents before me in the 1950s, is now 82 percent Latino, with an equal amount of its nearly 1,600 students on tax-supported meals.

But the ethnic cleansing is only half of it.

All three of my old schools today test dismally amid an already horrifically performing state system, despite hundreds of millions of dollars that Pomona Unified has thrown over the years into its blast furnace of curriculum and programs designed to teach the value of education to an immigrant population that comes from countries where education ranks somewhere between selling Chiclets on the street and bussing tables.

It wasn't always this way.

When I was a kid in Pomona, our fathers worked in the same plants together, our mothers shopped in the same stores, and our families grew to know each other. And we all spoke the same language in front of each other as well as mostly at home. Today, Pomona stands as a tribute to the remaking of Southern California as a region that is rapidly becoming ethnically homogenous, in reality a far northern state of Mexico, if remaining American in name only. Los Angeles County Supervisor Mike Antonovich told me in early 2008 that as many as two million illegal immigrants called the county home, an explosive figure that has almost certainly remained static even in the dismal economic climate and possibly even grown larger.

My old friend and colleague Charles Rappleye, a respected author and journalist, sees this epic demographic and cultural shift as nothing less than a positive development. Rappleye is a New England Yankee who first moved to Santa Barbara in the 1970s before finding his way down the coast to Los Angeles, where he still lives today in fashionably bohemian Echo Park. In an essay published in the esteemed *Virginia Quarterly Review* in the spring of 2007, Rappleye made his case that the tidal wave of refugees fleeing the failed state of Mexico is little more than the natural flow of indigenous peoples along their historic migratory routes.

It can't be stopped, he asserts. Nor should it be.

Rappleye cites my own history as a native Californian and my deep connection with the town of my birth throughout the essay, employing my perspective as ballast to give his argument some multi-dimensional nuance. He acknowledges the sense of loss that fellow baby-boomer Anglos like me are experiencing as we watch the literal remaking—Rappleye might describe it as a *"re-imagining"*—of the state we once knew into something we no longer even recognize.

"What of America?" Rappleye writes. "The future, of course, is impossible to predict. Our country is changing, that much is certain, and I think that is what spurs people like Pat Buchanan and my friend Mark alike. They want to alert the citizenry before it is too late, but they are trying to turn back the clock. What they see as realism, I see as nostalgia. The day of Mark's father, of the unskilled worker taking home a middle-class paycheck, is gone, and no amount of recrimination will change that."

A compelling writer with a penchant for flair, Rappleye views my distress over what I have witnessed, the end of California's golden era and its descent into an overcrowded and financially failed state that struggles to provide even adequate basic services for its citizens, as needlessly alarmist.

Perhaps, as my old friend suggests in his essay, I am nostalgic. But if so, then I am nostalgic much like the passengers of the RMS *Titanic* must have been as they boarded those too few life boats, stunned that such a glittering ship which seemed a mighty testament to a grand design was torn open, flooded, and sent to the bottom in short order.

As Rappleye sees in me a powerful yearning for a bygone era that will never return, I see in him the pie-eyed prayer for a utopian age that will never arrive.

His take on the largest sustained human migration that any nation in the history of nations has been forced to accommodate in such a short period of time is liberally embellished with politically correct cherries like "social justice" that ostensibly sweetens the dish for the American taste for benevolence. Yet in the cold air of reality that hangs outside philosophical dinner parties, such slogans have little real meaning.

To the African American citizens in south Los Angeles, who have watched as their neighborhoods and communities have been literally overrun with illegal immigrants (some high schools built to accommodate 1,000 students have grown to now house—yes, literally *house*, not *educate*—as many as 4,000 kids), there is a bitter irony in lofty progressive cant about justice for illegal immigrants even as Blacks find themselves again being pushed to the back of the economic bus.

Rappleye and his fellow travelers see no crisis in the staggering waves of illegal immigration, or the unsustainable population densities that it builds, because quite frankly, they don't suffer from its impact in the same immediate sense or on the same scale. Sure, they often face the crowded freeways and long lines that everyone else does in Los Angeles County, but they aren't fighting to maintain a precarious toehold above an existence of functional poverty. The stakes aren't an existential threat to them. They don't compete with illegal immigrants for jobs, they don't send their children to schools that are jammed beyond capacity, and they don't rely on a frayed safety net of social services that are perilously close to falling away completely in Southern California.

On a day-to-day basis, they simply live in a different, parallel universe.

Yes, I am saddened at the loss of the geographic and cultural esthetic that once defined my own hometown and much of Southern California, but my fear of what I am witnessing and my sense of outrage at those who are letting it happen—indeed abetting it—has a wellspring far deeper than merely the loss of something I was fortunate enough to have experienced. It is steeped in a sense of obligation to my fellow Americans, especially those who are struggling for a chance to attain the quality of life that many others of us enjoyed as a result of our parents' devotion to the American ideal.

Yet in Rappleye's world, that brand of American nationalism must seem as *passé* as flying the flag on the Fourth of July, a benign if rather quaint tradition—or "nostalgic," as he might say.

But my friend Charlie is at least candidly honest about his perspective of California and America's future, a refreshing if rare quality among many of those who share his views.

"Rather than fortify the border, another exercise in the failed, punitive mode, why not open it, granting open-ended visas to all Mexicans who apply," he offers in the *Virginia Quarterly Review,* "and, later, citizenship to any?"

Rappleye's suggestion may be effectively moot in a matter of another couple of generations if the present pace of mass immigration into the United States continues unabated, with the nation projected to reach a population of 500 million people by 2050 and perhaps a billion people at the dawn of the 22nd century.

Citizenship then may be as easily accessible as a counterfeit driver's license is now in the bustling bazaars of Los Angeles, Chicago, Las Vegas, and Phoenix that churn out the fraudulent documents that migrants now use to navigate the country they broke into. But by then, two or three generations deeper into this crisis, the real question will be what will that citizenship be worth? What cherished hallmarks will the designation "American" then hold?

Like the microcosm of Southern California, it will be a nation that is brimming with people struggling to survive and yet with even less of a cohesive sense of a national identity—of just what an American is—than at any other time in the country's history. Perhaps, as Rappleye suggests, the threshold for citizenship should be anyone who simply declares it, and thus the meaning of "American" will simply be whatever one wishes it to be. Instead of a bedrock sense of ideals and values it will be malleable, transitory, written in chalk.

Ironically, far from bringing more people closer to the "American Dream," that once-perennial hope which defined a country and provided more opportunity for its citizens than any other nation on Earth will now be further away than ever before for most of its people. So yes, I raise a nostalgic lament for a time that once was in California. Because it was a real time and place—there was a fundamental truth underpinning the California myth—before it slipped away into a smoldering memory. As with a fallen friend, I remember the good times and I honor them. It's important.

And California's grim fate should serve as a warning for the rest of the nation.

There are towns, counties, and states that are experiencing, like California in the late 1980s and early 1990s, exploding populations of illegal immigrants which are reshaping their communities, their culture, and their quality of life at a pace and on a scale that would have been unimaginable a generation ago. Fifteen years ago, it would have been hard to imagine that what was happening to California would in fact continue and grow worse. Californians thought that a compelling electoral consensus like Proposition 187, which passed with an overwhelming 60 percent of the vote in 1994, would stem the tide. Far from it; the cycle of mass Mexican immigration into the United States has continued apace, an exodus on a near biblical scale that has emptied entire regions of the narco-confederation to the south.

In places like Pennsylvania, Arkansas, and Georgia, the future is being decided today.

If American citizens cannot muster the political will to act decisively to preserve their overarching culture and the quality of life that was passed along to them after so much sacrifice across the 20th century, then they will find themselves in the same terminal condition that California is in today.

An inglorious ending for a nation whose lamps once burned so bright with promise.

HEY BUDDY, CAN YOU SPARE A JOB?

With real unemployment cresting beyond 20 percent and a budgetary meltdown that portends either a grim austerity program or bankruptcy—or both—a crowded and collapsing California foreshadows the nation's new normal.

Going down and out in the formerly Golden State in search of those "jobs Americans won't do."

First published in 2010

For a moment, it seems like it might be 1981 again.

I am standing in the lobby of the Carl's Jr. on Indian Hill Boulevard in Pomona, a fast-food restaurant that has managed to survive the socioeconomic convulsions the city has long suffered that has left much of the commercial property along the boulevard in a state of perpetual semi-blight; scarred by graffiti, etched windows, litter, loitering vagrants, and the decaying storefronts of businesses that have failed and those that are just hanging on. Even a McDonalds franchise died on this boulevard.

I have dropped in not to order a Super Star burger, fries, and a shake, but rather to ask for an application to make and serve them. I have come looking for a job, *any job*, that this restaurant in the fourth-largest fast-food chain in the country might have open. The guy behind the register, who looks to be in his late teens or maybe early 20s, offers only the briefest of pause when I ask for an application. It's a look that tells me he's perhaps concerned that he's seeing more people like me of late—middle-aged men and women looking for work as proverbial "burger-flippers" and other bottom-rung service industry jobs that serve as an economic lifeboat (or, more accurately, drift wood) until the rescue ship comes along to save them.

But he hands me the application with a polite smile and tells me the manager will be around most of the week so I can drop it back by pretty much any time during the day. "I don't know if we're hiring," he says, adding almost as an afterthought, "but you can try."

Of course, he couldn't have guessed that I wasn't really looking for this kind of work; not yet anyway. He didn't know that I wasn't fighting this desperately for my financial survival, but that I was actually a writer interested in exploring the whimsical adage that the U.S. Chamber of Commerce and their dance partner on the ethnocentric Left have spun together into a convenient "conventional wisdom" that is routinely played in high rotation by a mostly unquestioning media: *These are jobs Americans don't want and won't do.* It's this gospel that the advocates for open borders sing loudly against any suggestion that mass legal immigration into the United States be dramatically reduced to allow American workers and their communities some breathing room; and it's a chorus that grows only louder in the face of virtually any effort to secure the border and prevent illegal workers from taking jobs away from citizens. The corporatist suits of the chamber and the racialists of the ethnic-identity wing of the Left surely sing it for different reasons, but it's a song they routinely harmonize together on from Fox News to MSNBC.

As the second year of the Great Recession came to a close, I thought I might run that claim through some basic field-tests by revisiting some of the blue collar, entry-level jobs I had worked during my youth, positions that I had plenty of experience in, to get a better understanding of what actually happens when an American citizen does indeed want such work and is actively looking for it. So I again went looking for jobs as a fast-food cook, a delivery driver, a thrift-store pick-up driver, a busboy, a dishwasher, and more. And I branched out a little as well, looking for work in the ubiquitous carwashes of Southern California.

It didn't take long to discover what millions of Americans are going through on a daily basis: struggling to make it through a job search that is now far more crowded, chaotic, and desperate than any pie chart or government statistic will ever accurately reflect. And while many journalists are loathe to acknowledge it, the fact is that millions of out-of-work Americans are confronted with chronic joblessness even as millions more foreign workers who are in the country and on the job illegally are still employed. While perpetually having far more workers than available jobs is the nirvana of the U.S. Chamber of Commerce and its allies at the *Wall Street Journal*, it's a dangerous dynamic that breeds a volatile climate of resentment—a potentially explosive stasis in a country that allows approximately one million foreign workers to enter legally each year, even as its own countrymen struggle to find bottom-rung "survival jobs."

But it wasn't always this way.

***

Thirty years earlier, I had stepped into the same Carl's Jr. as a teenager looking for a job that might help out a little at home—which at the time was a small apartment about a mile away. Back then my mom was a single woman who had raised her two boys *sans* child support on a public school teacher's salary, which in the 1970s and early '80s offered pretty much a no-frills flight: enough money to keep a roof overhead, the lights on, food on the table, and shoes on our feet, but not much in the way of extras. So I rode my ten-speed over to Carl's Jr., filled out an application and, a couple days later, was back doing an interview; for which I had cut my hair and donned my Sunday slacks, collared shirt, and tie, all for a $3.35 an hour burger-flipping job. I don't remember much of the interview now, but it must have gone well since a few days later I was putting on my Carl's Jr. uniform, which was the first and last time I was ever excited about a job that required wearing a hat and name tag.

And so it began. For more than two years I worked the fryer and grill, I stood at the cash register and parroted the "suggestive sales" lines management had instilled in us— *"Would you like to try our new carrot cake with your order today, sir?"* I cleaned tables and washed dishes, I swept the parking lot, I prepped food for the following day's shifts, and I performed the nadir of any and all shifts, the one task that instilled absolute dread among the crew members: cleaning the bathrooms. You never knew what you were going to walk in to, but it was all too frequently a potpourri of disaster that left me convinced public restrooms had somehow evolved into an open invitation for humankind to revel in its most grotesque urges.

I had been well prepared for the job long before I was hired at Carl's Jr., as I had been working summer odd jobs for years, and in the fall of 1980 I landed an under-the-table gig cleaning tables at a beer-and-burger joint at the Los Angeles County Fair on weekends and school nights. Back then working was as much an adventure as it was a necessity and my job at the fair didn't disappoint; I watched hard-luck women mingle with hard-living stable hands and mopped up after the inevitable brawls. But I also cleared nearly $300 cash during that month-long fair, which was a stunning sum of money for a kid like me back then, as I usually saw Andrew Jackson's portrait on money only once a year, at Christmas, when some aunt or uncle's card would pay off like a lottery ticket.

My take-home pay for two weeks' work at Carl's Jr. was anywhere from $40 to perhaps $100, depending on how many shifts I worked around my school and sports schedule, but it was money we needed and the experience taught me many lessons, not the least of which was the sense of self-worth and accomplishment that menial labor can bring was short-lived and that the real value of such dead-end jobs was to engender a fear of becoming trapped in one. Any passing ambivalence I may have felt about college vanished every time I had to drain the grease vats or watch my manager—with his red pens secure in his vinyl pocket-protector—carefully inspect the floors I had just scrubbed for any flaw that might require a do-over, or worse (in his mind), a written warning for sub-standard floor scrubbing.

Even as a teen I could see how the blessing of such short-term jobs might turn into hellish drudgery for many workers if it were to become an employment destination. There's an underlying truth to the reason they call them dead-end jobs. But I also saw that such jobs provided at least a critical transitional income for those on their way up into a profession or skilled labor career, as well as a last-ditch safety net for those on their way down who had lost other, better employment. Through high school and until the end of my university studies, my job at Carl's Jr. was followed by a six-year succession of gigs that took me from delivering flowers to picking up used goods for a thrift store to bussing tables and washing dishes to parking cars. There's more than a little irony now as I recall how casually my peers and I took such work for granted—and for good reason—as such jobs were essentially available on demand. Throughout the 1980s, my friends and I rarely endured a job search that lasted more than a week or two, and they usually ended much sooner as it seemed someone always knew of a boss or business that was hiring.

If the availability of work in Pomona and its surrounding cities was different back then, so too was the complexion of the employment. Despite the recession that had plagued the later years of the 1970s, the Reagan-era arms build-up against the Soviet Union proved to be a boon for the substantial manufacturing base around the Pomona Valley, and defense dollars rippled out across the community. Thousands of skilled labor jobs in the local plants paid living wages that thousands of other jobs around the valley, in retail and service industries, ultimately relied upon. Back then a high school graduate could still work his way into a skilled trade with a reasonable chance of success and a shot at the proverbial American Dream, and it was only on a rare occasion that an older career casualty would end up working the grill or mopping the floors with my friends and me.

But you didn't need to be an economist to predict what would happen when the defense spending dried up following the end of the Cold War and the plants that once hummed with round-the-clock shifts began to be shuttered one after the other. The promise of a "peace dividend" that would redirect this manufacturing muscle into some other great national cause ended up bouncing like a bad check Washington wrote in the 1990s.

The last and perhaps most vicious cycle of the Great Hollowing of American Industry had begun.

***

I returned my application to Carl's Jr. a few days later and attached with it a cover letter, my resume, and a list of references. My cover letter explained that I had worked at the restaurant a generation earlier and was now in desperate need of employment. My application stated that I was willing to work any hours on any day during any shift. My desired salary was whatever they were willing to start me at. I was willing to take whatever position they might be hiring for, from cook to register clerk or whatever amalgam they used now.

I watched the cashier walk my application into the office where the manager was, where they said a few words to each other, then she walked back to the counter. "Okay, thanks," she said with a pleasant smile. "We'll let you know."

They were words I would hear repeatedly over the next few weeks as I made the rounds to the employers of my youth that were still in business. At Marie Callender's Restaurant, where I had bussed tables, washed dishes, and cooked, a manager read over my cover letter and scanned my application and resume in front of me, nodding intently. "I'll give this to my hiring manager and he'll let you know."

About a mile down Route 66 from Marie Callender's is the Domino's Pizza where I worked as a delivery driver in the late 1980s. They don't give out applications at the store anymore; prospective workers have to download them online—and it's a much more involved process to drive for Domino's these days, requiring the reading and completion of a 16-page application form that includes consent to a background investigation. I slid my application folder under the bullet-proof glass partition to a clerk who said the manager would get back with me if they were hiring.

It was a slightly more depressing story down at the Disabled American Veterans Thrift Store on Garey Avenue in South Pomona where I had driven a truck during summers in the mid-1980s. The store still sits in a dilapidated building on the east side of the avenue amid the grim remains of retail shops that probably haven't been viable in decades. It's in the heart of 12th Street territory, Pomona's oldest and largest street gang. There is the El Exito Market and across the street from that is another neighborhood store advertising "wire transfers, phone cards, and bike parts" as well as an income tax service on the second floor—I half expect to see Fred Sanford sitting in a chair out front. A few doors down is a liquor store, which makes three establishments offering off-sale alcohol hardly 100 feet apart.

The first thing I notice walking in is they have moved the checkout stands, which once were lined in a row like a supermarket, into the corner, and lines of mothers and their children spill across the lobby into the clothing racks as they wait to make their purchases. Everyone is speaking Spanish. I am the only Anglo in sight. A Black woman who walks past me quickly is the only other non-Latino or immigrant I see in the store.

A large American flag hangs above the front doors on the inside of the store.

I wait my turn and finally make it to the front desk, where I ask one of the checkers for an application. "Sure," she says politely, disappearing behind an office door. She returns with it. "Are you hiring drivers right now?" I ask. "Or for any position in the store?" She tells me I should speak to a manager when I return the application. Thanking her, I take a moment and walk through the old store that used to hum with the pitch of America's multi-ethnic blue-collar workers from Pomona and its working-class consumers. I am struck by how much has changed, and not just the disappearance of Black, White, and Chicano workers and customers. The store was always second hand—that was its charm and value—but its general manager was often fond of declaring, "We're a thrift store, not a junkyard!" That adage seems to have disappeared as I tour the general merchandise section, with shattered and battered goods seemingly tossed onto shelves. Among the items for sale is a bent California license plate, not an antique either, but a modern one that looks as if perhaps someone just found it in the street and brought it into the store. The California plate that was once synonymous with the quintessential good life; now bent, discarded, and unable to sell at a thrift store. How apropos.

A few days later I turn in my application package to an office worker, who informs me without looking at it that they aren't hiring—which is a little strange since they hadn't mentioned that when I picked up the application only days earlier. I ask her when I might be able to speak with a manager. "Just call back later today, or anytime tomorrow," she says. When I call back a couple hours later, the woman who answers the phone asks why I want to speak with a manager. I tell her I am following up on an application that I had dropped off earlier in the day. She puts the phone down for a minute, then comes back on the line and tells me that the manager hadn't received any application. I describe the folder it was in and the woman that I had handed it to. "Nope, it's not here. Sorry," she says. "You can come back down and fill out another one if you'd like."

***

The nadir came about a week later, when I stopped by the Pacific Care Car Wash in Upland, a bedroom community not far from Pomona. While I had never worked at the car wash before (I think it was a vacant lot or field when I was in high school and college), I had driven my car through it plenty of times and knew it was a labor-intensive job site, but one in which I couldn't recall ever seeing a White or Black employee working the line, and rarely an English-speaking one. It didn't take long to find out why. The woman behind the counter at the car wash seemed momentarily stunned that I was asking for an employment application but recovered long enough to direct me to the adjoining gas station, which was part of the same operation. The clerk there said he couldn't find any application forms, so he phoned the manager and explained the situation.

Hanging up, he gave me an awkward look and informed me, "My manager said not to give you an application. We're not hiring."

Now it was my turn to be stunned. "Well, you may not be hiring right now, but I'm sure you will be at some point and I would like to have an application on file for when you do," I said. But the clerk had his orders. "Yeah, but my boss said to not give you one. We're over-staffed today anyway." *Today?* "Well, I mean just in general," he said sheepishly, seeming to understand he had given it away.

It's fairly well accepted by the public, though apparently never admitted to by the employers, that the staff at most car washes around Southern California today are frequently illegal immigrant day laborers who are often working for tips alone. There is no application process in play here; just word-of-mouth referrals by amigos already working the line who vouch for who is a good candidate to work at no cost to the employer and who is not. Of course, it's pure speculation on my part that the dozens of Spanish-speaking men swarming over the cars with towels and squirt bottles may not be American citizens or have legal authorization to work in the United States. It would be absolute conjecture for me to assert that the reason the manager instructed his clerk to *not* give me an application for employment was because when he saw that it was a middle-aged, White, English-speaking dude who was asking for it, he saw trouble. Perhaps he correctly made the assumption that I might be aware of nuances like state and federal labor and wage laws, and have some sense of workplace safety standards, and thus could be a negative influence on the other workers.

But again, I would just be guessing.

***

And so it went. Applications, cover letters, resumes, references, handshakes, small talk, the inevitable "We'll get back to ya!" and then the silence. The phone calls and drop-back bys to follow up met by either casual indifference or being put off again to a later, evolving date. Or, as in the case of the car wash, I was outright denied even an application to wield a towel.

It's hard to explain the slow, draining effect this has, but I found myself increasingly facing a myriad of emotions as the slog dragged on: from initial alarm, disbelief, and frustration to a creeping depression and bouts of lethargy to finally a sense of fatalism imbued with a healthy dose of dark humor that's best summed up in two words: "Fuck it."

Over the course of more than two months my faux job search for the most basic types of employment—the kind that historically American teens have started their work histories with—proved to be an acid-bath that stripped away the notion that these kinds of jobs will always be around and available as a job-of-last-resort for men and women who lose their footing in skilled professions and college-required careers. They aren't.

Jobs that I picked up within a few days of looking 25 to 30 years ago aren't even calling back now for an interview. A dozen applications for minimum-wage jobs and even more inquiries at other potential entry-level service providers yielded not a single call back. My written and verbal offer to accept *any shift*, to work *any hours* and in *any capacity* for whatever their starting wage would be, didn't result in even one bite.

It got me to thinking what it would be like if I really did need this kind of job in short order. What would it be like if instead of searching for two months without a single offer, I had spent six months looking for any kind of employment and not received even one call back? What if it had been a year? Two years?

How angry would I have been walking out of the car wash then?

Anne Lennon knows the answer.

The 52-year-old Southern California native was born in Los Angeles and raised between the San Gabriel Valley and the Inland Empire farther east. Attractive, well-spoken, single and with no children, Lennon had established herself in the mortgage field, working for various brokers across the region for nearly 20 years. It was a career that had her earning upward of $50,000 annually during good years, a little less at times, but a reliable middle-class income nonetheless.

"I worked for firms that ran 'vanilla paper,'" she said. "These weren't firms that specialized in sub-prime lending. A lot of it was what we called 'niche for the rich,' essentially custom loans for people who could afford it."

But as niche as some of those loans might have been, the collapse of the mortgage industry and the cocaine-like frenzy of the housing market its chimerical lending fueled wiped out hundreds of thousands of jobs in the financial and real estate sectors, and Lennon found herself unemployed. Like many of her peers, the true gravity of the situation didn't immediately sink in and, believing that as an experienced professional she would have little trouble landing another job as soon as the market stabilized, Lennon said she decided to take a few months to decompress, travel, and see some family on the East Coast.

"After that, I got back and started to look for work," she said. "And it didn't take long before I began to discover that not only had a lot of the mortgage companies seriously downsized, but many companies were just gone altogether. And they weren't coming back."

As her savings began to disappear, Lennon she downshifted to looking for positions that she was overqualified for in the same industry to looking for jobs outside of her career field. "Then it became a matter of just looking for *a job*," she said. "Whatever I could find."

Just when it seemed that Lennon was on her last legs, she was hired by a security firm to work in its front office; but the experience proved both alarming and short-lived. "I was interviewing not only the guys that were coming back from Iraq that were looking for jobs, but I was interviewing guys from all walks of life that were coming in looking for work," she said. "These were people that had owned their own companies, ran their own businesses, and now they were trying to land any kind of work. I was in shock."

But she was in for another shock.

Lennon was laid off again and after suffering an injury had to turn to state disability to support her while she recovered and then began to look for another job. This second jag of unemployment she describes as a straight shot into the abyss of the recession—a bitter and debilitating lesson of just how overwhelmingly crowded the job market has become.

"I simply could not find work in the Inland Empire [which had been one of the fastest growing regions in the nation during the go-go housing boom], not by using the internet and not by dropping off resumes, which apparently is not what a lot of employers want anymore. They want to screen people online," she said. "I was looking everywhere, from chain stores to small mom-and-pop retail shops. From department stores like Macy's all the way down to very small family-run boutiques."

Lennon expanded her job search across four counties— Los Angeles, Riverside, San Bernardino, and Orange— grueling forays through the tangle of traffic-congested freeways of Southern California, in the process running up astronomical fuel bills. Her simultaneous search online didn't prove any more fruitful. "I did Monster.com and CareerBuilders.com," she said. "Those were just black holes. I still get depressed thinking about it."

Lennon said she began to experiment during her job searches; she stopped dressing up and when interviewing for office work would lower what her previous income had actually been. "I decided to lie about what I had been making before because I didn't want to scare them away by having them think I would expect wages higher than they were willing to pay. I was looking for full-time, part-time, temporary positions; you name it. I heard 'We're cutting back right now' so often it became cliché. I could say it with them as they started to say it," she said. "So I was out there, overqualified and selling myself short. I felt desolate, desperate, and depressed. I couldn't believe it was happening to me."

As the weeks turned into months, Lennon was forced into a cycle of downsizing, moving, and shedding her possessions; a spiral that appeared might end only when she was living out of her car—or worse.

Lennon said she knew she had a lot of company.

"If there was anything more frightening than what I was going through, it was some of the things I was hearing," she said. "I heard people tell stories about applying for a handful of jobs that a thousand resumes had been taken. Whether it was really a thousand or just a couple hundred, does it matter? I just knew that within a couple years I was now living in another world; one in which I got my ass financially kicked, and I couldn't recover."

As of this writing, Lennon still hasn't recovered, at least anything approximating the life that she once knew as a middle-class American.

Thanks to the graciousness of friends, Lennon has a place to stay for now. She also found two part-time jobs— at the Honda Center and Angel Stadium, both of them in Orange County—a significant commute from Riverside County where she has a room. She makes between $8.45 and $10 an hour. Her monthly gross is usually around $750.

"I don't pay rent and I don't buy clothes and I don't have any luxuries," she said. "I buy food and I buy fuel. Pathetic, huh? This is *so not normal* for me, but I am reading and hearing that this is the so-called 'new normal.' And you know what? There are so many people out there just like me, or are about to end up just like me, that the sad truth of it is—this is the new normal."

Lennon seems fairly apolitical, not much of an ideological water-carrier for either side of the aisle or for any side in the raging debate over continued mass immigration into the United States, and particularly illegal immigration. But she admits that her bitter job search has left her wondering what American leaders of all political stripes are thinking as more foreign workers come into the country at a time when so many citizens are out of work and can't find *any* job.

"The way that I am living right now, for a lot of these immigrants that is not only normal for them, but better than where they came from," she said. "I am struggling to handle it and [immigrant workers] are thinking, 'Hey, I live like this, no problem.' They have adapted to it. Of course the irony is they come to this country looking for a better life and to live like the way we lived, and now more of us are having to live like them."

Lennon has considered moving, possibly to a Rocky Mountain state or perhaps to Missouri, where she has family and friends. But after a recent trip back there, she returned to California unsure whether such a dramatic move would offer up much better results. Is she willing to leave the two jobs she has—that cover just enough to put food in her stomach and fuel in her tank—for the economic unknown of a distant state?

"I don't know what I am going to do," she said. "But I think one thing is certain: the California life that we knew, the life that was made possible by good middle-class jobs that offered healthcare and paid a wage where you could save a little money. That's gone for most people and I don't think it's ever coming back."

***

A strange thing frequently happens when considering the depth and scope of unemployment, when trying to determine what the *real* number of out-of-work Americans actually is, and how many more are part of the so-called "underemployed" and financially distressed. Amid the bureaucratic churning of lifeless facts and figures, stories like Lennon's are easily lost in the shuffle of statistics that roll out of Sacramento and Washington, DC and into the newsrooms across the country, where they are crunched and bleached by politicos and punditry who seem increasingly oblivious to the human toll on American citizens.

And they are even more reluctant to connect the dots to immigration.

It's surreal to watch *Newsweek's* Robert J. Samuelson hold forth about the emergence of essentially two economic realities: a relatively bright one for those who are university educated and a grim one for those who aren't—without so much as even bothering to mention that the chaotic scramble working-class Americans face for jobs has been greatly impacted by millions of foreign workers in general and illegal immigrants in particular.

And just as there is no urgency in Washington (or Sacramento, for that matter) to discern an accurate count of how many illegal immigrants are in the United States today, beyond vague assurances it probably is around 12 million people (though some credible studies have put the figure at more than double that number), there is likewise no rush to determine how many Americans are out of the workforce altogether, how many more find themselves in Lennon's position of barely surviving by cobbling together part-time or temporary employment? For all the talk about the legions of the unemployed during this Great Recession, and the even millions more "under-employed" workers who have staff jobs but can't get enough hours, there is another class of American worker that is routinely overlooked but rapidly growing: the *independent contractor*. These are the people who have work—just not a job.

In 2005, the Department of Labor's Bureau of Labor Statistics estimated that there were more than 10 million contractors in the U.S. workforce, a figure that some project will double by 2016. That's a vast demographic that touches virtually every employment sector in the country. The Labor Department estimates as many as 30 percent of companies misclassify employees as contractors—perhaps more than 3.5 million regular workers, according to one federal study. While the hit to Uncle Sam's cash register is considerable—more than $20 billion lost annually in taxes, according to the Government Accounting Office—the price paid by the worker can be even deeper. Beyond the pure financial considerations, companies realize another potent benefit when they classify workers as contractors: absolute leverage.

If China represents capitalism without the freedom, then full-time contractors represent work without the protection—kind of like an American citizen version of an illegal immigrant, except it's in their own country.

But you won't hear or read too much discussion of this in news cycles that regurgitate the meaningless figure of a 9.5% unemployment rate (meaningless when the actual, total number is quite likely more than double that figure), while giving air time and ink to political leaders who decry the great bleed-out of American jobs to offshore outsourcing while remaining silent about the mass importation of replacement workers—immigrants—by the millions. Thus, Senate Majority Leader Harry Reid can keep a straight face while telling a reporter during the campaign last fall that he prevented a vote on a bill that would have required employers receiving stimulus money to use E-Verify to confirm their employees had the legal right to be on the job because immigration reform had to be done in one grand measure, not piecemeal actions. Yet as soon as the election was over, Reid swiftly brought the so-called "Dream Act" to an ill-fated vote that he deemed as a down payment on a larger reform bill.

And Congressman Luis Gutierrez from Illinois can defiantly proclaim, amid the greatest economic crisis the American people have faced in nearly a century, that he has "only one loyalty—and that's to the immigrant community" (or more accurately, to Latino immigrants) and not worry about his job—a job in which he swore an oath of allegiance to the American people and their Constitution.

Political leaders from both parties can continue to step in front of the cameras to wring their hands in mock nervousness on cue over the staggering job losses America has suffered and the grim future that tens of millions of her citizens now face, but unless and until they are willing to honestly admit that millions of foreign workers pouring into the United States is undeniably devastating to the American worker and are ready to act decisively to end the practice, they are just playing to themselves.

And Americans, like so many Californians, will slowly come to understand that while their dream may be over, their long national nightmare has only begun.

THE NOTORIOUS P.I.G.

As America dies, the GOP's electoral serial killer Karl "Pig Man" Rove is still trolling the polls and positioning postmortem Republican political bodies all along his highway to hell

First published in 2021

Charlie Daniels once famously sang "The Devil Went Down to Georgia" and offered up during that summer of 1979 a semi-spoken word performance that sizzled with either America's casual confidence or her reckless disregard for risks and potential outcomes, depending on one's perspective. On the one hand, Johnny wasn't looking for trouble the day the Devil happened upon him, but on the other he didn't exactly skedaddle either.

And when Satan proffered his wager in Daniel's tune, Johnny didn't consider the odds and then step back from the pari-mutuel window and wave off a bet that offered either solid gold or the eternal abyss.

No, he put his collateral up and let Mephistopheles get the party started.

Anyone who remembers the tune when it first hit the airwaves recalls the invigorating outcome, with a simple country boy decisively vanquishing Old Nick at the song's crescendo and, in the best tradition of Southern hospitality, inviting Lucifer to come on back anytime he felt he needed some more of the same.

Karl Rove surely remembers the classic tune and as the disastrous year of 2020 came to a close with the Republican Party's majority in the Senate hanging by the political shoestring of two seats that would be decided in a Georgia runoff election the opening week of the new year, it must have seemed something like old times to the veteran political operative who by nearly every estimation didn't wager his soul as much as he outright sold it decades earlier on the altar of corporate globalism. While 1979 may seem like a political eternity ago, certain elements of the political landscape must ring a distant bell for Rove: in 1979, a feckless Democratic president from Georgia was in the White House and the GOP's presence in Congress was south of tenuous and stuck somewhere between frail and anorexic—with the Democrats holding a 58-seat majority in the Senate and a staggering 276 seats to the Republicans' 156 seats in the House of Representatives.

But as grim as those spreads appear now, it's worth remembering that more than 40 years ago the difference between most Democrats and Republicans in both chambers often ranged from minor to miniscule depending on the issue, a demarcation of a few simple degrees that would be unthinkable today amid the political peacocks and freak show power junkies carrying out their corporate looting and jihad for total control. The era of old salts like Tip O'Neill and Howard Baker and Bob Packwood and Alan Cranston making their party's case and jockeying for position inside the Capitol before retiring to Old Ebbitt Grill or Martin's Tavern to cut a deal that most everyone could live with over steaks and drinks has passed along with the nation's cultural cohesiveness that produced a functioning government symbolic of a fairly united nation. While men like O'Neill, Baker, Packwood, and Cranston surely did have political hills to fight over and perhaps ideologically perish upon, the definition of what constituted a man or a woman or whether a man can have a baby or if a seven-year-old boy should be chemically castrated so his mother can dress him up and parade him around as a "girl" or whether a blood libel against White Americans and peddled under the guise of "systemic racism" was the true arbiter of success in America weren't among them.

No, there was a very real fundamental and foundational consensus shared between the leadership and the rank n' file in both parties.

But that nation no longer exists as it once did, laid low by a long and dedicated campaign of sabotage and subterfuge and a populace's willing acquiescence to surrender a quality of life and cultural cohesiveness ultimately in exchange for a room full of cheap toys and mass spectacles.

Karl Rove harbors no illusions as to just how fundamentally changed—*indeed just how far gone*—the America of 1979 is when contrasted to what passes as "America" in 2021, as Rove is absolutely a high-profile political "person of interest" in the abduction, torture, and murder of the American nation-state as a functioning republic and a demographically and culturally cohesive enterprise. His greasy fingerprints are all over crime scenes that stretch today from the violent mass stampede across the border to the savage chaos exploding throughout the imploding cities to the deadly silence of the shuttered manufacturing plants that once hummed across the heartland and amid every kindergarten class to every university lecture hall where working White Americans are ritually defiled in theory as well as in practice.

One need not be a forensic technician to understand that *Karl Rove was there,* along with a Beltway brigade of his fellow travelers who are clearly no longer concerned about getting caught defiling the corpse in postmortem America, even if it remains forbidden to go off script and say so aloud now on Fox News Channel.

As 2020 came to an end, Rove surely understood that he was standing in the grave the GOP leadership has been digging for its own party for decades—a cozy little plot right alongside the pit that has been excavated for a nation that once shined brightly—but he dutifully made the rounds on FNC's shows nonetheless last winter, where he held his white boards aloft ever higher and insisted the Republican Party was poised for strategic victories yet to come.

And so it was Rove the GOP dispatched to Georgia to save the day at the dawn of 2021.

As Trump shrieked and wailed, Rove attempted to thread an impossible needle by keeping the populist movement of working White Americans who had tragically stuck (for the most part) with a do-nothing dolt named Donald and joining them at the political hip with the global corporate interests that operate the Republican Party's leadership.

The man dubbed alternately as "The Architect" or "Bush's Brain" among veteran GOP consultant circles—christened "Turd Blossom" by the very man he steered into the White House twice (albeit once effectively by court order)—but known colloquially of late by tens of millions of White working Americans simply as the "Notorious P.I.G.'" or alternately "Pig Man: The Swine of the Swamp," Rove went down to Georgia looking to make a deal that he apparently thought still could be brokered with voters on a campaign centered in corporate tax cuts and deregulation wrapped up in a simplistic but shiny bow of *"Vote for David Perdue and Kelly Loeffler or The Blob of socialism will devour your town, your state, your nation!"*

With Donald J. Trump's presidency reduced by December 2020 to a pustulating tumor oozing his reeking self-aggrandizing rage after having squandered his four years in office on masturbatory Twitter frenzies, leisurely golf weekends, and frenetic World Wrestling Entertainment political rallies all-about-him in lieu of actually delivering in any meaningful way on his campaign pledges to voters—a historic rank betrayal made even more pungent by his sickening sebum of negligence and utter incompetence dating to January 2017—Rove and his fellow corporate GOP honchos had their work cut out for them from the get-go in Georgia.

Loeffler and Perdue were two incumbent corporate cutouts who failed to cinch even 50% + .01 in the November election against two Democratic candidates who were far enough Left they wouldn't have come anywhere close to surviving their own party's primary a decade ago—when the state Democratic party still had some residual legacy of Zell Miller and Sam Nunn.

But if Trump was the weeping cyst on the face of the Republican Party, Rove is the cancer that still defines the deadly disease that resides in the decomposing core of its leadership.

The systemic rot of corruption that has metastasized throughout the GOP's leadership was on full display as Rove was found once again standing at the crucial nexus of a campaign that would decide how much longer the GOP might remain even remotely relevant as a national party before it's admitted to political hospice as it withers into a regional outfit with a stature more on par with the service clubs of yore such as Rotary, Lions, or Optimists, drifting onward to its date with oblivion.

That Rove Inc. was conjured forth to work the Georgia backwoods for every vote that might yet be squeezed out of them speaks volumes in itself, but the message that "The Architect" and his minions sought to tempt them with was even more revealing, as the Republicans went back to basics for the open-border, mass-immigration, business-class crowd: "It's the markets, stupid."

Rove was rushed in by the Republican National Committee late in the game to coordinate the Republican incumbents' last stand in the heart of Dixie via its Georgia Battleground Fund with its eight-figure budget, and Rove sought to convince a still convulsing Trump to keep chanting about the GOP's "great successes": corporate tax cuts, deregulation, Supreme Court appointees, and perhaps crow about "criminal justice reform"—the accelerating early release of thousands of dangerous criminals back onto the streets of America. And, of course, hammer home his apex achievement of moving the American embassy in Israel from Tel Aviv to Jerusalem—which Jared Kushner had assured Trump was a perennial priority for working Americans from Maine to Modesto even as the American homeland collapses in flames around them.

These were to be the key messaging points for Trump and the Republican power-players as they sought to keep Perdue's and Loeffler's Senate seats in GOP hands.

Long gone was any pretense of considering a moratorium on the mass immigration that has been literally trampling America underfoot for decades; there was to be no demand for an immediate cessation of immigration of every variety; from the H-1B and H-2B and other exotic visa schemes designed to eliminate American workers in favor of replacements from Southeast Asia who are imported as a precursor to the inevitable arrival of their extended families. Nor was there to be much made on the stump of the legions of garden-variety Rio Grande pole-vaulters to the caravan convoys slithering north from the failed states of Central America and South America that continue to slam with Category 5 hurricane force on every societal aspect of our most vulnerable American citizens, from housing to healthcare and education to employment.

As for the violent crime rates that have burned through America's Democratic-controlled cities and states with such ferocity that much of the middle class and upwardly mobile are fleeing in an exodus not seen in more than a half-century, Rove's playbook called for a passing mention at best of such deadly demographic drain-circling, and only with the qualifiers that Loeffler and Perdue first again denounce

"White supremacy," acknowledge again that they aren't racists and praise the so-called criminal justice reform that has poured tens of thousands of hardened criminals back onto the streets and into America's neighborhoods.

And Rove & Co. was damn sure that not a word should be uttered about the toxic brew of so-called "Critical Race Theory"—the fancy-pants terminology applied by academia to a crackpot ideology that at its core essence is an action plan for the defilement, dispossession, and disappearance of White America. Critical Race Theory is in no uncertain terms a daily demonization of working White Americans by an institutional class of elites entrenched across societal sectors ranging from the media to academia and corporations to government agencies.

Yet while Critical Race Theory is a multi-authored *Mein Kampf* of the 21st century, a surreal stew of fantastical historical rewrites and fabricated claims designed expressly as a blood libel that would escalate the hatred of White Americans to a breathtaking scale even while normalizing and rewarding it, Rove and the GOP suits were hell-bent that neither Loeffler nor Perdue seize on the psychotic philosophy as but a coming attraction of what the Democrats have in store for White Americans and offer a full-throated and full-throttle rejection of it.

Thus, come election day there shouldn't have been too terrible a shock when both Loeffler and Perdue were vanquished, with Jon Ossoff crossing the finish line with a margin of more than 50,000 votes than the stiff that is Perdue and Warnock rolling up a nearly 100,000-ballot margin to the talking mannequin Loeffler.

Karl Rove and the GOP's "victory fund" had struck again.

They may as well have poured the nearly $50 million that PAC raised for Perdue and Loeffler onto a beachside bonfire, as burning it would have generated more heat, light, and useful effect than Rove's brilliant strategy produced.

And that this was happening in Georgia at the dawn of 2021 was an indisputably brighter reflection of the fact that Georgia was going the way of Virginia before it just as North Carolina will soon go the way of Georgia. Arizona, Colorado, and Nevada are on their way to solid blue too.

This is the geopolitical, sociocultural transformation that takes place in one state after the next when one party plays realpolitik hardball as the other employs empty rhetoric while engaging in systemic self-enrichment while the getting is still good, coming up for air now and again to offer boilerplate complaints about the tactics of their adversary even as they refuse to confront them. It's hard to imagine that deep down in whatever constitutes Karl Rove's core—again, his *soul* has already been purchased—that he didn't understand he was running a dead party's errand down in Georgia, but there was money to be made and charades to be played whether it was Rove in the GOP's wheelhouse or not, so he was likely on autopilot.

Karl Rove was just doing what Karl Rove always does and always will do all the way to the end.

The implosion of the Trump presidency and the Republicans' failure to win back the House or even hold onto the Senate in 2020 produced another peculiar-if-familiar result: a surreal declaration of victory of sorts by the GOP's leadership—and only in the GOP today could coming in second in a two-horse race be considered a victory, with the Republicans awarding themselves a political trophy for "Most Improved" in the locker room as the Democrats stood Center Court and held their victories aloft like Bjorn Borg hoisting his fifth straight Wimbledon Cup.

The GOP leadership announced that their destruction at the polls in 2020 was merely prelude to victories yet to come, as the party was in the midst of a demographic refitting that would see it draw more Black and brown voters into its dominant base of White voters who would emerge as a multi-racial coalition that would wreak havoc on Democrats as the 2020s got fully underway. That approximately 92 of every 100 Black voters cast their ballots for Joe Biden in 2020 was of no never mind to them, just as Trump's loss of a few vital percentage points of working White males—enough to have turned the election decisively—was written off by GOP shills with a smirk and a shrug.

Such is the final dance of a dead party campaigning amid a soundtrack of its own delusional declarations.

The midterms of 2022 are now coming into focus on the horizon and the Republicans no doubt feel a sense of relief much in the same way a condemned man might feel upon learning a court had issued a temporary reprieve. The Biden presidency has, at first blush, stumbled badly from its opening night on Pennsylvania Avenue. The ongoing fiasco at the southern border; the frenetic pinballing of the administration on the protocols of the pandemic, from mask mandates to lockdowns to vaccine passports; the surge of violent criminals prowling the streets to prey at will upon law-abiding citizens; the legions of homeless zombies that have turned city life into a horror showcase of progressive accomplishments, and now the total and instantaneous collapse of the faux nation-state of Afghanistan and its resulting exposure of The Pentagon as a multi-trillion-dollar enterprise that hasn't produced a single strategic victory in three-quarters of a century—all of this and more seems to bode well for the GOP.

But again, only at first glance.

All of the violently chaotic dysfunction that is now endemic in so much of America shouldn't be misinterpreted as symptomatic of Biden's failure. To the contrary, it's a shining torch of the absolute triumph of the Democratic Party's agenda—as aided and abetted by the Republican Party's leadership. On his first day in office, Joe Biden accomplished more in his presidency than Donald Trump did in the entirety of his own occupancy of the office. With a blizzard of pen strokes across a raft of Executive Orders,

Biden struck mighty blows that advanced the Democrats to-do list, dropping atomic-grade sledgehammer strikes on everything from border security to energy independence.

And he did it on Day One.

So the GOP's estimation that Biden has botched border security is, as usual, nonsense based on the false premise that the Democrats want a border, let alone a secure one. The Democrats want the border effectively eliminated and Biden has clearly achieved that, with the five million or more immigrants who will have successfully crossed the southern frontier by the end of the year rightly viewed as a hallmark victory for progressives and one that portends the *tens of millions more migrants* who are on tap to enter America by any means necessary before the close of 2024.

While the Republican Party's mouthpieces on Fox News decry and bemoan this reality, what has the GOP leadership done to stop it? In a word: *nothing*.

Texas Governor Greg Abbott has taken to Fox News repeatedly to cry about how his state is being literally overrun, which of course is a matter of undeniable fact, but how many National Guard troops did Abbott call up and deploy fully armed to staunch the deluge? *None.* [Note: Abbott did make a show of sending several hundred guardsmen down to the Rio Grande with flashlights and first-aid kits, but in terms of anything meaningful that would halt the migrant flood and force a showdown with the Biden Administration, Abbott has done *nothing*.]

In California, once a reliable Republican redoubt that saw the GOP politically exterminated decades ago as result of a demographic repaving laid down by the very mass immigration the Republican leadership has long championed, the GOP's suits and soothsayers are playing make-believe once more with the looming fate of Governor Gavin Newsom, who faces a recall vote on September 14.

But again, Newsom's very real struggles to remain in office are not as they seem.

While the once Golden State is listing heavily under the sheer tide of humanity that has poured into it unchecked even as its former public schools have been converted into social service centers—in some Los Angeles "schools," more than 90 percent of "students" aren't proficient in math and a plurality are functionally illiterate in English—Newsom is counting on the very voters who largely populate those disaster zones to see him through this recall election.

In the crime-riddled No-Go Zones that were once called neighborhoods throughout California, where tens of thousands of career criminals now feed in frenzies of violence upon citizens fearless once again of any significant sanction, here too Newsom is counting on voters to vote "no" on the recall.

Despite the close margin of the polling as August burns into September in California, Newsom has a real reason to believe in a happy ending.

And it's the very closeness of the polls that is his silver lining.

Twenty years ago, Newsom would have been toast by now—and badly burnt toast at that. The perfect storm of crime, the official schizophrenia of lockdown and masking mandates, the sprawling encampments of World War Z urban berserkers all combined with his own very public habit of flaunting a *"rules for thee but not for me"* philosophy would have put the popular torch irrevocably to his reign as governor.

And that's to say nothing of his imperious death penalty embargo that spits in the face of every murder victim, their family members, and the long-suffering majority of California voters who have repeatedly confirmed their overwhelming support for capital punishment only to see the likes of Newsom and his fellow elites flip them the bird. Then there are the water restrictions, electrical grid failures, and traffic coagulation that are all accelerating and deepening even as developers are still enjoying

Sacramento's unequivocal support for a build-to-oblivion blueprint. Newsom is a high-density population-packing jihadist—with the black letter caveat that towers of affordable multi-family housing aren't to be built anywhere near his own home or family's portfolio of properties.

Newsom's GQ good looks and his Last of the International Playboys flair would have delivered him precious little on election day a generation ago.

And yet, in spite of all that, Newsom remains *ahead* in the polling on the first and foremost question that voters will answer: should he be recalled?

On that question, right now, Newsom is prevailing in most polls with 52 percent among the critical category of "likely voters." His margin is higher among "all voters." While his spread is within the margin of error—and California is known for its unexpected earthquakes of all kinds—that Newsom remains even a nostril above water among likely voters speaks far more about the fate of the GOP than it does of one Democratic governor who should be packing his bags but may not have to call U-Haul at all.

The GOP brand in California 2021 is so tainted that the state party chose *not* to endorse one of the Republicans seeking to replace Newsom for fear that doing so would hurt that candidate's chances of winning.

Even if Newsom is recalled, his removal from office changes none of the material facts on the ground for the Republicans in California, nor anywhere else in what remains of America.

The GOP is graveyard dead in California and will never rise again in this lifetime, its cadaver a testament to the Republican Party's commitment to nearly a half-century of mass immigration and an abandonment of critical cultural issues that amounted to, in cold actual fact, a political murder-suicide pact carried out at the behest of its donor class to destroy the Golden State—and kill the California Republican Party in the process.

If Gavin Newsom prevails next Tuesday, in his victory speech he ought to give a special shout out to Karl Rove, as well as House Minority Leader Kevin McCarthy and, of course, that GOP golden boy old David Dreier, the retired congressman from Southern California who spent three decades on his knees at the corporate glory holes until the state was in ruins and his district a deeply unwinnable blue.

Newsom should thank Rove, McCarthy, and Dreier by name and gleefully gloat that he couldn't have done it without them.

Because he couldn't have.

And as California goes, so too goes the nation for the Republicans as the GOP leadership and its key strategists like Karl Rove and Frank Luntz continue to manage the party like the private equity firm it has become, siphoning every dollar and dime that they can into the coffers of the cutouts and corporations that it long ago merged with.

Make no mistake; a Republican resurgence in the Congress come November 2022 will be utterly meaningless.

Even if the GOP does flip the House of Representatives, which this far out seems somewhere between plausible and likely, and manages to either hold its 50 seats in the Senate or perhaps pick up a critical seat or two and thus turn the chamber red once more—a much steeper hill for the party to climb—while it will ostensibly pump the brakes on the Biden Administration (presuming it's still the *Biden Administration* come the fall of 2022) it will still mean little more than a pyrrhic victory for the Republican Party.

In pure electoral terms, it will be the GOP's Battle of the Bulge, a short-term tactical breakthrough that will do nothing to alter the strategic balance they now confront. The Rubicon was crossed years ago, the die has been cast, and the demographic denouement the Republican leadership wrought upon the nation itself will soon consume its own political host organism.

And yet Karl Rove, the Notorious P.I.G., will continue to work his treasonous tradecraft from the Beltway to the bayous, from the boardrooms to the boardwalks as he's paid fat stacks to draft campaign messages that are increasingly dead letters to a fantastical 21st-century coalition of voters that will never appear.

Rove will urge Republican candidates to steer clear of "divisive social issues" such as the national grooming of school children's sexual and gender identities. He will appeal to the GOP roster to resist vocally supporting the death penalty for convicted murderers while imploring them to deny being racist as a stock-opener and demand they denounce "White supremacy" before diligently declining to stand up for working White Americans or challenge the lies that have been leveled against them.

And most critically, Rove will assert to the Republican bench that another mass amnesty—messaged as "comprehensive immigration reform" on the campaign trail—is the most vital goal for the GOP and its benefactors. Talk of walls, enforcement, E-Verify, and deportation is antithetical to the capitalist foundations of America and unpopular with Americans, Rove will assure them.

Accordingly, Rove will demand that any effort to discuss let alone introduce an across-the-board moratorium on any further immigration into the United States for at least a decade—a pause to let the nation catch its breath, so to speak—must be muzzled immediately, proactively denounced as xenophobic fearmongering that weakens the bedrock of liberty.

The imprint and impact of Karl Rove on the Republican Party's orthodoxy, to which its leadership remains devout, cannot be overstated.

And it can be best witnessed in the deafening silence its congressional host hews religiously to when working White Americans are assailed in vitriolic terms across virtually every platform and actually assaulted in accelerating violent attacks across the nation. When Nancy Pelosi proclaimed during a February 2018 speech on the House floor that her six-year-old grandson's birthday wish was to not be White, not a single word of consequence was heard from the Republican majority that then controlled the chamber. There was no thunderous rebuke over how perversely pathetic such a declaration was—as it was either a brazen lie Pelosi sickeningly fashioned on the back of her own grandchild or, more ominous still, it was all too true and a glaring-if-unintended confession of disgusting child abuse occurring amid Pelosi's progressive family.

But no matter, Pelosi could have reached deep into her Jonestown People's Temple ideological roots and shouted from the rostrum, *"My six-year-old grandson's birthday wish is that White America be wholly exterminated in a campaign of righteous genocide that they themselves are forced to fund!"* and as the Democratic caucus jumped to their feet to roar their jubilant approval, the Rove Republicans would remain seated in cathedral silence, waiting politely for their turn to speak on the benefits of the carried interest loophole, the importance of new tax cuts for developers, and why environmental regulations were hurting the American economy.

The Pig Man has prevailed.

Like the Los Angeles County Fair's classic mascot "Thummer"—an anthropomorphic pig sporting some snazzy duds and lugging a suitcase advertising his destination—Rove is already looking well beyond his 2022 GOP prospects and over the horizon to the 2024 election that is increasingly likely to represent the formal burial of the Republican Party as a nationally relevant party.

And you can bet, just like Satan on those old Georgia backroads, Karl Rove will be on hand and at head of the rest of the corporate hogs, his corpulent face aglow and smeared with the decomposing detritus, as the filthy swine dine on the lifeless body they once long possessed.

THE CATTLE BELL OF ACCOMMODATION

It's not jobs or economic opportunity alone that inspire millions of immigrants to come to America illegally, but rather an unsustainable culture of complicity

First published in 2011

It's an early spring night in downtown Los Angeles and I find myself poolside at the venerable Hotel Figueroa's Veranda Bar, sharing a table and some cocktail conversation with a legal professional in her early 30s. Flashing a radiant smile, penetrating eyes, and natural beauty, she might be something of a poster child of the generational evolution among LA's business class, blending a pseudo-bohemian edge (replete with strategically-placed tattoos) and social activism with power suits and a daily grind all rather seamlessly. Sequestered amid the candlelit tables with a cool breeze rolling in from the coast as searchlights frantically crisscross the night sky above the garish LA Live entertainment complex south of Olympic Avenue, our talk drifts from pleasant observations to the banalities of the obligatory resume recitations and my ears pick up as she ticks off her "social justice" bona fides, including work in support of "the undocumented" and "paperless people," particularly those who have run afoul of the law beyond their illegal immigration status, whether it's a drunk driving or domestic violence charge.

"The immigration system here is fundamentally racist," she says, proffering that indictment as casually as she might offer an observation of the weather. "It targets and punishes Latinos that come here to work. It is essentially a war against Mexicans."

Intrigued, I ask her how is it that a "racist system" that she feels reflects a "racist society" that is waging a literal "racist war of hate" against Mexicans is, in actual fact, responsible for the most liberal immigration policy in the history of the modern nation-state and one that continues to inspire and facilitate the migration of millions of people annually from the southern hemisphere. For all the wild-eyed hysterical hyperbole by mass immigration advocates who draw morally outrageous comparisons between today's immigration enforcement measures like those in Arizona and humanity's 20th-century nadir of the Holocaust, the hard historical fact remains that Jewish people desperately sought escape from the murderous clutches of Nazi Germany, while literally tens of millions of Mexicans dream of coming to America and every year, millions seek to turn that dream into a reality.

Not many people are eager to run into a burning house, let alone risk humiliation, degradation, and death to break into a country that ostensibly has declared war on them.

The incongruity of her one-dimensional description of the country and the sheer numbers of people seeking entry to our shores weighs on her only for a moment before she dismisses it with more casual aplomb, however contradictory it may be: "They come here to work. That's the *pull factor*. If Americans don't like it, then they ought to focus their energy on helping these people improve opportunities for them in their home countries. If these people had jobs *there*, they wouldn't be coming *here*."

I marvel at the almost evangelical certainty with which she wields the crux of her position, the fine simplicity of it, smooth and undisturbed by any nuance that might lead to a different, less clear conclusion. Yet there is something quite alarming about listening to someone who knows better—indeed, someone who is practiced in the art of argument—reduced to cheap sloganeering not so much in pursuit of a valid point as in spite of not having one. There is a disturbing undercurrent to it, like watching educated people chant in unison at a political rally, offering mantras to whatever truism they need to have.

Of course, as the night wears on I find that my disappointment in her use of slogan-based arguments that are so simplistic they make Sarah Palin sound like Charlie Rose lost in digression to be increasingly ameliorated by her electric personality and beauty. The way it should be.

It's time for another drink and to let the conversation drift into more universal pursuits. The way it should be.

***

It's now an article of absolute faith among those who support continued mass immigration into the United States that immigrants, both legal and illegal, come to this country for a better life, one that will be provided by employment here that simply doesn't exist in their home countries. They tell themselves, even as they watch the unemployment lines grow deeper with citizens across the nation, that immigrants are merely filling jobs that Americans simply no longer want to do, from the fields to the factories. The ease in which immigrants, and particularly illegal immigrants, can find work in certain industries such as light manufacturing, construction, hospitality, and landscaping is often characterized as the primary "pull factor" that lures, like a siren's song, millions of men and women to risk their lives in an increasingly desperate effort to make it surreptitiously across the American frontier. And of course it's not difficult to see the powerful attraction that even minimum-wage American jobs would have over workers in a country like Mexico and many others, where the average wage amounts to little more than five dollars a day; a literal pittance relative to what even a busboy can make in a single hour in the United States.

In late 2009, well into the Great Recession's epic job bleed-out in America, a poll showed that one out of every three Mexicans—nearly 40 million people—wanted to move to the United States given the chance. Imagine what those numbers would be throughout much of the developing world, across all continents.

That mass exodus-in-waiting has nothing to do with job prospects alone.

There's no question that the practical prospect of escaping the brutal grind of poverty and the dead-end of subsistence living that is its hallmark burns far brighter for immigrants than any poetic assurance that can be glimpsed in the torchlight of the Statue of Liberty, whose lamp now lights a golden door that many corporate executives seem to believe reads "Employees Only."

But the suggestion that tens of millions of illegal immigrants have streamed across the Rio Grande and into many other ports of entry over the past generation primarily for jobs is a simplification in the extreme, a radical shoe-horning of reality into a more convenient narrative that discards wholesale a range of fundamental factors that motivate immigrants—and it verges on the very anti-intellectual charge that proponents of mass immigration all too frequently level at their critics.

The fact is that mass immigration into the United States, and particularly illegal immigration, is driven by a now well-established and pervasive culture of accommodation, of which the prospect of employment is only one element and not even the determinate one at that, since being unemployed in America still offers immigrants far more ultimate promise than life with a meager job in their home countries. From subsidized healthcare, education, food, and housing to a civic landscape that is largely free of the corruption that is endemic in their homeland, making landfall in America by any means necessary for most immigrants is to essentially find themselves in Oz—a vast, surreal land of immense wealth that has created an enviable middle class and established a sense of functional order that they can hardly imagine existing in their home countries.

All things considered, the United States isn't so much a land of mere employment opportunity as it is a tangible place of sweet deliverance from the dysfunctional and violent misery they are seeking to escape. And like a dream come true (as indeed immigrants often describe the services and opportunities made available to them as dream-like), upon arrival they are effectively feted in much of the media as the engine that is sustaining and revitalizing America— even as millions of American workers fall further into debt and despair—and ritualistically deified by a Latino pan-nationalist identity movement that seeks demographic hegemony at virtually any cost, including undercutting the most at-risk and in-need Latino Americans (along with everyone else) by exploding the labor pool and dramatically escalating demand for services. Central to the canonizing of illegal immigrants is the constant assertion of their martyrdom, the cult of their perpetual victimization which takes on a surreal air as illegal immigrants are effectively sheltered from the worksite to the college classroom and beyond while simultaneously being held up as a people under endless siege amid a racist nation that's aligned against them.

The inherent and obvious conflict with reality that is rife within the popular illegal immigrant narrative matters not, as credibility isn't the point. The story line just needs to permeate the media climate consistently enough to reinforce both a heightened sense of threatened cultural identity among immigrants (which is particularly useful to ethnic-identity groups that peddle "us against them" scenarios; whether they are White, Latino, or Black) and a sense of equity entitlement (i.e., if immigrants built this country you have an intrinsic right to come here regardless of any laws enforcing "capricious borders"), both of which in turn help fuel the cycle of mass illegal immigration.

Thus, American citizens have become accustomed each spring to the spectacle of watching hundreds of thousands of illegal immigrants take to the streets in major cities throughout the nation in May Day protests that accuse America and its people of the most heinous of racist crimes—all while vowing they will not leave and, actually, want in on the party.

Even among media outlets where the illegal immigrant story narrative is the most carefully managed news coverage, these protests sometimes result in the jarring images of cheering illegal immigrants waving Old Glory (which they had been given for the photo op) while activists denounce America as a vast corporate gulag populated by rednecks who enjoy nothing so much as a weekend of "hunting immigrants." If their own estimation of the United States were accepted at face value, it's difficult to imagine just what pull factor would really have to exist to tempt even a handful of immigrants to illegally cross our frontiers and risk attempting to build a life here.

But the stage show of mass protests are simply the street pageantry of a coordinated production aimed at reinforcing illegal immigrants' sense of a cloistered community that is under constant siege and threat.

If only more reporters would more closely examine the world these immigrants return to when the protest is over. It's a world unlike anything they ever could have imagined in their home countries.

***

In Southern California, as in many other parts of the country, there is perhaps no better or immediate example of the immense benefits that are extended to immigrants in America regardless of their legal status than the public education system. It's a system that, in California at any rate, has seen its mission in many communities transformed amid the tsunami of illegal immigration from providing a quality education to serving as the delivery point for a host of subsidized social services, including providing meals, healthcare, daycare, English-language courses for parents, and the ever nebulous "parenting classes" for people who have lots of children but seemingly few of the skills needed to raise or provide for them.

In but a generation, California's once vaunted public education system has become a frontline clearing house for services often extended almost exclusively for the benefit of immigrants here illegally; and it has collapsed in large part as a result of it. The near total academic implosion of not only the Los Angeles Unified School District (LAUSD, the second largest school district in the nation) but of numerous other large- and mid-sized public school districts throughout Southern California is simply indisputable—no matter how heretical saying so has become. Public schools were simply overrun and swamped by mass immigration in the 1990s and the earlier part of the past decade. One didn't need the gift of an oracle to see what was happening as the fine lawns and open spaces at schools built to comfortably educate several hundred students were suddenly filled with portable classrooms and trailers in a desperate effort to accommodate enrollments that swelled campus populations to triple their intended size. Classroom instruction suffered dramatically as teachers—even if they were bilingual in English and Spanish—scrambled to effectively teach their American students while at the same time helping immigrant students who frequently were multiple years behind their class level and came from families with functionally illiterate parents and a culture that placed little sustained emphasis on the importance of education.

Not too long ago, a childhood friend of mine who went on to become an educator in the Pomona Unified School District where we both attended public schools in the 1970s and early '80s invited me back to my old junior high school. More than 30 years after I had walked its halls, it was simply no longer recognizable as the school I once attended, from the most obvious distinctions to the most fundamental. The relative racial balance that Emerson Junior High School, and the district itself, had achieved by the mid and late 1970s between Blacks, Whites, and Chicanos had been completely erased by the seismic demographic shift, with Black and White students all but disappearing amid a student body that according to the California Department of Education (2008-2009) is now nearly 90 percent Latino, of which 91 percent qualified for taxpayer-subsidized meals served at the campus. Half of the students are classified as "English language learners." These figures roughly mirror the entire PUSD, whose more than 17,300 students are 82 percent Latino, of which seven percent are eligible for state-subsidized meals, according to the National Center for Education Statistics.

The number of students at Emerson Jr. High has close to doubled since I attended, now hovering around 800, according to district statistics and the school, a surge that was met by peppering its open space with portables. But perhaps the most stunning difference I was confronted with as I sat in on some classes and watched the students in the halls was the sense of low-boiling chaos that seemed omnipresent, running the gamut from lethargic disinterest to constant distraction. I asked one class of eighth graders what time they went to bed on school nights. The answers ranged from "I don't know," to "It depends where I'm staying," to "Midnight," to "Whenever I feel like it."

Even accounting for the bravado of puberty, the reality of a constant level of relative chaos in the students' home lives was immediately apparent. And for teachers it's an exhausting prospect, particularly as they struggle to help students who are dramatically below their assigned grade level.

"If I have a class of 24 students and perhaps three or four of them are a class level behind where they should be in their studies, I can handle that. I can successfully instruct the majority of the students in their course work and still help the other students catch up," my friend said. "But if I have a class of 24 students and 18 of them are not one, not two, not three, but actually *four grade levels* below where they should be, what the hell am I supposed to do with that? Baby-sit, that's what. And that's what a lot of us are doing here, baby-sitting. Providing daycare. We've got eighth graders walking in here from Mexico that are on a third-grade level, maybe, and we're supposed to meet the test standards? That's a joke."

But the joke has been on the American citizen, and particularly the working class, who have watched the public education system that once provided a pathway to a better future literally be overwhelmed at their expense. For middle-class families throughout Southern California, the tidal wave of immigration that crashed into the schools fueled their flight from public education altogether, resulting in an effective double taxation: taxes to support public schools they won't send their children to—plus steep tuition fees for a private education. Either that, or they simply moved.

But what has been a long-running catastrophe for the American working and middle classes has been a godsend for millions more illegal immigrants and their children. Despite the death-spiral of public education in California, at least by the standards of developed nations, the K-12 schools here appear like shining Taj Mahals when contrasted with what was available to the vast majority of illegal (and legal) immigrants in their home countries, which, simply put, was little to nothing. And the array of services made available to them through the schools—at no cost to them—is the gift that keeps on giving.

So, there is no overstating the lush irony that hangs thick in the air of the "ethnic studies" courses that are taught in public high schools today, classes that all too frequently serve more as ideological proving grounds for sociopolitical indoctrination than the legitimate curricula approved by districts. Two years ago, students at Jordan High School in Watts launched a series of protests in June after the LAUSD refused to renew the contract of Karen Salazar, an untenured English teacher at the campus. The LAUSD—not exactly a bastion of gold-hoarding, bunker-building Glenn Beck sycophants—determined that Salazar had veered wildly into blatant ethno-political indoctrination of her students. While Salazar presented a reasoned defense of her standards and practices in the classroom for the media, video footage showed her standing in front of the school clutching a bullhorn and declaring, "Historically, the school system has been used as a project of colonization to rob students of their identity."

Her students were even more blunt.

"She goes out of the curriculum and teaches us our history," one student said at the time, "instead of that [expletive deleted] U.S. centrism they teach us in our history class." In another video clip the same student declares students are being "hunted down and treated like terrorists" at schools that are really prisons.

The reality that public schools are just one element in a network of services and benefits offered to immigrants regardless of their legal status—where millions of immigrant children and the children of immigrants in the country illegally are fed breakfast and lunch every day on the taxpayer's dime and plugged into a host of other services, along with an effort to actually provide an education—is either lost to them or cynically ignored. In high irony, the American people have subsidized the creation of entire academic departments that are openly hostile to them.

Perhaps most amazing of all, even as the public education system in California collapsed, even as tens of billions of tax dollars have been feverishly shoveled into epic failures like the LAUSD—Superintendent Ramon Cortines's 2010-11 budget reported total annual funds from the years 2006 to 2011 ranging from $10 billion to $12 billion annually—it became a matter of not only policy but pride that no effort was made to even quantify the direct impact of mass illegal immigration on public schools, let alone staunch it.

To the contrary, it's accommodated and as such, encouraged.

***

Along with public education, the healthcare system in the United States has proven to be a powerful lure for illegal immigrants, another part of the benefit package. And like public education, it's one that has developed a self-perpetuating dynamic to it, like a flywheel that sustains its own momentum, albeit one at a devastating cost to public treasuries, particularly in states like California and Texas, where in some hospitals along the Texas-Mexico border, births to illegal immigrants now account for more than half of all babies delivered. The depth and consistency of subsidized prenatal care alone that's offered in the United States is simply non-existent for most immigrant mothers and families south of the border. Mothers who might otherwise have given birth at home with no doctor or even a nurse-practitioner to oversee the delivery of the baby and all the attendant risks of childbirth are able to access state-of-the-art maternity wards in the U.S., as well as virtually the entire host of neonatal medical services available to the child once it's born.

A few years ago in Texas, a network news crew conducted a bedside interview with an illegal immigrant from Mexico who had just undergone a C-section delivery of her baby, who is an American citizen as a result of taking his first gasp of air on American soil, all covered by Medicaid payments. The mother had illegally crossed the border only months earlier, very pregnant, along with her husband and two other children. She felt no need to be bashful as to why she and her family took the risk of crossing the border illegally: she wanted to give birth in America. "I am very glad he was born here," she said through a translator. "That is why I came here; so my children, my husband, and I could have a better life."

Not a better *job*, but a better *life*.

Emergency rooms and county clinics, which are rightly bound to treat people regardless of immigration status, ultimately offer a gateway into a broader healthcare system that while increasingly nightmarish for many American citizens is a dream come true for most illegal immigrants. And this isn't something that illegal immigrants discover through happenstance once they arrive in America; it's well known throughout the dusty warrens and shantytowns throughout much of the world, often simplistically—though with laser-like accuracy—reduced to the concept that in America it actually pays to have babies.

And as in the case of public education, the tidal wave of illegal immigration that slammed into public hospitals and clinics throughout the American Southwest in particular did so with staggering costs of so-called "uncompensated care" and with devastating consequences to the American working class and the native indigent that watched as funding and services designated for them—and often already stretched thin—was swamped by a seemingly endless tide of immigrants arriving illegally.

And like public education, the instinctive American reaction was one of total accommodation; even as the emergency rooms filled as they became de facto non-emergency treatment centers, all while county clinics closed and hospital administrators streamlined processes to admit and treat patients with no Social Security numbers, no valid identification, and no ability to pay for treatment.

***

Despite the superheated rhetoric that claims America is waging war against immigrants, the culture of accommodation has even metastasized throughout the criminal justice system, resulting in people who have no legal right to be in the nation frequently getting a pass that allows them to stay once they have committed some other crime.

In California, the stories of illegal immigrants who have been arrested and released only to commit some other horrific crime are so ubiquitous that they have lost some of their intrinsic power to enrage citizens for more than a few embittered passing moments.

Such was the case of Humberto Higareda Robles.

In the mid-afternoon on the Fourth of July in 2008, Robles, an illegal immigrant from Mexico with active warrants out for his arrest, was drunk and behind the wheel of a 2001 Ford Aerostar van as it sped along the streets of south Pomona. Robles slammed the van into another car, seriously injuring two people, then sped off into a residential neighborhood, where he lost control of the van again, causing it to jump the curb and smash into a utility pole, shearing its high voltage lines. Though Robles fled on foot, he was tracked down by police, arrested, and transported to the hospital for treatment of his injuries. As he was being treated, police said Robles laughed when informed of the people he had injured and cursed the officers, in English.

Booked on multiple felony charges and already carrying arrest warrants stemming from domestic violence charges filed against him 2002, Robles had an ICE hold placed on him that prevented him from being bailed out and set the stage for deportation proceedings following the adjudication of his case. At least that's what was supposed to happen. What actually happened was the Los Angeles County District Attorney's office chose to file *misdemeanor* charges against Robles instead of pursuing the felony counts, and as a result the immigration hold was dropped.

One week later, Judge Judson W. Morris Jr., a veteran of the bench, sentenced Robles to 51 days in county jail after Robles took a plea deal on two misdemeanor counts. Less than three days later, due to overcrowding in a county jail system that has also been swamped by illegal immigration, Robles walked back on to America's streets a free man. Despite being in the country illegally for years, despite being a repeat offender with active arrest warrants for domestic violence, despite nearly killing two people while driving drunk out of his mind, despite costing the American taxpayer almost certainly hundreds of thousands of dollars, Robles not only walked free, but he hardly broke a sweat.

Far from fearing even enforcement of the law—let alone the waging of some war of terror against immigrants— Robles displayed all the confidence that the system would actually work for him, not against him.

His confidence wasn't misplaced. The system; as administered by veteran jurists and prosecutors, didn't disappoint him.

And there are thousands, tens of thousands, maybe even hundreds of thousands of Humberto Robleses roaming California today; from vicious gang members who deal death to rapists to drunk drivers—all seemingly unaware or unafraid that there is a war of oppression being waged against them, and all too often literally laughing their way through the system right back out onto the streets again.

The virtual collapse of immigration enforcement even among criminal suspects is a pull factor of the most ominous kind, with some of the most tragically deadly results.

***

It's a Friday evening during peak rush hour as I make my way out of downtown Los Angeles, crawling east in the stop-and-go traffic along Interstate 10 as part of the now iconic daily mass commuter migration to and from suburbs that stretch over the Cajon Pass into the high desert boom-and-bust towns like Victorville as well as deep into the eastern reaches of San Bernardino County. The mind-numbing, unsustainable insanity of three-hour commutes by hundreds of thousands of single-occupant automobiles apparently remains beside the point during Southern California's continuing implosion in 2011—it simply continues on its own momentum.

I have ridden and driven this stretch of freeway since the late 1960s and the spasms of growth and decay that have blossomed and withered along its corridor are engraved in my mind. Each time I drive it, I am confronted with some memory of what it was that stands in sharp contrast with what it is—all in grim prelude to what certainly is coming to this megalopolis of 15 million people jammed into a desert.

It will make the inevitable ghost town fates of Phoenix and Las Vegas look like a matinee before the main feature.

My quiet marveling at the slow burn of teeming humanity that is so evident amid the epic sprawl of Greater Los Angeles from the air-conditioned confines of my Saturn VUE is brought to a sudden end with a literal bang. In a single instant I hear a loud, sharp smashing crash and look up just in time to see the car behind mine hurtling into what

I instantly know will be impact with my Saturn. *Bang!* My VUE is thrown violently forward but fortunately doesn't strike the car in front of me.

What follows over the next hour in the aftermath of the accident perfectly exemplifies a small but critical piece of the larger culture of complicity that is now indeed the pull factor for millions of immigrants streaming illegally into the United States.

As the three cars involved in the accident limp over to the shoulder of the freeway, the car that triggered the accident by slamming into the car behind me pulls ahead of us and the driver, a middle-aged Latino man, leaps out of the vehicle once it comes to a stop, runs to the passenger side of the car, and gets in, settling into the passenger seat. The woman who had been in the passenger seat slides over into the driver's seat, then nonchalantly gets out of the car, walks back to where I am standing with the driver of the car that was first rear-ended and hands us a driver's license.

"Here's my license," she says without batting an eye.

"You weren't driving the car. He was," says Brenda, the middle-aged Black woman who was first hit. "We need to talk with him."

"No, I was driving the car. He doesn't drive," says the woman, whose driver's license identifies her first name as Lisette. "I was driving."

"Look, the guy in your car was the guy behind the wheel. We all saw it; we watched you play musical chairs. Now get him out of the car and tell him to come talk with us. We need his information," I say, as Brenda begins to call 911.

"He doesn't have any information to give you," Lisette offers somewhat sheepishly. "He has no license, no ID or nothing like that. He doesn't speak English." She then informs us she doesn't have insurance either.

As we wait for the California Highway Patrol to arrive, the guy finally gets out of the car and walks back to where Brenda and I are standing next to our cars. He lights a cigarette and moves around our cars looking at the damage, then says a few things to Lisette in Spanish. She looks at us and says, "His brother runs an auto body repair shop and he says if you take it there he and his brother will fix your cars for you. That way we can get going." I get the sense that he's thinking about splitting either way.

I remind her the cops are on their way, the accident has already been reported, and I will be going through my insurance company to handle the repairs. She relates this to him in Spanish. He shrugs and walks back over to their car. A metro emergency tow truck arrives to see if we need anything. The tow truck driver, a middle-aged Chicano, asks us what happened, then goes up to the other guy, speaks to him in Spanish, and comes back to us shaking his head.

"You know the score," he says to me. "No license, no papers, no *nada*. I see it all the time out here. Wadda ya gonna do?"

He checks with dispatch and inquires as to when the CHP officers may arrive. "They're *still* on their way," he says with a wave. "It's busy out here tonight. Good luck!"

The CHP finally arrives nearly an hour after the accident, and the officer works the scene with a cool, proficient professionalism, taking each of our statements. I describe the accident and the musical drivers that played out in its immediate aftermath. The officer actually breaks into a bemused chuckle. "Yeah, I figured as much, but that's not what they're telling me, of course."

He finishes taking my information and statement and then lets me go on my way. As I merge back into traffic that is still moving little more than a slug's pace, I get a final look at the driver of the car that triggered this three-car collision, noting that he seemed remarkably cool for someone who is almost certainly in the country illegally. In spite of the relentless hysterical rhetoric from the proponents of mass immigration and the network that supports and sustains millions of illegal immigrants that America is waging a "war of racist terror" against Mexicans—this illegal driver/ immigrant seemed as cool as a cucumber. As if he knew he had little if anything to actually fear.

And by almost every measure, he doesn't.

He seems to know, perhaps by previous experience, that he will not be taken into custody for driving without a license, registration, or insurance. In all likelihood, he wasn't arrested for providing false information to an officer at the scene of an accident. And even if the CHP officer did impound the vehicle and take him into custody, unless he has a previous arrest and conviction for a violent crime already in the system, he probably knows there is a better than even chance he's simply going to be released back onto the streets in a matter of days, if not hours.

The result has been unfolding in real time across Southern California for years, as tens of thousands of immigrants climb illegally behind the wheel and head off to jobs (employment they have no legal right to hold either, but have learned they have about as much to fear at the worksite as they do in the driver's seat of their car) in what in some neighborhoods looks like a cross between bumper cars and a demolition derby on the streets.

Throughout the past decade, law enforcement and emergency first-responders have reported surreal traffic collision scenes where they arrived to find smashed up cars abandoned. One officer I know described them as "Rapture crashes," where the cars collide and the people in them suddenly vanish. Motorists and passersby throughout Southern California have long been witness to sporadic crashes that end with numerous people from one or more vehicles simply jumping out and running scattershot in every direction.

The long-term effect of this chaotic wave has been a slow, corrosive tide of attrition that has now permeated virtually every element of society in California, soaking it in a malaise of exhausted acceptance. As the tow truck driver noted with a shrug: "You know the score… wadda ya gonna do?"

The answer has consistently been "nothing" for a long enough time by local, county, state, and federal officials—from the highways to the hospitals to the worksites to the schoolyards and everywhere else—that a logical, enforceable sense of order has simply been overrun to the point where it's now in many respects nearly erased, rubbed away to a new order of a culture that lives largely in the moment, and only from one moment to the next. It's simply a world in which producing a license, registration, and proof of insurance at an accident scene is, well, beside the point.

Those aren't just cars that are crashing, but actual worlds that are colliding.

And as high irony would have it, it's the American cultural foundations of reliable order, accountability, and responsibility that are being totaled and written off, one by one, a little more each day.

For the two Americans standing on the side of the freeway that evening, producing on demand the documents that we are legally required to have, it was a blistering indictment of a system that has collapsed into a cynical impotence that ultimately caters to the illegal immigrant. We pay thousands of dollars annually for insurance and to register our vehicles, fees that a now perpetually broke Sacramento legislature continues to jack up in endless efforts to staunch the state's financial bleed-out. We play by the rules despite the continually escalating costs that we can barely afford; and yet at such accident scenes, we are treated to a front row presentation of the consequences—or lack thereof—of people who not only don't play by the rules, but who in fact are encouraged to ignore them.

For us, it wasn't just our bumpers that were crumpled, and it was far more than our nerves that were shaken. No, the damage runs far deeper than that; and it's far more fundamental. For every American citizen involved in such an accident, or waiting it out in a swamped emergency room, or whose children have been crowded out of the neighborhood school, or who are waiting for their unemployment checks to run out even as they drive by worksites where only Spanish is being spoken, the lasting injury is the emotional one, the psychic wound that leaves us with a deep scar of betrayal.

These sorts of wounds are now festering all over the nation, deepening an already dangerous chasm between the working middle class in America—long its stabilizing social rudder and engine of its progressive programs—and a government that seems increasingly unresponsive to the demands of its own citizens.

It only takes common sense and an intellectual willingness to step outside the shouting matches, the politically correct No-Fly Zones, and the cultish sloganeering to grasp that the United States simply can't continue to absorb the waves of immigrants that it has been accepting legally and otherwise over the past four decades while at the same time even pretending to offer a better future with more opportunities for its own citizens. Playing make-believe that endless mass immigration is what really fuels America's economic growth (versus our ingenuity and exceptionalism), which in turn supports the entitlement programs for the nation's seniors, will not make those hard facts and bottom-line limitations any less so.

Ultimately, the United States is facing the consequences of its own historically unprecedented success: never before has one nation offered so many people such real opportunity, prosperity, and freedom for so long. The proverbial American Dream became a reality for enough of its citizens that the power of its global brand is now indisputable—and that is the ultimate pull factor. The proof is evident in the millions of people who are planning—not dreaming, but planning—to come here, legally or otherwise, even as you read this. The pull factor isn't a job in a lettuce field somewhere outside of Bakersfield or an assembly line in

Mississippi or a construction site in Pennsylvania. No, the pull factor is that America is a fundamentally benevolent, wealthy nation that simply offers more hope on its worst day than these immigrants' home countries do on their best day.

It's simply delusional to suggest that illegal immigrants—a population that may well now number close to 30 million men, women, and children—are willing to voluntarily return to countries that many of them risked humiliation, extortion, dehumanizing brutality, kidnapping, and even death in merciless treks in order to escape. The vast majority of illegal immigrants harbor no intent or desire to return to countries where they had lost all hope. But before America can have an honest national conversation about how many people here in violation of our laws will have to leave, there first should be an open discussion as to how many more people the country can take.

If we wait until the quality of life in America—its true pull factor—has corroded to the point for the majority of its citizens that its glow has finally dimmed across the world stage and mass immigration begins to naturally decline in significant numbers, then the game will have been long over for most Americans, to say nothing of the legion of new arrivals.

California, once the window display of the success of the American way of life from higher education to healthcare, should now serve as a three-bell fire alarm as the Golden State buckles under unsustainable mass immigration and growth while its tax base shrivels.

As daunting as the task may seem given government intransigency and the visceral attacks from some supporters of mass immigration that are rooted in a highly balkanized, stridently ethnocentric agenda; the challenge of staunching mass illegal immigration from its present flood to a trickle of insignificant numbers pales in comparison to the grim future most working Americans will face if we continue to accommodate it.

A FENCE BETWEEN FRIENDS

There may not be a wall on the border, but illegal immigration is building barriers in personal relationships all over the country

First published in 2006

The high-voltage debate over illegal immigration that is crackling across America isn't just dividing Anglos and Latinos, conservatives and liberals, Democrats and Republicans, the House and the Senate.

No, it's getting increasingly personal between friends, especially those of us on the Left.

So I recently discovered when I began writing for Californians for Population Stabilization (CAPS), a non-profit think tank based in Santa Barbara that has focused on the state's population spike as a result of illegal immigration and the resulting impacts on the environment, American culture, and our collective quality of life.

While I have never been much for slapping generic labels on people or their viewpoints, it's fair to say that my politics have been practiced primarily on the left side of the aisle for the better part of the past three decades. I cut my teeth in the anti-nuclear movement of the early 1980s; volunteered as a foot soldier for Sen. Alan Cranston; professionally consorted with faux progressive Larry Flynt and socially cavorted with the real McCoys like Sen. George McGovern, Cesar Chavez, and renegade tripper Timothy Leary.

I supported Dennis Kucinich in 2004 and when his quixotic campaign ended, I voted Green that November.

Perhaps that is why I have watched the blood drain from the faces of more than a few of my friends, cohorts, and fellow journalists as I explain that I signed on as a "Senior Writing Fellow" for CAPS and am now wielding my figurative pen in support of seriously cracking down on illegal immigration—that sustained human wave I have watched erode the social services, job opportunities, and quality of life in Pomona, CA, the working-class town of my birth and where I have lived virtually my entire life.

The response from my cohorts, stretching from LA's bohemian Echo Park and the chic Westside all the way up to the Golden Gate, has been fast and more than occasionally quite furious. It seems my position, however steeped in concern for the environment and quality of life for the American working and middle classes, has crossed some ideological red line, a cultural No-Fly Zone.

I was no longer just sleeping with the enemy (I admit I have something of a fetish for Republican women); I had now *enlisted* in their cause. My long history as a contributor to the *LA Weekly* was suddenly recast more in the light of "infiltration."

When Rush Limbaugh read one of my columns for CAPS on the air during his drive-time morning show, almost immediately I could hear air-raid sirens blaring from my email account. The bombing had begun.

"I don't know whether to laugh or to cry," one friend announced in a mass email.

"Believe me, I'm crying," replied another. "I am really surprised by your vehement disdain for so many things Mexican."

"I'd like to congratulate you, but I can't bring myself to do it," advised an old colleague and friend, before going for the backhand slap: "You've been called many things in your colorful career, but 'Tool of The Man' has never been one of them." Until now, that is.

Another sounded more like a disgusted parent: "Rush Limbaugh!? Are you proud of yourself?"

Some friends have dropped off all together, offering the proverbial cold shoulder.

In short order, it seems I have devolved from a maverick Liberal into a pawn of The Man, a mere dupe of the GOP's Machiavellian scheme to divide and conquer the electorate with yet another wedge issue. I have become a political heretic, joining the anti-Mexican, Nativist, xenophobic, saliva-drooling Gabacho mobs hyped up by "hate radio" and eager to prey upon proud but vulnerable immigrants whose crime is working in American fields without papers.

I would be lying if I said some of the flak wasn't distressing to me, especially the toxic suggestion that CAPS is some "creepy anti-immigrant group" with a "final solution" approach to population control, as one of my Lefty friends put it.

I found myself countering such claims by telling any of them who would listen that CAPS, in fact, is made up of former Sierra Club activists, respected academics, and good people hailing from the full range of American political identities, brought together to confront what we agree is a crisis. I told them I found it refreshing to be working with Democrats, Greens, and—*gasp!*—Republicans on the issue of overpopulation, which is like AIDS twenty years ago: a crisis politicians won't talk about.

I repeatedly offered my own background of being raised on the multi-ethnic, working-class streets of Pomona, cataloging the history of my deep, real-world friendships with Latinos and Chicanos, which stands in stark contrast to the dinner party multi-culturalism that still conveniently passes as hard currency in some Left circles.

And I shipped some of what I received, telling my friends that they reminded me of a low-calorie version of Mao's Red Guards, indulgently playing make-believe revolution and bravely shouting, "*Viva la causa!*" from their barricades at Starbucks. "No person is illegal" plays well on their Volvo bumper stickers, until of course it's *their* job, property value, emergency room, or neighborhood school that is SRO with impoverished refugees.

Then I realized I was just playing a time-honored game, one that's increasingly employed against people with honest opposing points of view in order to force them to defend their character personally—and their motives politically—against a wide variety of insidious smears, rather than argue the issues on the basis of fact and genuine disagreement.

So now I feel far more liberated than hurt and I can thank some of my friends for confirming just how paper-thin their tolerance truly is for ideological diversity.

Indeed, the reaction by some of my friends and colleagues has splayed open to the bone just how intellectually bankrupt many self-declared progressives can be when frantically clinging to politically correct orthodoxy on the issues of illegal immigration and overpopulation.

And just how bitterly personally they can take a dissenting point of view.

The good news is that real friendships are based on far more than being faithful political bedfellows, and they will survive accordingly.

I suspect there will be a mild culling of my larger social roster this summer, with my name conveniently vanishing Soviet-purge style off a few invite lists. Well, so it goes.

My close circle's reaction has encompassed all the stages of a sudden trauma: shock, denial, anger, and among some, the slow drip of a begrudging acceptance.

I saw the glint of this social détente at a barbeque in Echo Park the other day, where I took (and gave) some lighthearted jabs before being handed a plate of ribs, beans, a cold beer, and a place at the table.

As my Uncle Lorn used to say, "Here's to champagne for my real friends, and to real pain for my sham friends."

The way it should be.

SACRED COWS IN THE CITY OF ANGELS

When it comes to reporting on illegal immigration, some journalists just stick to the script

First published in 2007

As an active member in "good standing" of both the Los Angeles Press Club and the Society of Professional Journalists, I was quite confident last summer that my offer to organize a panel discussion of a hot-button issue would be readily embraced by both associations.

I proposed that we assemble a group of reporters and media wonks to dig into an issue at the core of the illegal immigration debate and its coverage in the news: the ubiquitous practice of labeling opponents of illegal immigration as "racists," "xenophobes," and other toxic terms that smacks of a new McCarthyism.

Do reporters have an ethical obligation to weigh the validity of such accusations of racism?

Or do our professional standards release us from anything beyond slipping the charge between quotation marks and letting the reader sort it out? Is there any threshold of authenticating the claims of an accuser leveling these charges? Is there any burden upon the person making the charge to demonstrate that the person they are calling a bigot actually is one?

What news value is brought to the reader by merely passing along such polarizing rhetoric?

It's a hot issue, it's a great opportunity to explore an ethical question that's central to how we do our jobs as journalists, and I was volunteering to help put it together. I was looking forward to hearing all perspectives on the matter. I figured it was a no-brainer.

That was in August.

Going on five months later, I am still waiting to hear back—even a courtesy "no thanks"—from Anthea Raymond, a reporter for NPR and the president of the Los Angeles Press Club, to whom I directed my pitch.

Just to make sure my proposal wasn't lost in the shuffle, I followed up repeatedly as the weeks and months rolled by via certified letters, emails, faxes, and phone messages taken by the press club's executive director Diana Ljungaeus— who assured me that Raymond had indeed received my proposal and follow-up correspondence.

"I don't know why she hasn't replied," Ljungaeus mused.

Well, I think I do.

As the head of the dominant press association in greater Los Angeles, I suspect that Raymond is really just *doing her job* by ignoring the proposal and its central question. An open, freewheeling and, God forbid, critical analysis of how the media is handling this issue is simply not in the cards. It's nothing personal.

That stonewall deftly displays the arrogant contempt that is deemed mandatory in much of the media today at even the suggestion that the press is out of touch with the rest of America on the issue of illegal immigration.

Raymond's silent treatment is the outward expression of that contempt: the very premise of the proposal is unworthy of even a response, let alone honest consideration. She may not have personally bristled at my request, but Raymond clearly feels comfortable enough that the Los Angeles Press

Club is in ideological lockstep enough on this issue that she could safely discard it without so much as a reply.

And that says a lot.

You would be hard pressed to find a more sacred, gilded cow among much of the traditional media today than that of the "undocumented worker." Conventional wisdom at news desks and among editorial boards across the country clings desperately to the central tenet that the illegal immigrant living in America today is oppressed and impoverished, indentured and abused.

As the cliché goes: illegal immigrants are "living in the shadows."

Accordingly, the heavy in this storyline are the citizens, particularly of the White variety, who dare to speak out against illegal immigrants and the corrosive impact they are having on local and state budgets, the environment, and the quality of life in working- and middle-class neighborhoods.

By definition alone, White citizens in this media production tend to be mean-spirited and bigots by association, if not at heart. It's a script that has been in circulation so long throughout newsrooms that I am surprised it hasn't been codified in the AP Stylebook. Yet.

In Los Angeles, this schematic is now as fundamental to reporting the issue of illegal immigration as learning the "inverted pyramid" style is to students in Journalism 101.

Unlike Raymond over at the LAPC, the Los Angeles chapter of the Society of Professional Journalists did manage to respond, after a couple of months and several follow-ups on my part in an effort to shake an answer out of them. Chapter President David Dow, formerly of CBS News, informed me that my proposal had been scheduled for discussion, but was then put on hold since the SPJ "diversity chair" wasn't at the meeting.

Raised at a later meeting of the SPJ board, Dow emailed me to say that the board determined that my proposal was "a legitimate part of a broader discussion of journalistic coverage of race-related issues." Dow thanked me for taking the time to pass my proposal along and noted it would be kept on file for possible use at a future date.

As the saying goes around Hollywood: "Don't call us, we'll call you."

Whether Raymond's icy silence or Dow's polite brush off truly reflects an attitude prevalent among the national press associations was at least partly answered last year by a cover story in *The Journalist*, the glossy trade magazine published by SPJ.

Entitled "The Immigrant: Spirit of America," the cover photograph features a father with his small daughter sitting on his shoulders, both grasping an American flag. It's a great shot that evokes powerful symbolism.

But journalist Brian Grow's story gives light to the message behind the cover photograph, which is yet another depiction of Caucasian citizens as one-dimensional racist caricatures. Grow compares illegal immigrants to the African Americans who struggled for their constitutional rights (conveniently skipping the part about Blacks being American citizens), evoking Martin Luther King and violent Freedom Summers.

Then, on cue, the modern-day descendants of Sheriff "Bull" Connor make their appearance.

"[T]here is an ugly side," writes Grow, a reporter for *BusinessWeek* in Atlanta. "Those seeking a crackdown muster their forces to patrol the southern border, blame immigrants for disease, report them to police, and harass them at job sites."

In case you missed the point, Grow brings it home by noting, "The anti-immigration cabal will rail that the nation is being overrun with freeloaders, leaving schools burdened, jobs poached."

Grow's closing summation suggests that if America succumbs to actually enforcing its immigration laws and protecting both its sovereignty and its citizens, it's the Klan that will have prevailed.

It's not that the inspiring stories of immigrants—both legal and illegal—should *not* be told in the media. Nor is the problem that writers like Grow unabashedly embrace them to the point of intentionally stilting the portrayals of those opposed to illegal immigration in such a poisonous manner that it becomes propaganda—not honest journalism.

The problem rests, journalistically, when the same storyline is recycled again and again, at the expense of other competing and often contradictory stories. While the struggling undocumented worker has approached mythic lore in the media, Americans and particularly Whites are left wondering whether their stories of economic hardship and displacement matter; whether their views on illegal immigration count?

Increasingly they have reached the conclusion that they don't. While right-wing pundits tend to view Grow's perspective as a pathetic manifestation of "White guilt" that runs abundant in an overwhelmingly liberal profession, they overlook the more potent vein of class status that courses deep through such stories.

Reporters radiate such disdain for the White working and middle classes—and therefore so easily affix the dismissive label of "bigot" upon them—because they tend to view them as losers; as embarrassments; as a rabble of distant relatives better to be avoided.

Championing the huddled masses of impoverished, illiterate economic refugees fleeing the failing nation-state of Mexico and yearning to breathe free makes these same journalists feel better about themselves; even as it reinforces their own quiet notions of superiority. Listening to Whites describe their frustrations, struggles, and hardships as a result of the impact of illegal immigration is simply counter-intuitive for many reporters. They just don't go there.

Indeed, the dirty little secret among reporters in major metro markets like Los Angeles is that the White working class that still dominates the nation's heartland is viewed as little more than a tribe of red state cavemen who hunt, drink beer out of cans, listen to country music, failed their GEDs, and sadly cling to outdated religious values that are based upon superstitious concepts like "good" and "evil."

In the minds of many major metro scribes, the great geographical sweeps of White America is truly The Land That Time Forgot. They deride it as "fly-over country," a place that's better viewed from 35,000 feet while *en route* to the coasts.

So, when Anglos living in the seemingly cosmopolitan oasis of Southern California take a position against illegal immigration, it immediately evokes a visceral reaction from news desks and editorial writers alike.

And thus, when a story is written about White activists opposed to illegal immigration, the inclusion of a quote or two from a Chicano studies professor or a Latino activist calling them racist hate-mongers becomes standard issue. Even if the action proposed by the anti-illegal immigration activists is seemingly benign, their personal motivation, as a result of their whiteness, is always suspect.

Deep-seated anger over the one-dimensional portrayals of Whites in the media and their total exclusion from having an ethnically identifiable voice on the editorial pages is the jet fuel that has propelled talk radio in LA, making KFI 640 and KABC 710 twin outlets for largely working- and middle-class Whites' views.

Not surprisingly, the stations have been dubbed "hate radio" by a media establishment furious that Anglos might demand some semblance of equal time given to their perspective on the issues.

This journalistic orthodoxy has ruled at a price for some traditional news outlets in the City of Angels. The *Los Angeles Times* has hemorrhaged readers and credibility for years, in no small part as a result of its editorial page view increasingly dictating how it covers illegal immigration and race relations on its news pages.

The newspaper that legendary publisher Otis Chandler once pushed into greatness recently suffered a devastating left hook from the *LA Weekly*, which exposed the *Times*'s soft-peddling an explosive story of three Caucasian women who were victims of a brutal hate crime.

Of course, the *Times* didn't have much to say about the *Weekly*'s detailed evisceration of its anemic and slanted coverage of a story that would have dominated the *Times*'s front page every day with multiple bylines and shrieking headlines—if only the victims had been the *right color*. Or more specifically, had *more color.*

Like Raymond's official silence on behalf of the Los Angeles Press Club, the *Times* brooks few questions over the editorializing of its news coverage, but instead marches stoically back to a Leftist variant of its pre-Otis roots, when the newspaper was little more than a cheap shill that served California's then-powerful right wing.

Perhaps I am being too hard on Raymond and too suspect of Dow at SPJ.

After all, I have long known that both professional associations, in Los Angeles anyway, are frequently nothing more than a tax-deductible reason for journalists to dress up and party down.

And perhaps the only thing reporters love more than a hosted bar is an award with their name on it, thus both clubs work feverishly to fulfill those needs.

When I renewed my SPJ membership late last year, I received a DVD in the mail of the group's annual awards bash. A few weeks later, SPJ sent me a survey about the DVD, apparently in an effort to devise an even bigger and better awards show that members can watch over and over again.

Yet I can't believe the SPJ fete could top the Los Angeles Press Club's annual orgy of self-congratulatory indulgence: the Southern California Journalism Awards. A glitzy night held in elegant ballrooms, the LAPC's awards blowout allows reporters to bask in a low-watt version of the Oscars, complete with emotional acceptance speeches bathed in the glow of spotlights.

Such fleeting recognition may indeed be well deserved by reporters who nail a great story, but as a profession we should demonstrate our accountability to a higher standard through tangible actions, not just rhetoric from the dais.

While the courtesy of a reply would have been, what's the word—*professional*—I suppose if Anthea Raymond can raise enough money to pay for the annual bash and its shiny trophies, well, I guess that's enough.

Oh, I did finally get a letter from the Los Angeles Press Club last week, albeit a photocopied form letter. Raymond and the board thanked me for renewing my membership.

Not to worry.

As Groucho Marx was fond of saying: "I'll join anyone for a drink."

But sometimes that's about all this press club is worth.

A LIBERAL'S BURDEN

When it comes to illegal immigration, Flagstaff hears Hollywood calling

First published in 2004

An acquaintance of mine—let's call her "Lisa"—who lives in a nice spread in the University Heights neighborhood of Flagstaff (about as swanky as that small mountain town gets) is what I would consider to be a quintessential liberal of the Hollywood-cum-Malibu breed: young, Cosmo pretty, educated, world-traveled, vibrant, and flush with dead presidents buried in her bank account.

She also employs an illegal immigrant.

Settling in for a drink with her not too long ago on the balcony at the legendary Zane Grey saloon, I listened intently as Lisa explained that as a single mom she needed the extra help taking care of her year-old son, so she hired "Rosario" as a nanny/maid to lend a full-time hand around the house.

While the flood of economic refugees from Mexico has long roiled California's political waters and set the stage for numerous showdowns in Texas, Arizona is now taking the brunt of the illegal migrant flow, with as many as a million refugees now living in the state.

With hospitals closing their trauma centers and social services collapsing over the strain, the wild west of Arizona is now facing a showdown on the issue.

Arizonians are scheduled to cast their ballots on the "Protect Arizona Now" initiative in November, which will require proof of citizenship to vote and to access a range of social services. Bearing shades of California's Prop. 187, the PAN initiative comes as a last-ditch effort to staunch the human tidal wave of Mexicans pouring into the state—the government reports that 2,300 illegal immigrants were captured daily in the Tucson District alone for the past five months, 95 percent of whom were Mexican.

The high-octane debate has finally highlighted corporations which hire illegal immigrants to drive down wages and grind as much profit from an exploited workforce, but private citizens like Lisa who hire the undocumented at home continue to skate along undisturbed, enjoying the same dynamic of exploitation that the corporate greed freaks indulge, just on a smaller scale.

Not that they would ever admit it. No, people like Lisa will offer downright egalitarian motives for passing over fellow Americans in favor of hiring illegal immigrants.

As the wind whipped wisps of her brunette mane across her beautiful face, Lisa blathered on about the wonders of having her son raised bilingually and "totally exposed to other cultures."

It sounded nice, I suppose, but we both knew what her decision to hire an illegal immigrant was really all about—money and power.

The irony of listening to a fashionably bohemian, six-figured corporate headhunter who protests the global disease of corporate excess blithely explain away her decision to personally employ an illegal immigrant was… well, entertaining, to be charitable about it.

When I asked her why she didn't hire an American—perhaps even an unemployed American struggling to find a job—she shrugged and simply said she couldn't find any citizens suitable for the job.

I had a feeling that she didn't exactly search far and wide.

The fact is Lisa hired Rosario for reasons that have nothing to do with broadening her son's cultural horizons or even finding good house help. If it really was about her son, then what kind of background check did Rosario go through? Did Lisa vet Rosario's employment history or conduct a criminal history check and mental health backgrounder to ensure the safety of her child?

Of course she didn't.

What it seems Lisa does know about Rosario—and it's all she knows—is that she lives in an apartment off Lake Mary Road that is crowded with other illegal immigrants, an assortment of family members, her lover and his family from Mexico, and other children he has had with another migrant. Fourteen people jammed into in a two-bedroom apartment.

Far from being an altruistic endeavor to help Rosario, I suspect that Lisa enjoys the fact that she isn't bound by minimum wage requirements, overtime rules, unemployment and disability insurance, and Social Security taxes—to name a few legal responsibilities of an employer.

And what recourse does Rosario have with Lisa, should any disagreement over a work-related issue arise? In a word: none.

So what's the difference between Lisa and thousands of other Arizonians just like her who hire illegal immigrants and the corporate giants in retail, restaurants, hotels, auto body shops, agri-business, and dozens of other industries that also pass over American citizens in order to squeeze every drop of profit possible out of migrants?

There is no difference, except maybe that people like Lisa insist on playing make-believe when they discuss their rationale for breaking the law, spitting in the face of Americans looking for work and exploiting economic refugees from Mexico.

So they dress it up with every excuse from insults like Americans "don't want these jobs" to absurdities such as increasing "cultural awareness" in their home.

Perhaps the most telling moment in my dialogue with Lisa was when I asked her if she was going to help Rosario become legal and work her way toward citizenship.

"No," she replied. "She doesn't want to become an American, she has no interest in being a citizen or learning English. She just wants to stay up here and work."

How convenient.

While many people would understandably like to see the estimated nine million illegal immigrants living in this nation deported home, I would equally like to see plantation owners like Lisa marched off to a Zen center—the kind surrounded by fences and razor wire—for a year or two of hard meditation.

BUREAUCRACY OF BETRAYAL

Government's calculated complicity in driving Americans out of their jobs is exposed in Pomona

First published in 2010

Some of the best busts, veteran cops will often tell you, sometimes begin by sheer happenstance: a broken taillight, an unhinged license plate, a careless gesture by a suspect, a slip of the tongue.

At The Watergate back in 1972, it began when an alert security guard discovered the lock of an office door had been taped open.

At Pomona City Hall earlier this fall, it began when the cops found a door wide open.

If Watergate became synonymous with the criminal enterprise that Nixon and his henchmen were running out of the White House, then what Pomona Police officers uncovered at their civic center is a small but glaring example of the low-grade treachery that is now pervasive throughout our government—from the Oval Office to city halls across the country—even as millions of Americans are hungry for work.

Pomona Police officers discovered the open door at City Hall on the Sunday morning of September 27, 2009, during a routine check. The building's alarm hadn't been triggered.

Inside, the cops found a woman carrying a few cleaning supplies.

The woman, who said she didn't speak English, told one of the Spanish-speaking officers that her name was "Esminda Giles," that she was 34 years old, and that she was part of the janitorial staff that cleans City Hall. The woman said that her son was really supposed to be working the janitorial shift, but that he was at a soccer game and so she was covering his shift.

But the cops knew this didn't look right. In fact, it looked very, very wrong.

"She had no uniform, no employee badge or contractor identification on her. She had no driver's license, no state identification card, no passport, nothing that would identify her; not even a Matricula Consular card to present us," said a police source familiar with the incident. "She was asked if she had any of type of identification at home, if she had left some form of ID there. She said 'no.' It wasn't much of a stretch at that point to assess that she was likely an illegal immigrant."

The woman told police she had been cleaning Pomona City Hall and other city facilities for more than five years. When officers summoned an on-call city facilities employee, he told them he had seen her cleaning City Hall during previous years—but told them he had no idea who she was either.

An electronic swipe-card is needed to gain access to City Hall without triggering the alarm, but the woman told officers that she didn't have a swipe-card. "When she was asked how she got into City Hall, she said she didn't remember," the police source said.

But one thing police said the woman did have in her possession were the keys to the city's offices, including the city attorney's office, the police department's administrative offices, human resources, the city clerk, planning and the water department; offices that contain confidential information of city employees and residents of Pomona.

"She effectively had the entire run of City Hall and everything in it to herself," the police source noted. "She had the keys to the kingdom and no one had even half a clue as to who she was."

Police photographed her, took her thumbprints at the scene, gave the City Hall keys to the facilities employee, and sent "Esminda Giles" on her way.

While she may well not have been committing any crime in City Hall that Sunday morning, the system that allowed her to be there—indeed the Pomona city government that effectively made sure she was there—is guilty of jettisoning standards and safeguards that protect American citizens and workers.

And they have been doing it for years.

In 2007, Pomona's contract for the outsourcing of its janitorial services for all city facilities came up for bid again. It's a job that includes cleaning City Hall and its council chambers, the city library, the police department, the city yard, and assorted satellite buildings belonging to the city.

According to city documents, eight "competitive bids" were received from contractors, with the Monrovia-based Haynes Building Services the high bidder at just over $318,000. Skyline Building Services in Torrance bid the work at more than $187,000, while Diamond Contract Services in Burbank offered to take the job for $178,665. Reliable Building Maintenance in Los Angeles bid more than $150,000 to clean Pomona's facilities.

Then there was the low bid, tendered by United Maintenance Systems, which had the original contract in Pomona dating back to 2001. United's bid was under $98,000—or more than three times lower than the Haynes bid. It was also nearly $90,000 less than the second highest bidder and more than $50,000 cheaper than the mid-range bid.

Pomona awarded United the contract, again.

"This company has provided janitorial service in Pomona for the last five years and has done a satisfactory job," a city staff report states. "Public Works staff has determined, due to their qualifications and experience, as well as the fact that they submitted the lowest responsible bid, that they are capable of continuing to perform this service."

"... as well as the fact they submitted the lowest responsible bid..."

Pomona City Manager Linda Lowry said in an email this week that an investigation has been launched into the incident.

The city should investigate and perhaps indulge a little municipal soul-searching as well, as the incident raises serious questions of whether Pomona is intentionally turning a blind eye to brazen violations of the terms of its own contracts as well as intentionally ignoring whether state and federal labor laws are being followed.

It also raises the question of just how a janitorial firm can offer such a low bid on a large worksite and still turn a profit?

According to city documents, Pomona's City Hall and other facilities covered under the janitorial contract—but not including the police department—account for nearly 125,000 square feet of floor space that needs to be cleaned Monday through Friday, along with 76 sinks, 97 toilets, and eight showers that must be scrubbed.

Daily duties for janitorial staff also include polishing of mirrors and frames, polishing of metal fixtures, disinfection of sinks and commodes, cleaning of water fountains, maintaining of bottled water dispensers, sanitary napkin dispensers emptied and cleaned, stairways and landings swept. And that doesn't count a separate weekly list of cleaning chores for janitors.

Then there are the police headquarters and other police facilities, which account for nearly 60,000 square feet of more flooring to be cleaned in a staggered schedule throughout the week, work that includes scrubbing 32 sinks, 44 toilets, and seven showers.

That's a hell of a lot of labor to cover, as well as all the cleaning supplies, which the janitor service must also provide.

Calls to management at United Maintenance Systems went unreturned.

"In today's competitive business environment, cutting costs is essential," the company's website states. "At United Maintenance Systems, we are firmly committed to developing ways to increase efficiency and quality of service, while striving to save you money on your janitorial expenses."

Angie Zavala, a vice president at Haynes Building Services, which lost its bid for the Pomona contract, said that Haynes hires only citizens or legally documented immigrants and starts their workers at $10 an hour, well above the state's $8 an hour minimum wage. Zavala said the company pays higher wages to ensure a reliable quality in their labor force and meet the standards that contracting cities expect.

"You get what you pay for," Zavala said.

Haynes handles the janitorial services for Rancho Cucamonga, a city of comparable size to Pomona, and Zavala said that her firm always maintains bilingual lead supervisors at worksites if their workers at the location aren't fluent in English.

In fact, the contract that United Maintenance Systems signed with Pomona requires that "on-site, supervisory personnel of a high professional caliber, including bilingual communication ability if any contract crew member does not have a working knowledge of the English language."

The contract states that janitorial services are to be provided during weekdays at City Hall, not on Sunday.

The contract also states that United Maintenance Systems must comply with the city's building security regulations "... in such a way as to safeguard the city's personnel, equipment, and property."

Yet on the face of it, when Pomona's officers discovered "Esminda Giles" roaming City Hall unsupervised, without any identification, unable to speak English, and on a day when janitorial workers aren't supposed to be in the building, that constitutes a serious failure of the system.

Rob Baker, president of the Pomona Police Officer's Association, said the incident was likely a disturbing side effect of slashing budgetary costs. "I believe it's simply a matter of contracting services to the lowest bidder and having no mechanism in place to ensure quality control," Baker said in an email.

The police association raised the issue with Pomona Police Chief Dave Keetle several days after the incident. "We explained our concerns and asked if confidential information is stored in a secure manner within City Hall," Baker said. The head of Pomona's Human Resources assured Keetle that confidential information is kept in "locked rooms" that janitorial staff cannot access, according to Baker.

Yet another police source familiar with the incident was incredulous at any suggestion confidential information is being protected.

"Who are they trying to kid? She was in there with the keys for offices throughout City Hall," the police source said. "She could have been anyone, with any agenda whatsoever. Mexican Mafia? An identity thief? Or maybe she was just who she claimed to be: an immigrant mother covering for her son? The point is we don't know because the city doesn't check. And that puts us all at risk."

Baker knows just how deep and real that risk can run.

"The incident on September 27 wasn't the first 'episode' involving contract janitorial services," Baker said. "In fact, there was an incident a few years ago where a close relative of an outstanding murder suspect had gained access to the police department and was performing janitorial duties for a 'family member.' This caused grave concern for investigators and prompted an immediate change in service."

Baker suggested that perhaps the only way to elevate standards and accountability is for Pomona to return to hiring its own janitorial staff as city employees. "The downside is the cost involved," he said, "which during this time of national economic crisis is a very real consideration. The question now is: 'What price is too high for the security of confidential information?'"

Whatever they feel the answer may be, one must wonder whether the City of Pomona will start conducting compliance checks anytime soon on its various contractors to ensure that even basic security protocols are being met and that all wage and labor laws are being enforced.

Or perhaps to cut costs even more, the city could dispatch employees to swing by Home Depot each day and hire the city's janitorial crew right out of the parking lot, doling the jobs out as daily "piece work" like the old company towns of the Great Depression. Pomona could offer a dime for every sink cleaned, a quarter for every toilet scrubbed.

But whatever Lowry and the rest of the management team that runs Pomona does from this point forward, one thing is certain: they can no longer say they aren't aware of what actual practices are occurring in the city, regardless of what their policies state.

This is important because on the day that a real city employee is attacked by an unidentified person roaming around City Hall; or as soon as city residents begin to have their identities stolen by some ghost-like pseudo janitor working an unauthorized graveyard shift; or as soon as an "Esminda Giles" slips and cracks her head open as she works alone in City Hall—when the lawsuits start to fly—the city can't say they didn't know what was going on.

They know damn well what's going on, because they're in on it.

On that Sunday morning back in September, a couple of Pomona cops didn't just come across a well-meaning but unauthorized janitor trying to cover for her soccer-loving son. No, they turned the lights on an insidious bureaucratic betrayal that is now endemic across California and much of the nation. It's a silent treason that has forced millions of citizens from their jobs and replaced them with the outsourced sweat of exploited illegal immigrants who toil for dimes on the dollar at the expense of unemployed Americans and financially strapped taxpayers.

It's the active and conscious complicity of our elected and appointed governing officials in corrupting the integrity of our system, weakening the security of our communities and abetting the dry rot that is eating away the very foundation of our nation.

AMERICA JUST SAID "NO"

Vox populi prevails on immigration

First published in 2007

If you listened carefully in the moments after the immigration bill was killed for a second time, a bitter gnashing and rending could be heard from the Senate floor all the way to the editorial boardrooms at the great metropolitan newspapers across the nation.

As the death of amnesty was announced Thursday morning, its most fervent supporters in Congress and the self-styled "mainstream media" began a hysterical meltdown that will slowly ebb to a simmering boil over the next few weeks as the post-mortems fly and payback is plotted.

The 46 votes that the architects of the legislation were able to garner to end debate on the bill was cold evidence that the unthinkable had occurred yet again: the American people's voice had risen above the control of the anointed gatekeepers and its furious echo rattled enough of the exclusive Senate to effectively kill the amnesty plan.

The rage that will now flow like lava in the aftermath of this bill's defeat will not surprisingly pour down upon talk radio, which gave voice to the vast sea of discontent that has been building among the American working and middle classes for years.

The true scope of the disconnect between the power structure inside the Washington beltway and its corporate media cohorts and the vast majority of America's working and middle classes will again be laid bare.

Rather than concede that there never has been any significant support for this bill among the American people, the bipartisan purveyors of mass amnesty will decry the caustic influence of a medium that is perhaps the last great forum for the opinion of the ordinary American.

Talk radio reaches deep into the proletariat because it only requires a dime store transistor radio and occasional access to a phone—much less than the blogosphere's threshold of a computer, an internet connection, and some web savvy.

Since *vox populi* is at its most pure and raucous form on the AM band, those senators who are the targets of the anger vented over the airwaves increasingly choose to dismiss the entire medium as "hate radio."

Over the past two weeks, senators as ideologically diverse as Hillary Clinton and Trent Lott have denounced the audacious nature of talk radio, hardly bothering to conceal their contempt for those unwashed masses who listen and participate in its daily roundtable.

And since they believe the medium *is* the message, the architects and media proponents of a bill that was brokered in the shadows of the Senate cloakrooms will now lash out against talk radio, hoping to silence it in advance of some future drive for mass amnesty.

Yet the venom they spew only betrays their entrenched sense of entitlement.

Consider that when the bill was first derailed several weeks ago, the reaction from the Senate floor to the editorial pages was swift and visceral.

Both *Newsweek* and the *Los Angeles Times* declared senators voting against this bill to be hostages of a radical "know-nothing fringe," a characterization that kept with the carefully scripted narrative rampant in both editorials and news coverage of the debate.

The editorial board at the *Wall Street Journal* claimed opponents of the legislation had a "cultural" agenda (that's an anemic way to call Americans "racists") and the *New York Times* has long been swinging for the fences in its denunciations of opponents of the amnesty bill.

But it was Geraldo Rivera who took that contempt over the top, shamelessly declaring on FOX News Channel that voting against the immigration bill was akin to Nazi street thugs who roamed German cities, pulling the pants off men they suspected were Jewish to see if they were circumcised. Yes, Geraldo stooped that low.

If there is any analogy to be made between the epic struggle of World War II and the atmosphere surrounding the immigration debate in America today, it isn't Geraldo's truly sick evocation of the Holocaust.

Rather, a better comparison would be of our federal government and the Vichy government that administered occupied France for the Nazis. Smug and self-serving senators telling working Americans that this bill was the best deal they could expect indeed carries the echo of a Vichy collaborator: accommodate surrender while pretending to preserve some shred of national sovereignty.

And like those collaborators a half-century ago who chaffed at the underground press of the resistance for exposing and chronicling their betrayal, official Washington and its courtier of media elites are truly whistling past their mutual graveyard if they actually believe it's the medium of talk radio that is the problem.

Talk radio is indeed the medium, but the defeat of the immigration bill is a triumph of the American people's *message*.

And that message will be ignored at Washington's peril.

SEE NOTHING, SAY NOTHING

A California health official loses his job for speaking out against illegal immigration

First published in 2007

Dr. Gene Rogers had a pretty good idea of what was coming when he saw his supervisor and a county security officer arrive at his office door. His supervisor was holding paperwork; the security guard was holding an empty box.

Rogers knew what they had come to do, and why they were doing it.

As the medical director for Sacramento County's Indigent Services program for the better part of the past decade, Rogers has waged a long fight against the central California county's practice of providing non-emergency medical care to illegal immigrants—a policy he says violates federal law and results in the poorest American citizens being denied the care they deserve.

Last week, that fight cost Rogers his job.

In a two-sentence memo to Rogers, the county's Health and Human Services Director Lynn Frank informed him that he was fired but thanked him for his services. No reason for his termination was offered, but then he didn't really expect one.

"Sacramento County knowingly violated state and federal laws, misappropriated taxpayer revenues, and diverted funds designated for indigent citizens to pay for services delivered to illegal aliens," Rogers said. "And they did so even as they cut the budget."

Rogers is the latest casualty on a frontline in the struggle over illegal immigration that's often overshadowed by mass street demonstrations, chaotic protests, and the widespread outrage sparked by the tragic deaths of Americans at the hands of illegal immigrants who should have been deported. It's a battle that has simmered throughout the government agencies and offices, from the courthouse to medical clinics to public schools and the frontline social program administrators who confront the reality of illegal immigration every day.

Many government employees remain silent in the face of what's happening; fearful for their jobs and perhaps doubtful they would make a difference. But Rogers, a Vietnam veteran, felt compelled to become a conscientious objector to the status quo.

The local cost of the medical treatment provided to illegal immigrants is small when contrasted to the billions of dollars the state and federal governments spend every year on the "undocumented," but the numbers have grown dramatically. According to county health officials, the hundreds of illegal immigrants who were being treated through the indigent program in the mid-1990s have now grown to thousands of people, with the annual cost to taxpayers swelling into the millions of dollars.

Ironically, when Rogers, 67, took the position of medical director for the indigent services program back in 1999, he arrived in the Central Valley with hardly a clue (let alone an opinion) about illegal immigration and its impact on social services. He had one goal: provide the best care possible for those who need it most.

As the years went by, however, that egalitarian perspective began to be tinged with cynicism as he watched poor citizens get squeezed out of the system even as illegal immigrants gleefully manipulated it, all while bureaucrats facilitated the rampant violations of the very laws they were entrusted to enforce.

"I've seen cases and case histories of patients who essentially have come up from Mexico for the express purpose of being treated here and then leaving to return home," Rogers said. "I've watched illegal immigrants brazenly demand free, non-emergency health care that was meant for our poorest citizens. I've heard them and their families complain. They feel entitled to it."

Rogers filed a lawsuit against the county in 2003 after county officials "stonewalled" him when he questioned why they were cutting budgets while still providing non-emergency medical treatment to people who have no legal right to be in the country. Rogers recounts staff meetings where the agendas had legal residency requirements listed under the euphemism "parking lot items."

"Basically, that was their way of saying leave it outside, you know, that it wasn't even to be broached," Rogers said. Considering he served in Vietnam as a forward-deployed doctor treating horrifically wounded soldiers, Rogers wasn't exactly intimidated by politically correct etiquette.

The lawsuit he filed was dismissed on a technicality and is currently under appeal in federal court, but its impact was felt in the state capital, causing a nervous Latino Legislative Caucus in California to push through a bill by State Sen. Deborah Ortiz last year that explicitly allows counties to "opt" to provide non-emergency medical care to illegal immigrants.

Feeling that he had exposed a bureaucratic conspiracy that silently circumvented the law for more than a decade and continues to subvert the will of the people, Rogers continued his quest to ensure that citizens and legal residents had priority at the front of the line when it came to medical services for the poor.

The county responded, Rogers said, by seeking to alienate him from his prior relationships with county medical staff and by methodically preparing to fire him—with a little humiliation thrown in along the way.

On one occasion, Rogers said, he was forced to sit through a staff meeting in which his supervisors asked case management nurses, one by one, if they had any issues or problems with him. None said they did, but it was a humiliating experience. Rogers said his job was then reclassified after eight years last fall and new duties were assigned to him. New benchmarks were assigned that he was expected to meet in short order. Then in May, he was given a letter of reprimand for referring to the program's patients as "lawful residents" as opposed to "eligible patients."

"I am concerned that you continue to focus on patients' immigration status," Program Manager Nancy Gilberti said in the letter. "Which is outside your and [the] program's purview."

And that's the problem: it's *always* "outside the purview."

Gilberti's remarks are indeed a fine reflection of a prevailing culture that has now emerged in many arms of government, a culture that will not tolerate anyone who dares to draw a distinction between American citizens and illegal immigrants. It's a culture that, in California at any rate, now pervades police departments, public schools and universities, social services, and healthcare. It's difficult to imagine Rogers being ruthlessly drummed out of his job if he had been advocating for illegal immigrants to receive free medical care.

But when someone like Rogers speaks up to question the impact on citizens of such allocation of funds for health services like those in Sacramento—the response is clear: sit down and shut up, or else.

The federal government sought to make examples out of Border Patrol Agents Ignacio Ramos and Jose Compean with a prosecutorial sledgehammer that sent them to prison for more than a decade each after they shot and wounded an illegal immigrant drug smuggler whom they caught bringing more than a million dollars of dope across the border. In Rogers's case, the message is less drastic but equally clear. They seek to eliminate his voice and intimidate any other public employee who might also question this policy of drawing no distinction between citizens, legal residents, and those who are in the United States illegally.

But considering that a young Dr. Rogers started his medical career trying to save the lives of American soldiers in the jungles of Vietnam, the county's apparatchiks are seriously mistaken and have picked the wrong target.

For Gene Rogers himself, his crusade is deeply rooted in those grim battlefields he found himself on more than 30 years ago: the young men he watched fight and die; men who sacrificed all for the very distinction that citizenship brings to Americans.

It's a distinction that Sacramento County and so many others may choose to ignore, but for Dr. Rogers, that loyalty is a sacred trust he's determined to keep.

HOLLYWOOD'S HYPOCRISY

The writers' strike reveals Left Coast outrage hinges on whose job is at stake

First published in 2007

What's the difference between an illegal immigrant on a job and a "scab" who crosses the picket line? After all, aren't both merely seeking work where they can find it? Aren't both willing to toil at a lower wage in an effort to feed their families?

The difference—at least in the ongoing strike by the Writers Guild of America—is Hollywood liberalism and the bi-coastal 213/212 area code universes that ideologically feed it.

For what the strike by the WGA has revealed yet again is that outrage among the Los Angeles-Manhattan intelligentsia over corporate greed, unfair labor practices, stagnating wages, and vanishing job security is directly related to the income and education level of those threatened.

Consider for a moment the hundreds of thousands of American workers in California alone who have been forced from jobs in construction, landscaping, auto body repair, cable installation, and a host of other jobs by an alliance of greed-driven employers and an ethnocentric lobby that's hungry for demographic power.

These aren't crop picker or dishwasher jobs that Americans allegedly won't do, but rather entire skilled and semi-skilled industries that have provided the butter and bread for the working-class table.

Where is the outrage within Hollywood's fabled "Thirty-Mile Zone" for these displaced workers?

If there's any anger at all, it's actually directed at the American workers and their supporters for daring to speak out against the employers and the illegal immigrants who brazenly break the law to replace them on the job. They are belittled as bigots and dismissed as protectionists unable to adjust in a global economy.

But when college-educated writers earning six-figure incomes that are padded with residuals take a bottom-line hit, the blood-curdling rage can be heard from Malibu to Martha's Vineyard.

The writers have taken to the streets for increased profit participation in the DVD and internet-based markets. Those who have crossed the line to continue work have been labeled far worse than just "scabs," and Ellen DeGeneres has faced the scalding wrath of the guild for daring to continue her show through the strike.

Now imagine what would happen if the studios decided to break this strike by using Canadian writers—by the thousands—who were coincidentally in the country illegally. And imagine if the political establishment then turned on the striking writers in support of the Canadians, labeling the American writers as hate-fueled "xenophobes."

The Canadian government, in cooperation with the networks and the entertainment lobby, might set up a web of advocacy groups staffed with legal teams to support the Canadians who were, after all, simply writing for wages that Americans considered too low.

Perhaps then Hollywood would release a satirical film entitled *A Day Without a Canadian* that mocked the plight of its former American writers by noting that Tinsel

Town would collapse if the government started enforcing immigration laws.

As outlandish as those circumstances may seem, that's pretty much what has happened over the past two decades in a wide array of industries that provided critical paychecks for the American working class. Blue-collar communities have faced greater competition from workers illegally in the country while simultaneously watching their access to education, health care, and other social services suffer as a result of overcrowding and limited resources.

On the Left Coast today, illegal immigrants who replace blue-collar American workers are portrayed as heroic, "hard-working immigrants." But the very moment they were to take a job from a privileged class of Americans (screenwriters, for example) you can bet they would get an instant Hollywood makeover into job-poaching "scabs."

As they scream about the networks' greed and unfair practices, it's a safe bet that many of these writers—who earn an average of $200,000 annually—have a nanny at home who doesn't speak English.

How many of them are paying their nannies overtime? How many are covering their payroll taxes, disability and unemployment insurance? Do they get paid time off? Do they offer health insurance?

Hardly. And that's precisely why illegal immigrants get the job.

In a fine touch of irony, the so-called "reality" television shows, which are cheaper non-union productions, may actually provide the networks with enough fresh programming to prevail in the strike.

If that happens, the guild's writers will get a small taste of the bitter reality show that working-class Americans have been subjected to for years.

DIVERSITY'S DEATH RATTLE

Public schools in Los Angeles offer a glimpse of our ethnically homogenous future

First published in 2008

Global warming may be the marquee issue of the moment among progressives, but greenhouse gases don't elevate body temperature to the fever that strikes many White liberals when the topic turns to racial and ethnic diversity. Indeed, few issues spark the passion that's evident as they praise the multiple benefits of racial diversity. Daring to question that politically correct orthodoxy in progressive circles is akin to administering a patellar reflex test—sure to prompt a knee-jerk reaction. That's when the kicking starts.

So it was a little strange that a stunning set of ethnic statistics provided by the Los Angeles Unified School District that appeared in a news story about school sports earlier this month were greeted with hardly a whimper.

It's surprising because the data demonstrates the virtual ethnic homogeny that has settled across a school district that loves to glory in its alleged diversity.

The death rattle of diversity can be heard wheezing from the schools across the failing LAUSD, even as it struggles to provide basic instruction amid basement-level test scores, exploding dropout rates, and the violent chaos that has gripped many of its campuses.

In contrasting demographic snapshots of LAUSD schools in 1980 and again in 2006, the sheer magnitude of the human tidal wave of sustained illegal immigration is inescapable. Latinos aren't just the dominant ethnic population on campus; they are now practically the *only* ethnic group at many of these schools.

Schools that were marginally weighted between Black, White, and brown students a generation ago are now approaching ethnic exclusivity; boasting Latino student bodies that eclipse every other group.

In 1980, Banning High had more than 1,100 Black students, 1,200 Latinos, and more than 400 Whites on campus. Today the school has 135 Black students, 59 Whites, and more than 3,000 Latinos.

Canoga Park High School had almost an equal Black and Latino student body in 1980, with both populations close to 300 students each. White pupils on campus numbered approximately 1,300. Today, Whites and Blacks combined on campus don't even total 300 students, while Latinos now number nearly 1,500 students.

At Fremont High, the ethnic makeover is as stark as the growth of the student population is staggering. In 1980, the school had more than 2,300 Black students, just over 100 Latinos, and three White kids. By 2006, Blacks numbered less than 500 students and the school was down to two White pupils, but Latinos had pushed well past 4,000 students on campus.

These three high schools reflect what has happened across not only LAUSD, but in school districts throughout Southern California, which have been forced to absorb such a massive wave of illegal immigration that it has effectively erased the tangible ethnic and racial diversity that had finally been achieved in public schools during the 1970s and '80s.

Even more intriguing is the ethnic composition of the public schools on LA's Westside, which is predominately Anglo, upscale, and viewed as politically progressive.

Yet neighborhood schools such as Walgrove Avenue Elementary and Mark Twain Middle School—which should be drawing significant numbers of Caucasian students from surrounding neighborhoods—instead are comprised almost entirely of Latino students.

According to the California Department of Education, during the 2006-07 school year Mark Twain had a student population that was 80 percent Latino and four percent White. Nearly half of the school's students were "English language learners" and 97 percent of these students spoke Spanish at home. More than 80 percent of the students at Mark Twain were enrolled in the school's free lunch program.

At Walgrove Avenue Elementary, the student population was 64 percent Latino and 13 percent White. More than a third of students were English language learners and 84 percent of these students spoke Spanish at home. Nearly 70 percent of the students at Walgrove were enrolled in the free lunch program.

The numbers betray a reality that all the sugary, feel-good rhetoric about diversity cannot conceal: White parents in liberal enclaves aren't willing to sacrifice their own children's education to schools that are overwhelmed with cultural and linguistic barriers that both drain resources and corrode the focus of instruction.

But politically correct orthodoxy dies hard, even in the cold face of facts.

One Westside mother recently used a popular online message board to recount the visceral reaction that a handful of White parents drew from the Latino parents who had been bussed in for a meeting at Mark Twain Middle School this fall.

"It was such a horrendous scene," the woman wrote. "They looked at us with such contempt and hatred."

Yet even as she recounted being shouted down, she couldn't help but praise the school's "wonderful diversity." White students at the school now number about four percent.

In the comment lines that followed her post, fellow Westside parents were quick to empathize with her—while noting they will be sending their kids to private schools.

KEEPING CNN HONEST

The most trusted name in news plays the race card

*"Be honest about what you see, get out of the
way, and let the story reveal itself."*

CNN Anchor Anderson Cooper

First published in 2008

As a journalist who has written about immigration and
population issues for the past several years, I was intrigued
when a reporter for CNN called and asked for an interview
about the issue of race and its ramifications in the discussion
over immigration, both legal and illegal.

Given my exploration of the politically correct
parameters that dictate how the issue of race is presented by
the media in the immigration debate, I figured this was an
opportunity to candidly make a variety of points that aren't
often heard on broadcast and cable news networks.

I wanted to specifically point out that the groups
which frequently label opponents of illegal immigration as
"racists" ironically tend to be the very same organizations
and individuals who routinely make brazen racial appeals to
their own ethnic constituency.

In short, I wanted to tell Anderson Cooper that I thought
it was pretty rich for people peddling strident Mexican
nationalism and shrieking *"Viva La Raza!"* to accuse anyone

else of being racist. Since CNN brands itself as "the most trusted name in news" and given that Cooper enjoys telling his viewers each night that he's "keeping them honest," well, I figured mine would be a welcome viewpoint—if only to expand the discussion.

That was my first mistake.

Gary Tuchman, a national correspondent for CNN, assured me over the phone that the special to be aired on Cooper's *360* show would be an honest exploration of the issue. They were looking for someone to address the oft-repeated charge that bigotry is fueling opposition to illegal immigration, Tuchman told me.

A few hours later I was on camera and Tuchman started to ask his questions, which were fairly generic at the start. But it didn't take long at all before Tuchman was essentially asking me, in a polite if incredulous manner, "So, how long have you hated Mexicans?"

And just when did I stop beating my wife.

I probably wouldn't have minded as much, were it not for the fact that he clearly was not interested in *anything* else I had to say—but rather was only looking for a White guy whose role in CNN's pre-written narrative was to deny being a bigot. He thus asked me essentially the same question repeatedly—*isn't it because they are Mexican and not Scandinavian that's really behind all this anger!?*—fishing for the appropriate sound bite.

It was a journalistic equivalent of a car dealership's "bait and switch" skullduggery.

So when the report aired, I wasn't exactly shocked to see the narrative unfold along a very tidy, PC plotline: Whites bemoan a "changing neighborhood," enter immigrant activist Angelica Salas who declares that racist "anti-immigrant" groups are pressuring presidential candidates to attack poor Latino migrants and then, on cue, I appear for literally five seconds to declare that we aren't really hate-mongers.

The irony is that Tuchman's reportage did indeed highlight just how race plays a part in the debate over immigration, in a way he and Cooper never intended: it laid bare how many reporters have given Latino activists and so-called immigrant rights groups a free pass to tar anyone who opposes their agenda as a racist.

It's quite simple: Latino activists and their surrogates make the charge to a media shill; Anglo opponents are then forced to deny them. And obscured in the contrived rancor is any substantive debate over the staggering impacts that a surging population of illegal immigrants has brought our communities—exactly what the immigrant activists want to avoid at all costs.

Noticeably absent from Tuchman's report was a Black perspective. In Southern California, long-established African American communities have been virtually overrun by illegal immigrants, forcing working-class Blacks to compete for already scarce resources, jobs, and affordable housing.

But I suppose Blacks decrying the impact that illegal and mass immigration has had on their everyday lives would have been corrosive to the script Tuchman had already produced for Cooper's newscast. Indeed, Salas might have had trouble with her lines had she been called upon to label Black opponents of mass immigration as racists.

After he got his sound bite, Tuchman told me he would call and see what I thought of the special report after it aired. Going on a week now, he still hasn't rung.

But now I understand why Cooper can't stop talking about "keeping them honest"—it's a Freudian slip.

Me thinks he protests just a little too much.

THE GREAT GUESSTIMATE

What's a few million people when counting illegal immigrants?

First published in 2010

For the past 25 years, politicians and activists have played it fast and loose when it comes to estimating the size of the illegal immigrant population in the United States. Before the 1986 Simpson-Mazzoli Act, proponents of the amnesty insisted it would cover about 900,000 people in the country illegally.

By the time it was over, more than three million illegal immigrants had taken advantage of its provisions.

With President Obama and Congress vying this summer for politically safe footing in the treacherous terrain of immigration policy, one might assume that accurately assessing the true scope of the problem would be an urgent federal priority.

But it isn't; nor is it likely to be any time before the so-called comprehensive immigration reform that the president is pushing comes to a vote, as the one thing the Obama administration doesn't want to do is spread panic.

In other words: keep the victim calm.

The 1986 amnesty triggered a land rush across the southern border that has resulted in a staggering population of illegal immigrants in the country today, though its massive size is acknowledged more in the way it's felt anecdotally across communities, through classrooms, emergency rooms, and jail cells.

No one seems quite sure precisely how many millions of illegal immigrants are now here, least of all journalists covering the issue.

Earlier this month, the *Los Angeles Times* published a figure of 11 million illegal immigrants in one story, and then a few pages later in the same daily edition, used a figure of 12 million illegal immigrants in another story. That's two news stories in the same newspaper on the same day identifying the same population—with a margin of error of a million or so people by the newspaper's math alone.

Other newspapers and magazines of record have used figures as wildly divergent as seven million to 15 million people when projecting the size of the illegal immigrant population.

Oh well, what's a few million people—give or take—when counting illegal immigrants?

While think tanks ranging from the Pew Hispanic Center to the Center for Immigration Studies have estimated the number to be close to 11 million, Bear Stearns published a detailed study in 2005 that concluded the population of illegal immigrants could be as high as 20 million people.

The obvious if unspoken reality is that no one has any reliably accurate figure of precisely how many millions of people are illegally in the country. While that's partly due to the clandestine nature of illegal immigration, much of this dearth of information is a result of government malfeasance and journalistic complicity.

Government at all levels has made it its responsibility to *not* count the numbers of illegal immigrants pouring into schools, hospitals, jails, and the fraud-infested ledgers of its welfare rolls. With the threat of being accused of "racial profiling" hanging over their heads like a Sword of

Damocles, government agencies have been conditioned to simply look the other way.

And many journalists, whether by ideological concurrence or sheer professional laziness or some mixture of the two, now provide more cover than critical examination.

This can be seen in the reflexive use of the figure of 11 million illegal immigrants in stories around the country, a figure that has remained oddly static in much of the media over a period of years, as if there has been no discernable net growth in this population even as Mexico continues to dissolve into a morass of violent chaos and corruption.

Journalistic complicity can also be seen in the unchallenged declarations from the White House about its "unprecedented" efforts to secure the border, allowing Homeland Security Secretary Janet Napolitano to offer vague assurances that "the numbers are all going the right way" when discussing interdiction and deportations.

It's a complicity that allows politicians to piously declare a humane solution must be found for the millions of illegal immigrants who have established deep ties with American communities, without being challenged by questions of what should happen to the millions of other illegal immigrants who have arrived here over the past few years, who have no deep or truly enduring ties.

Should they not be identified and deported? It's a yes or no question, but one that is simply not asked. And what of those illegal immigrants who have ignored deportation orders, disappearing again into America? Should they not be found and shown the door?

These questions aren't raised because the answers from the White House and the Congressional leadership are likely to further scare and enrage an already frightened and infuriated electorate. The result is a credibility gap that makes the dynamic between LBJ and the American people during the Vietnam War look like a simple misunderstanding.

Even in the absence of reliable data and in the face of journalistic acquiescence, the American people can safely bet on two things regarding an immigration reform bill: the problem is far larger than Washington will ever admit before the vote; and that illegal immigrants here just 15 minutes—let alone 15 years—will indeed be granted amnesty.

SUNLIGHT IN THE SHADOWLANDS

Actual background checks for illegal immigrants is pure fiction

First published in 2008

Those who bristle at the American people's refusal to support yet another mass amnesty for illegal immigrants frequently cite the need to bring them into the sunshine of the system in order to determine the true identities of the millions who, as the cliché has it, *live in the shadows*.

We are going to document the "undocumented," they say.

Background checks, we are told, will be conducted on all comers who step forward and essentially turn themselves in for having broken into the country. Once illegal immigrants are properly vetted and determined to have committed nothing more egregious than violating laws that govern American sovereignty, the logic goes we will all sleep easier.

This pitch is now universal in the movement that favors amnesty and mass immigration; from the ethnocentric Latino activists who see unchecked migration as the fast-track to demographic hegemony, to the corporatists at the U.S. Chamber of Commerce and the *Wall Street Journal* who represent those intent on importing indentured servants into their company town.

It's virtually certain that whichever of the senatorial triad of Hillary Clinton, Barack Obama, or John McCain wins the White House this fall, they will make background checks a centerpiece of whatever security elements they claim to support.

Yet the prospect of actually conducting legitimate background checks on illegal immigrants is, in fact, the absolute pinnacle of the bald-faced lies that typify the security assurances offered by the proponents of amnesty.

Journalists who have conducted investigative research into the background of individuals know that it's a time- and resource-intensive enterprise—one that can be incomplete if reliable data is lacking on a person. And these are background checks that are conducted into the lives of people who have legitimate, discernable footprints in our society: credit histories, educational backgrounds, property records, employment references, family history, civil litigation, and, sometimes, criminal records.

The vital connective tissue that runs through a real background check is an *authentic* primary identification. An incorrect spelling of a name, the lack of a middle name, no date of birth, or the absence of other corroborating identifiers can render any resulting profile of a person useless.

Even under the best of circumstances, it's not hard to miss something.

Thus, if researching established citizens can pose significant challenges, then putting together a factual background on people who use multiple aliases that are based on counterfeit documents obtained throughout a highly transitory life while in the U.S. illegally is all but impossible.

When considered on the scale of a national amnesty, it becomes a cynical joke.

Yet proponents of immigration reform insist that the tens of millions of illegal immigrants who will step forward to claim a chance at legalization can indeed have their histories adequately researched. Some have even suggested that background checks on illegal immigrants could be conducted in a similar fashion to the so-called "instant" background checks that are used to screen potential gun buyers.

This fiction slips into the public discourse so easily simply because too many reporters have become stenographers, transcribing comments by rote and declining to challenge or analytically explore such sweeping claims.

Fundamental questions about these proposed background checks remain unanswered—because they aren't asked: What agency will conduct them? What universe of source material will be researched? What is the scope of the search? What is the criterion for approval or denial of the immigrant's application? What is the budget for this mammoth undertaking?

And here's the biggie that Obama, Clinton, and McCain are all loathe to answer: Will illegal immigrants whose background checks are flagged and applications for legalization denied face immediate deportation?

Should the American people be asked to believe that Mexico—the corruption-riddled narco-state that is responsible for seven out of every 10 illegal immigrants in the United States today—will provide adequate information about its citizens that may result in their deportation home? Or is it more likely the Mexican government will do whatever it takes to ensure they stay in America and continue wiring billions in hard cash back to Mexico?

At the end of the day, those pushing immigration reform would be better served if they just dispensed with the nonsense about background checks and admit that we have no way of knowing who these illegal immigrants really are, whether we legalize them or deport them.

Deporting them is to choose caution; legalizing them is to hope for the best.

Pretending we can determine just who they all really are is as phony as the Social Security numbers on file in the HR Departments at food processing plants, general contractor offices, and hotel chains across the nation.

SANCTUARY, BLOODY SANCTUARY

San Francisco's arrogance provides a brutal reality check on illegal immigration

First published in 2008

If Americans needed another horrifically bloody testament to the absolute chaos the federal government has allowed our immigration system to collapse into, the "sanctuary city" of San Francisco has delivered it again in spades.

The outrage over San Francisco's policy of hiding illegal immigrant drug dealers by sending them to a safe house in Southern California (where many of them simply walked away) had just settled to a low boil when the story of Edwin Ramos came to light earlier this week.

Ramos was arrested on three counts of murder in June following the shooting deaths of Anthony Bologna and his two sons, Michael and Matthew. The three died in a hail of gunfire as they returned home from a family picnic.

As details of the story have emerged this week, it's hard to imagine a more damning indictment of President Bush, the commander-in-chief who has absolutely refused to secure the nation's borders and assert federal jurisdiction over immigration enforcement in our cities and towns during a time of war.

While it might be difficult to envision Bush working hand in hand with San Francisco Mayor Gavin Newsom, in fact both executives are directly responsible for the conditions that led to the murder of the Bolognas—and God knows how many other Americans.

On Newsom's end of this Faustian bargain we have the alleged killer Ramos, an illegal immigrant gang member with multiple felony busts under his belt in the Bay, including being taken into custody for attempting to rob a pregnant woman and savagely attacking a bus passenger. As a hardcore member of the MS-13 street gang, Ramos benefited from San Francisco's policy of shielding illegal immigrant criminals who claim to be juveniles—even though there is no way of independently determining the actual age of the criminals. But since Ramos told authorities he was 17 years old at the time, he was protected from deportation.

The nadir came in June, when a clearly adult Ramos was yet again released back onto the streets after being arrested instead of being held for deportation. That arrest came as a result of a traffic stop in which police recovered a gun traced to a double homicide. Free to roam the streets of San Francisco, police say Ramos opened fire and slaughtered Anthony Bologna and his two sons after the car they were in had briefly blocked Ramos's car on a narrow street.

While Newsom didn't create the sanctuary policies in San Francisco, he championed them with a righteous zeal, ridiculing those who opposed them as dangerous and wrong-headed. The fate of the Bologna family is the direct result.

But the blood is even more indelible on Bush's hands.

San Francisco's policy lays bare the president's willful surrendering of federal jurisdiction over this crisis, which is a cold-blooded abrogation of Bush's sacred responsibility to defend Americans.

Bush's dereliction of duty in the face of mass illegal immigration into the United States comes as we face an enemy that crosses our borders not with armored divisions, but individual by individual, where violent criminals blend in with economic refugees, just as Al-Qaeda seeks the cover of civilians. Just what is the difference in the blood spilled by Al-Qaeda on Sept. 11th and the slaughter perpetuated by illegal immigrant gang members like MS-13?

In the not-so-distant past, a defiant challenge to federal authority like San Francisco's sanctuary policy had swift and certain consequences—occasionally delivered at bayonet point—as Southern governors George Wallace and Orval Faubus discovered the hard way.

But strange bedfellows as they may be, it's clear that Bush and Newsom share a common goal: the subversion of immigration laws at the behest of a coalition that includes big business interests and ethnic lobbying groups.

The price of such subterfuge and betrayal is to be paid by the American people.

The depth of the tragedy that has befallen the surviving members of the Bologna family almost defies comprehension, and one need only listen to the absolute agony of Danielle Bologna as she describes taking her 16-year-old off life support to understand that part of her has been killed as well.

But the spilled blood of the Bologna family is little more than cheap wine to officials like Newsom and Bush.

Indeed, Newsom may be the poster boy for sanctuary policies, but he's hardly the only elected official engaged in promoting them. Mayors such as R. T. Rybak in Minneapolis, Richard Daley Jr. in Chicago, and Antonio Villaraigosa in Los Angeles, among others, have all publicly declared their desire to undermine federal enforcement of immigration laws to varying degrees.

These mayors of sanctuary cities sleep easy knowing that if Bush does anything, it will be to use a debacle like San Francisco's protection of illegal immigrant, drug-dealing gang members as an excuse to again call for a mass amnesty under the guise of "comprehensive immigration reform."

As the enforcement of immigration laws continues to evaporate and with them the fundamental safety that Bush swore on a Bible to deliver, it's not hard to imagine the day when deporting virtually anyone for any criminal act will be considered by officials such as Newsom and soon John McCain or Barack Obama as passé, if not nonsensical.

After all, just where does a nation without borders deport someone?

LA GANGA MADRE

One woman with thirteen kids delivers deadly chaos

First published in 2008

If the total dysfunction of America's immigration system has a name, that name is Maria "Chata" Leon.

A 44-year-old illegal immigrant from Mexico who until recently lived in Los Angeles, Leon apparently made landfall in the United States in 1985 and in short order began having children in spite of her poverty.

Twenty-three years later and the highlights of Leon's story flow with all the cadence of a rap sheet, quite literally: She's the mother of at least 13 children fathered by five different men, a maternal feat accomplished despite being arrested at least 14 times so far, including multiple felony busts.

As a dope hustler on the street of a once quiet neighborhood nestled in the shadow of Dodger Stadium, Leon made rank as a gang mom as her brood took up the family trade. One son was sent to prison for narcotics sales. Another was busted as an immigrant smuggler.

Yet another of Leon's sons was killed by LAPD last month after a wild gun battle in the neighborhood left another man dead. The police said Leon's son jumped from a car firing an AK-47 assault rifle at them when they returned fire.

News reports that followed the carnage brought Leon's story to light; and in the process it offered a stark portrayal of how cynically our nation's immigration laws are manipulated to devastating effect on our cities' streets.

Leon was part of a stream of illegal immigrants who poured into Los Angeles from the town of Tlalchapa in the Mexican coastal state of Guerrero. Many of the impoverished migrants were fleeing what they described as a violent, corruption-riddled homeland.

And yet as Leon's story illustrates, far from escaping the bloody chaos of Mexico, they brought it with them.

Over the past few weeks, news reports have detailed how refugees from Tlalchapa have settled into the "Drew Street" neighborhood dating back over four decades. As the population density surged, apartment buildings rose in place of demolished single-family homes and the quality of life in the neighborhood spiraled.

By the early 1990s, according to one former resident quoted in a news story, the neighborhood was governed by "the law of the revolver."

As tranquility on the neighborhood's streets evaporated with the collapse of the rule of law, to illegal immigrants like Leon it must have seemed just like old times back home: no job, no discernable structure of a lawful authority on the street, and a carefree reproductive regimen that jibed with a culture of day-to-day subsistence living.

Before too long, Leon was peddling dope and getting arrested.

Yet thanks in part to "Special Order 40" in Los Angeles, the fact that a blossoming career criminal like Leon was in the country illegally didn't result in her immediate deportation on the numerous occasions when she found herself in jail.

In 1992 alone, Leon was arrested twice for selling drugs, including PCP, but for whatever reason wasn't charged by the district attorney, according to news reports. Instead of getting on a bus for the ride back to the border, Leon got a ride home to her Drew Street neighborhood, where business was booming.

It wasn't until a decade later, when police raided Leon's home and found cocaine, assault weapons, explosives—and six children under the age of 10—that Leon finally faced a lengthy prison sentence and federal immigration officials.

And guess what happened? Nothing.

Sentenced to more than six years in prison, Leon apparently was given credit for just 259 days served and then, according to news reports, she was finally handed over to immigration officials for deportation.

Whether she was shipped back to Mexico is unknown, since Immigration and Customs Enforcement officials have refused to comment on Leon's case.

What is crystal clear is that if Leon was ever deported, she's back—and currently living in a two-story home in the Southern California desert town of Victorville.

While police say she and her family of gang members are still players in the drug trade, and while reporters from local newspapers had little problem contacting Leon trying to get interviews, Uncle Sam seems a little confused as to what to do about her.

Despite her son's fatal confrontation with police and the news stories that have followed, there apparently has been no hurry—let alone *shame*—from ICE to move aggressively to find and deport her.

So, she's back in the States and back in business.

Those who support open borders and continued mass immigration describe criminal immigrants like Leon as but a fraction of the swelling numbers of the "good, hardworking" people who come to America to better their lives and benefit our nation. The reality is that while Leon is indeed not representative of most immigrants, legal and illegal alike, she is by no means an anomaly either.

There are hundreds of thousands of Leons all over the nation today, wreaking violent havoc on the communities they call home and costing taxpayers a fortune in medical care (it's a good guess that all of Leon's 13 kids were delivered on the taxpayer's dime) and incarceration costs.

Given the incompetence of immigration officials and the reluctance of local, state, and federal leaders to move decisively to secure the borders and ruthlessly prosecute and deport illegal aliens like Leon—it's no wonder she and her ilk are drawn here.

It's now indeed just like home.

POISONED WELLS

Our future depends on a sustainable population

First published in 2008

As the looming crisis of dwindling long-term water supplies hangs over the American Southwest like vultures circling for dinner, the alarm bells are finally starting to be heard from academia to the media.

National news magazines this month have featured articles on growing water shortages across the nation, with one analysis showing most of California has "moderately to severely overused" its ground water supplies.

Dr. Brian Fagan, UC Santa Barbara professor emeritus of anthropology, wrote a column this week in the *Los Angeles Times* that contrasted human flexibility in adapting to sustained aridity in California a millennia ago with the challenges we face developing water sources today.

"The future is truly frightening," Fagan writes.

Indeed it is, and all the more so because elected officials and even many experts in science and the environmentalist movement have been cowed into silence when it comes to addressing the elephant in California's living room: population growth.

While Fagan ticks off a compelling list of warning signs, including a projection by Britain's Hadley Centre for Climate Prediction that 40 percent of the planet will be in a state of "extreme drought" by the end of this century, the professor only makes a passing reference at our surging population.

That glaring omission isn't accidental. It's a matter of self-preservation.

One of the casualties of the super-heated debate over immigration into the United States, both legal and illegal, has been the ability to openly discuss the growing impacts of our population growth. Since immigration—and particularly illegal immigration—has been the engine driving the sustained population growth in California and the U.S., to discuss population growth is to wade into the immigration debate.

Thus, academics, environmentalists, and elected officials alike run the very real risk of being tarred "racists" by immigrant advocacy groups if they dare to suggest seriously slowing population growth.

The chilling effect this smear campaign has had on the issues surrounding population growth is evident in the increasing calls for new water-use policies, tougher restrictions on developers, beefed up land-use regulations, and investment in research and development of technologies that will ameliorate the discomfort of our crowding; *anything but* a reasoned call for slowing our population growth and then reducing it to replacement levels over the next century.

It's politically correct to call for dramatic reductions in consumption, whether it's fuel, water, or arable land, but it's verboten among political and academic circles to discuss the root of consumption run amok: population growth.

This whistling past the graveyard has taken on an absurdist hue in various environmental groups, where it remains chic to warn against global overpopulation but absolutely unacceptable to discuss the immigration that is fueling America's population surge.

I was treated to an example of the depth of this intellectual charade not long ago while speaking with a

Sierra Club representative who was working an information booth at a park for the venerable environmental group.

We chatted amicably for a few minutes about the runaway development in Southern California that in a generation has erased the open space that once demarked "city limits" and in the process created a mammoth suburban sprawl which simply isn't sustainable. She seemed pleased as punch to meet a fellow traveler on the issue of sustainable growth.

Then I dropped the "pop-bomb" into the mix, asking her about the Sierra Club's view on population growth and its impacts on the environment. She quickly downshifted her pleasant banter into a stock, monotone recitation of the challenges posed by global overpopulation.

When I pointed to the dramatic strain of critical resources in California, such as water, and contrasted that with the state's continued population growth that has us on track to hit 60 million people by mid-century, her response was immediate: she lifted her hand up in front of her, like a crossing guard ordering cars to halt, while sternly intoning, "No! No! No!"

And that was the end of that; conversation over.

But the serious discussion on California's population growth has yet to begin. It's absolutely intellectually dishonest for academics like Fagan to proffer "adapting" as a solution without confronting population growth.

Academics, scientists, and elected officials—and the media—must find the courage to address the issue of overpopulation in the face of the insidious smears they rightly anticipate they will suffer.

We no longer have a choice.

The longer we put off launching that discussion, the faster Fagan's projection of a "frightening future" is going to become a reality.

BREAKFAST WITH AGUSTIN

The *Los Angeles Times* serves up a professional race card driver

First published in 2000

One morning each week I have breakfast with a man who has taught me much—and who I have learned to respect less and less in the process. Like millions of other Angelenos, I have stared at him while sipping my cup of coffee, drinking in the smug grin that defines his cherubic face.

Of course, it isn't his face that bothers me. It's his words. More specifically, it's what he doesn't say that often sours my morning. I call this weekly ritual "Breakfast with Agustin" and like many of *Los Angeles Times* columnist Agustin Gurza's readers, I find his terminal affliction of Latinophilia (a symptom of which seems to be using the word "Latino" at least 45 times in each column, or three times in each sentence, whichever is more) to be everything from predictable to outrageous.

Unveiled as part of the *Times*'s manic "Latino Initiative," Gurza's column was met with the usual jeers and cheers any columnist can expect from readers, albeit much of the jeering falls on the Anglo side of LA's constantly grinding ethnic fault lines.

Most columnists worth their salt should be wearing a flak jacket at work, and Gurza quickly earned his stripes.

He wasted no time drawing heavy fire by pushing all the easy buttons by castigating Anglos for their anxiety over immigrant issues. While his goal may indeed be noble, his approach has been predictable and unfortunate: he advances a position and then implies that opposition to it is nothing less than—surprise, surprise—"racist."

From Orange County school districts to the supporters of Proposition 187 to the boogey men (or is it Storm Troopers?) of the dreaded *La Migra,* Gurza has found plenty of blue-eyed targets in his sights. Of course, he isn't alone. The *LA Weekly*'s cartoonist Lalo Alcaraz, while often right on the money with his straight-up artwork, seems to live in a black-n-white world filled with familiar, one-dimensional Anglos: evil White cops, evil White INS agents, evil White politicians, evil White businessmen, evil White _____ (fill in the blank).

Since the race card seems to have no limit with the media in LA (and the *Times* in particular, especially when it comes to *La Raza!*), it's small wonder self-anointed "community activists" constantly use it to motivate the masses. But when a featured columnist at one of the largest and most influential daily newspapers frequently resorts to employing it time and again, one wonders if he really believes in the idea he embraces—since he so fervently defends them by smearing any detractors in advance.

Yet the most glaring, perhaps even damning, shortcoming Gurza has displayed as a columnist thus far hasn't been who he has attacked, or even how he has attacked them, but rather who he has turned a blind eye toward. One would hope that columnists at least try to adhere to Abbie Hoffman's classic Yippie adage that "sacred cows make the choicest hamburger" and are willing to take on whoever needs a public thrashing.

But Gurza has made it clear that the targets of his columns are virtually, as the old signs down South used to read: "Whites Only." Indeed, Gurza has been MIA on a host of incidents and issues in which blatant racist hate has been embraced and employed by Latinos.

When an Anglo principal was beaten down by Latino thugs in the San Fernando Valley (lacing their blows with a "Whites out!" harangue), Gurza was silent. When Latino parents marched their kids around Los Angeles schools holding signs that read "I Hate Miller" (a sentiment dedicated to Los Angeles Unified School District's chief executive Harold Miller, whose crime was to be an Anglo tapped by the school board to head the beleaguered district), Gurza looked the other way. When Latino students at Cal State Northridge attacked the campus newspaper last fall for daring to run an editorial favoring tough academic entry requirements—an editorial position they deemed "insensitive" to Latino students—Gurza evidently couldn't find his voice or pen.

To be sure, Gurza has occasionally used his column to highlight the common bonds that bind all cultures, such as when he writes about his family experience. Yet even then he has gone off the deep end on occasion. But the nadir came when Gurza reached hard to equate the roiling political debate over illegal immigrants with the persecution and systematic genocide of Jews in Nazi Germany.

Not surprisingly, Gurza sought the cover of comments made by Anti-Defamation League attorney Sue Stengel, who noted her offense at the Anaheim Union High School District's plan to symbolically bill Mexico for the cost of educating illegal immigrant students. Still, I have to wonder how Jewish readers felt when they read Gurza's theft of their poignant, blood-soaked reminder of "Never Again."

Flashpoints of Latino racism abound in Los Angeles, though it's unclear if Gurza can see them or just conveniently looks the other way. Yet I think it was hard to miss the "Pete Wilson Must Die!" signs that dotted the crowds during the height of the Prop. 187 hysteria or the former governor's effigy being burned. Perhaps Gurza hasn't heard that scores of veteran Anglo teachers across Southern California were demonized as racist xenophobes for supporting Prop. 187, or for putting an end to the state's disastrous bilingual education program.

And maybe he hasn't been following the continuing war between Latino and Black street gangs, which has all the ethnic trappings of a Balkan conflict. As a crime reporter in the mid-1990s, I covered a Latino street gang's brutal campaign to drive Black families from the neighborhood they controlled (one family was literally burned out of their home), but I doubt such race-based hate on the part of Latinos is of much concern to Gurza.

No, Agustin is too busy keeping an eye out for transgressions both real and perceived against what he likes to call "the poor and the powerless." It's quite a romantic notion that he fancies for himself; too bad it's delusional.

And that is his greatest failure. Eager to fight the good fight, he ignores the fact that the revolution for social justice has a cancer on it. While I don't believe that Gurza is a racist himself, I do believe that he's a hypocrite. He's not a watchdog; he's a lapdog, one who has a long walk uphill to the moral high ground.

As long as he chooses to focus solely on the Anglo side of the problem, as long as he chooses to remain silent in the face of hate that's the same color as his, as long as he cannot summon the guts to call Latino racism exactly what it is—racism—then he's as guilty as any of those he attacks.

He has been given a unique opportunity and he has squandered it as surely as a politician who rides into office with the best of intentions but then blows it by shamefully pandering to his core interest group. Indeed, like a fearful politico, Gurza tells the masses (as well as his anything but powerless political allies) what they want to hear—not what they need to.

And that's a shame.

THE DARK AGE OF DENOUNCEMENT

From campus commons to company water coolers to celebrity-ruled media channels, an insidious culture of social surveillance, digital show trials, and public vilification spreads across the nation

First published in 2017

America may be rudderless on a turbulent sea of discontent, but she isn't in uncharted waters.

For all the societal headwinds, rogue waves, and squalls that seem to explode around our ship of state on a daily basis now, the cultural storm that appears ever closer to enveloping the grand design of the American enterprise and disappearing her to the bottom has plenty of historical precedent, just not entirely of the sort that is so conveniently framed in one-dimensional terms by much of the establishment media that has been cynically sounding general quarters since early last year.

The pathetic imagery of a hundred or so White supremacists brandishing tiki torches as they stomped and chanted across the campus of the University of Virginia one night three weeks ago might have evoked a modern Nuremberg rally in the sad imaginations of the Neo-Nazis, but the unvarnished reality is that they are merely garden-variety social miscreants who number far fewer in our nation today than in many eras past and they matter even less.

Their chants weren't a dying gasp, merely an irrelevant one.

But in our hyper-connected, outrage-dependent world, why let such an inconsequential moment go to waste when the "news cycle" can be fed with breathless declarations that The Boys from Brazil have come of age once more and are marshaling new corps of *Schutzstaffel* to converge on America's vital national arteries in a menacing redux of the Munich Putsch? Such non-moments are what memes and Twitter were made for, no? That social media microwave that converts the mundane margarita sitting on a table into a brilliant insight on the meaning of life can also transform a motley rabble of social cripples into a frothing tidal surge of National Socialists that is rolling in a sinister hiss across our nation.

Thus, the radically absurd amplification of a dismal attempt to hijack a statue one night on the campus of UVA became but the latest opportunity to turn a dud into dynamite and explode something else altogether.

On cue, the black-garbed street goons who claim some affiliation with the mainstream Left for now (something about the useful idiocy of the Democratic Party's leadership) hit their usual marks as they have consistently over the past eighteen months or longer, in startling produced stagecraft that has turned entire downtowns into grim spectacles of organized violence dressed up as "social justice" (a watchword employed today with all the panache of "ethnic cleansing") but who are actually as transparently nihilistic as the homicidal antics of the equally black-clad freaks of the Islamic State.

But again, this is nothing new. We have indeed been here before as a nation, in both our recent past and at various points throughout our historic evolution as a democratic republic. Despite the historic precedents throughout the

19th and 20th centuries, the rapidly unraveling social fabric today is dangerous—and our perseverance through tough patches and dark days in the past is of little assurance that America will survive this current turmoil.

Of course, some don't care if the country recognizably survives, wagering they will be fine come what may (a bad bet if there ever was one), while others clearly hope that it does succumb, and in the death of a nation lies their mad joy.

As disturbing as the violent social upheaval has been, it's far from the most ominous sign that America truly is in deep-water trouble of the sort that is imperiling the functional cohesiveness of the country and perhaps mortally wounding it. Amid the ugly street violence, the shattered glass, the acrid smoke, the burning flags, the broken bodies, the gutted buildings, the chanting mobs, and the armored-up police formations that seem stuck on pause on the sidelines of it all, a more odious virus continues to spread unchecked.

We are now living in another dark age of denouncement.

Where the McCarthy era had its Hollywood blacklist and the televised witch hunts of the House Committee on Un-American Activities with its poisonous inquiries that often pinnacled with its infamous query, "Are you now, or have you ever been, a member of the Communist Party of the United States?" the crucible of today is a digitized web in which not screenwriters, actors, and union leaders find themselves under the klieg light of official suspicion, but rather the average American citizen (a demographic that itself is now a risky strata to claim in certain circles) who can find themselves suddenly tangled up amid shrieking accusations that they believe in an *"ism"* and thus must be an *"ist."*

From cake-makers in their bakeries to delivery drivers on their routes, from airport gate attendants to professional athletes, from students at Halloween parties to professors strolling the campus grounds, all are but one iPhone (or a hundred) away from being charged with a violation of, intentionally or not, some "social justice" penal code section and find themselves facing a lightning-speed trial on social media and subsequently sentenced to terms ranging from hostage-like apologies to eviction from the dorms to expulsion from the academy, from being run out of business to being forced into the unemployment line to being forced into hiding.

For all the well-founded fear of the growing power of surveillance being placed in the hands of an overbearing American government, precious little objection or even sustained contemplation has yet been offered in the face of not a dozen intelligence agencies snooping on Americans but rather, legions of people self-deputizing and patrolling virtually every aspect of everyday life, keenly on the lookout for anything they find suspiciously impolitic or offensively not in line with their own personal dogma.

Around urban and suburban America today signs have gone up that read, "If you see something, say something," but a more appropriate advisory in the era we now live might be: "If you see something you don't like, capture it on your iPhone, post it immediately online with a shrill denunciation of the culprit(s) and faster than a flash mob, a drumhead court will be in session on social media and simulcast across the cable news networks."

While traditional and new mass media weren't the lone carcinogens that created this latest mutation of a social malignancy, various members of media dependents both fuel and feed from the spreading cancer that is today's culture of denouncement, their every finger-pointing, *j'accuse!*-shouting moment another crack-hit high of self-righteous moral ascendency. The cult of accusation in this age of denouncement produces a never-ending need for more, just as it did in the McCarthy era. As the high of accusation crests and then ebbs, the accusation-armed enforcers crash into an existential despondency, one remedied only by another hit of denouncement, so they load another indictment of someone, somewhere, for something (fictionalizing as needed) into their little digital glass pipe for another toke that sends their eyes rolling back into their skulls as the rush sends their sense of purpose soaring.

As Shakespeare might have observed: they denounce; therefore, they are.

And thus we have Sheriff Lena Dunham who was recently on patrol at 3:00 a.m. at JFK eavesdropping on a conversation that she claimed to be objectionable—or perhaps just not suitably applaudable enough—and accordingly documented herself springing into action as she reported the suspects to American Airlines in real time on Twitter. It was almost dizzying enough to make one forget that Dunham had recently declared in an interview that she was simply exhausted from being a poster girl of the social justice movement and wanted someone else to carry the banner, but then again that was like so five minutes ago. Almost as quickly forgotten was American Airlines' official response that it couldn't corroborate a single element to Dunham's claims, but that was clearly beside her point.

Then there's ESPN's Max Kellerman taking to his cable pulpit to alert his sporting parishioners that he was keeping a close eye on all the White players in the NFL who weren't suitably sitting down or kneeling in protest of the playing of the national anthem, a not-so-subtle memo to the pigskin platoons that *he* saw something, *he* said something, and now *they* better understand that Max Kellerman Is Watching. Kellerman had taken Dunham's self-stylized culture policing to its next logical progression: it's not something that the White players in the NFL were doing that he found objectionable and, moreover, worthy of denouncement, but rather what they *weren't doing*.

Four years ago this week at Michigan State University, Professor William Penn in the university's Department of English in its College of Arts & Letters demonstrated the surreal circular nature of the informer network: Penn stood at the front of his lecture hall on the very first day of school and sneered at the students in his creative writing class that Republicans were nothing more than "dead or dying White people" and then issued this ominous warning: "I am a college professor. If I find out you are a closet racist, *I am coming after you.*"

But while Penn, who has held forth at MSU for three decades and whose annual salary of $146,510 (in 2013) is funded by taxpayer money, menacingly boasted of his professional bona fides as a Thought Detective who was experienced at discovering and outing "closet racists" and then harassing them, he apparently was unable to deduce that a student was videotaping his threats on his iPhone, the footage of which promptly went viral and resulted in the good professor being suspended for the rest of the semester. Of course, due to the magic of tenure and a brazen political double standard that has long since been institutionalized in American academia, Penn was able to return to his classroom the following semester after he issued a pro forma apology that was as vague as it was insincere and a fingers-crossed promise to keep his Roy Cohn routine to a low froth as he went back to ferreting out any suspicious looking/sounding/thinking students.

Karma catching up with Penn and his threats aside, however, it's hard to not also see the inherent danger in students now routinely taping their professors or even high school and junior high/middle school teachers in class. Under constant if casual social surveillance, for every educator revealed to be using their classroom as a personal political soapbox by students looking to add a little octane to their social media pages, how many more professors and teachers will feel that every class is now a dance through a minefield and simply mute the free and candid discourse they are supposed to be fostering?

The stifling fear of being publicly denounced has been a hallmark of police states and oppressive cultures since time immemorial, from the Inquisition to Salem, from Nazi Germany to North Korea, where official apparatuses of enforcement are supplemented with volunteer social compliance squads that denounce suspected heretics. In such toxic atmospheres, among the most damning evidence of an enemy within the gates is not overt objection to a party line or a cultural truism, but rather insufficiently expressed and unconvincing agreement. In Pyongyang, Kim Jong-un had his uncle, Jang Song-thaek, executed in 2013 for failing to clap enthusiastically enough while in his presence. Initial accounts reported that Jong-un ordered Thaek blown to smithereens by anti-aircraft guns, but *The Independent* later reported on Chinese accounts that Jong-un literally threw Thaek to the dogs—120 of them—who ripped him and five of his aids to pieces in front of hundreds of party apparatchiks required to watch. It took about an hour. It's enough to make Saddam Hussein's eerily filmed public denunciations and dispatching of Baathist officials deemed no longer sufficiently politically reliable seem rather quaint.

No, we're not *there* in America, nor are we anywhere even remotely near it.

Despite all the manufactured and disingenuous hysteria over the presidency of Donald J. Trump and the fantastical allusions to the rise of a fascist dictator, Congresswoman Nancy Pelosi and Senator Charles Schumer aren't going to be dragged out of their seats and hauled out of the Capitol during the next State of the Union address, nor are Congressman Paul Ryan and Senator Mitch McConnell going to be stripped to their boxers or briefs and paraded around the Washington Mall before being shipped to Guantanamo for political rehabilitation delivered through what the CIA might describe as "electroshock therapy." And the last time a group of Americans were stripped of their rights *en masse* and forced at bayonet-point into prison camps was 75 years ago under President Franklin Delano Roosevelt, the iconic liberal whose visage still looms large during Democratic National Conventions.

But America's government need not descend into the depravity of despots in faraway lands nor sink once more into the shameful crimes of our own past like that which was perpetrated on Japanese Americans for the nation itself to utterly disintegrate today. If the culture of rabid intellectual correctness long prevails, however, and its vast veil of suspicion that only fuels the need to indict ever more violators and publicly immolate them in gleeful fulfillment of the old adage "First they came for..." continues unabated, then it can and most likely will completely torch the framework that still holds the nation together until it implodes and disappears into deadly and irreversible balkanization.

While America has emerged from past tempests intact, whether and how she makes her way out of this one isn't clear at all and perhaps it's that deep uncertainty of the outcome that feeds a creeping sense of dread across much of the nation that the worst is yet to come.

And perhaps it is.

In which case, real resistance to many Americans might increasingly look like a small cabin in the woods or perhaps a farmhouse out on the vast plains of the heartland, a quiet place where unplugged rustic austerity is complemented by printed books, firelight, a proper provision of wine, and a security system no more elaborate than a rifle, a sidearm, and an unflinching determination to live in peace.

Come what may.

THE ENEMY WITHIN

Celebrating America should mean defending her in public schools

First published in 2008

For most of America, celebrating the 232nd anniversary of our republic's declaration of independence from the British Empire inspires at least a moment of reflection of what brought our nation to greatness.

If the national revelry indeed has any deeper purpose at all beyond binging on hotdogs and beer, it must be that we acknowledge our ancestors' strong work ethic, their bloody sacrifice, our unique national sense of exceptionalism, and our bedrock respect for the rule of law.

But once the fireworks are over, Americans would be wise to take note that our national holiday isn't seen as something to celebrate by significant and growing numbers of students at public high schools across the Southwest. In school districts from Tucson to Los Angeles, advocates of a radically ethnocentric agenda are expanding their reach into the student body and the curriculum, teaching a core message that holds the United States is a racist police-state bent on the oppression of Latinos and other ethnic minorities.

Students at Jordan High School in Watts launched a series of protests in June after the Los Angeles Unified

School District refused to renew the contract of Karen Salazar, an untenured English teacher at the campus. The LAUSD determined that Salazar was engaged in blatant ethno-political indoctrination of her students.

Salazar recently went on PBS's *Democracy Now!* to offer a reasoned defense of her teaching, noting that she used district-approved textbooks and taught them in compliance with state-mandated standards.

In the vacuum of a PBS studio, her explanation sounded like she was indeed the victim of an overly cautious administration.

But then there's the footage of Salazar standing in front of the school clutching a bullhorn and declaring, "Historically, the school system has been used as a project of colonization to rob students of their identity."

And judging from Salazar's students outrage over her firing—which was captured on video and posted on YouTube—just how much fundamental grammar or writing skills was being taught in her classroom is questionable.

One female student, with a penchant for calling her classmates "comrades," seems to confirm the basic premise of LAUSD officials' decision to fire her.

"She goes out of the curriculum and teaches us our history," the student says, "instead of that [expletive deleted] U.S.-centrism they teach us in our history class." In another video clip the same student declares students are being "hunted down and treated like terrorists" at schools that are really prisons.

One of her "comrades" chimes in that Salazar "teaches us how to be strong and not let nobody oppress us." Well, so much for English standards.

Ethnic studies courses used as academic cover to brazenly indoctrinate students with a racially-based, anti-American perspective comes as no surprise to John Ward, a former history teacher in the Tucson Unified School

District. Ward, who is of Latino heritage, was tapped to teach a history course at Tucson High Magnet School.

Ward said he was comfortable that the course featured a Mexican American perspective—but what he didn't know was he was expected to only assign grades, a bureaucratic loophole that allowed the students to be lectured by advocates without teaching credentials.

The coursework was steeped in hard-edged anti-American rhetoric.

"They declared students were living in an occupied, colonized land," Ward recalled. A central tenet of the instruction was that White Americans oppress Latinos, and that the education system was a tool of White oppression.

The impact on students, Ward said, was dramatic.

"By the end of the class, they were very pessimistic and angry about America," he said. "They were convinced that anyone who isn't brown is out to get them, to oppress them."

When Ward challenged the angry, one-dimensional instruction students were receiving through the class, he said his own Latino heritage offered no protection. "They called me a racist, a tool of the oppressor, a 'vendido,' which means 'sellout,'" he said. "They replied that all education is politically charged and that they must combat the dominant culture's view of history. They believe non-White kids need an anti-White curriculum."

If Ward was hoping that administrators from TUSD would intervene, he quickly learned otherwise. "They didn't want to pick this battle," he said. "They were White administrators that could see the writing on the wall if they tried to defend me. They'd immediately be tarred as 'racists.'"

Ward eventually resigned his position and now works for the Arizona state auditor. He said the radicals who lectured his class now have their credentials and are teaching "Raza Studies" at TUSD. The program is set to be expanded throughout the district.

In Los Angeles, Salazar's students and activists continue their efforts to pressure the school district into renewing her contract and it's almost certain she will find herself back in a classroom somewhere.

If Americans are unwilling to defend their national heritage to the emerging generation in its classrooms, then the fireworks this Fourth of July will really have been just flares illuminating a mighty nation that is sleepwalking to its own demise.

OVERPOPULATION DENIERS

Climate change isn't even the half of it as failed states collapse into violent chaos unleashing human tsunamis across a planet that's been bled dry, gutted, and boned

First published in 2017

Denial is a powerful sedative.

I am reminded of this every time I listen to politicians or elected leaders of any political persuasion or ideological stripe start plucking the harp strings of promises to act today with responsible policies so that younger and future generations will inherit a brighter tomorrow.

Sometimes I suspect it's a dark goof offered with an absurdist's tip of the hat to the obvious, much like a stand-up comedian would deliver a punch line with a straight face before breaking into a grinning advisory of, "But seriously, folks, your kids, your grandkids, and future generations? Yeah, well, they're totally screwed."

But other times I think some of them actually may feel they're not being completely dishonest as they tick off their multi-point policy plans for a better tomorrow, at least to the self-hypnotic extent that *Seinfeld's* George Costanza once explained: "It's not a lie if you believe it." So perhaps they have talked themselves into a mild trance that allows them, however briefly, to believe or appear to believe their own sugar-frosted pablum they regurgitate for public consumption.

Yet whether the bipartisan political leadership in this country or bureaucratic suits running the Western world actually believe their own hype about the promise that tomorrow may yet hold is ultimately immaterial to the grim tide of reality that is now unfolding across the planet.

The End isn't near. It's already here. The only question is how long will it last before the bright lights of humanity suddenly go dark?

And while the sirens wail throughout the world's capitals over the climate change that is indisputably manifesting across the planet, there is only the accompaniment of crickets in the halls of power to the rising sea of people. It's a strange juxtaposition watching world leaders breaking into cold sweats about a warming planet even as they offer little more than blank stares of befuddlement when confronted with a human population that has far outstripped the carrying capacity of the planet and is adding corrosive multipliers with every monthly net gain of humanity.

The science is clear and compelling and confronts us with challenges that are already overtaking humankind's historic ability to adapt and evolve to navigate shifting environments and new threats. Throughout modern human existence, our innate resourcefulness and inventive nature has been able to keep us enough steps ahead of danger to not only preserve our species but propel it into absolute ascendance above all others on the planet, a dark meteoric rise that continues to lay thousands of other species low in our wake.

But even the blinding pace of technological advances in the adolescence of the 21st century will not be enough—not even close—to pull a rabbit out of the hat of salvation yet again, even if that is the laudanum being peddled and passed out now to the masses. The snake oil of 2017 is the idea that brilliant young minds who are busy writing code and developing apps even as you read this are going to save the day.

No, they are not.

Not because they aren't young, brilliant, and possibly even visionary, but rather because they are facing problems too vast, too deep, and multiplying too rapidly to overcome in time to prevent collapse.

The most dangerous times during a flight on a jetliner are during takeoff and landing, in part because the pilots are actually flying the plane at those points, which increases the odds of "human error," but also because the lack of altitude presents pilots with precious little time to assess and react to correct the problem if possible. Altitude equals time. The human population on the planet today is at about 1,000 feet off the deck with an airspeed of 400 knots and the jackscrew is about to snap on the elevator.

The accelerating collapse of wild habitats, depletion of vast ground water aquifers, clear-cutting of vital forests, billowing dead zones in the oceans, and the globalization of the food supply chain has all unfolded against a backdrop of an endless surge of human population growth.

Yet can anyone recall a single question being asked or perspective being offered about human population growth, both across the planet, the hemisphere, and the country, during Election 2016? Or Election 2012? Or Election 2008? Or...

You can't recall a question or an answer on the issue of overpopulation—even to challenge the argument—because the global governing elites who got us into this mess over the past century by their failure to seriously address it at numerous critical junctures during the past half-century are now steadfastly locked into a non-disclosure agreement with the media, a dutiful routine of "don't ask, don't tell."

They are overpopulation deniers.

And yet the rapidly accelerating consequences of overpopulation are now unavoidable.

The frenzied mass migration of tens of millions of people fleeing the civil wars and societal collapse across the Middle East and Africa is an obvious symptom of what tomorrow and the day after that holds much more of, but it's hardly the only one. In an above-the-fold, front-page feature article published in Sunday's national edition of the *New York Times,* reporter Michael Kimmelman offered a stark portrayal of the day-to-day reality for a vast sweep of the 21 million people who are now jammed into the crumbling megalopolis of Mexico City. Headlined "A Parched and Sinking Capital," the article's subhead advises readers that "Mexico City's Water Crisis Pushes it Toward the Brink."

But toward the brink of what exactly?

Mexico has already achieved all the hallmarks of a failed state: historic and endemic corruption of an archaic and malignant patronage system that pervades virtually every level and branch of its municipal, state, and federal governments; spiraling street violence and narco-cartel battlefronts that have claimed hundreds of thousands of lives and "disappeared" thousands more people, sometimes busloads at a time; and a non-existent or crumbling infrastructure, a stunted public education system, and a vast disparity of not just wealth but even the dim hope of economic opportunity altogether. More than two decades after the passage of the North American Free Trade Agreement (NAFTA) that was supposed to lift workers' financial boats north and south of the Rio Grande, the average *daily wage* for Mexicans in Mexico continues to hover around five American dollars—or about half of what a busboy can make in a single hour in the United States.

A report published by *Business Insider* in 2015 declared, "Mexico's wage crisis is so bad that it violates what's stipulated in [its] Constitution," and noted that 20 percent of Mexico's population had an average net worth of $80. And another front-page story published in the *Los Angeles Times* on Sunday explored how Delphi Automotive eliminated 20,000 jobs in America in 2006 and moved their plants to Mexico, where the company today pays its Mexican workers $1 an hour for the same work it had paid American workers $30 an hour to do a decade ago. While Americans poured into unemployment lines and extended economic misery, many of the Mexican workers were only advancing from abject squalor to dirt poor.

Kimmelman's story in the *New York Times* offers vivid snapshots of just how bad daily life has become in Mexico's teeming capital, reporting that around five million of its residents—or a population larger than that of Los Angeles—do not have access to clean water at any given time. Simply put, when more than five million residents of Mexico City turn their tap, whether it's actually in their home or somewhere else on the block, nothing comes out. When there is actually water coming out of the taps, it's often a yellow hue that looks like another liquid altogether and makes the drinking water scandal in Flint, Michigan look like a simple mistake that's a quick fix. The dwindling supplies of drinking water have forced many among the impoverished masses of the capital's inhabitants to devote much of their daily lives improvising ways to acquire water. Kimmelman describes the plight of Diana Contreras Guzmán, a young single mother in the Xochimilco district who shares a single-room cinder-block shack with five other adults and four children. While the five other adults all work full time to earn a combined monthly income of $600, Guzmán watches over the children at the shack and is responsible for obtaining several hundred gallons of water each week that are brought into the neighborhood by delivery trucks and donkeys. She's also tasked with guarding whatever water is on hand at their shack, since water theft is a daily threat in the district.

Another resident of Mexico City, Virginia Josefina Ramirez Granillo of the Iztapalapa District, put it bluntly: "We wait for hours to get water that doesn't last a week, and usually there aren't enough [privately-owned trucks selling water]. Sometimes there is violence. Women sell their spaces in line. If you are from the wrong political party, you don't get water."

The detailed and unflinchingly frank reporting of Kimmelman's story is at once a testament to the power and importance the tradecraft of print journalism still retains even as it exposes its fundamental flaws and ultimate impotence to prevent or even long delay the reckoning that is pulling into the station.

While Kimmelman's story again brings into focus the catastrophe that is taking shape and building in strength like a perfect storm in Mexico City—to say nothing of dozens of other massive urban population centers that are imploding under their own weight across the globe—he's careful to carry the water of the *Times* editorial orthodoxy and not connect the dots of climate change, accelerating chaos, and an unsustainable human population.

In fact, throughout the entirety of his feature news story, Kimmelman made not a single direct reference to overpopulation as a root cause of the crisis that is now unfolding. While he certainly set the table well enough to clearly understand the connection, he apparently dared not quote even one source that openly explored whether the vast and still growing population of the Mexican capital was the explosive component being packed into another human population time bomb. Or perhaps Kimmelman did indeed diligently report on how an unsustainable human population directly correlates with squandered and vanishing vital resources such as fresh water, but the *New York Times* editorial equivalent of the NKVD redlined those passages into obscurity for being "politically inappropriate."

Either way, unsustainable human overpopulation is peppered like cancer cells between the lines through Kimmelman's bleak report.

In 1950, Mexico City covered approximately 30 square miles. Today, its vast footprint sprawls across 3,000 square miles in a portrait of what author Mike Davis had warned of more than a decade ago in his book *Planet of Slums*. In what Davis called "humanity's final buildout," the human population on the planet hasn't been fleeing cities that can no longer provide basic services, but rather are getting sucked into them in a vortex-like gravitational pull of a dying star. In 1950, when Mexico City was a mere 30 square miles, there were 86 cities across the globe that had populations of more than one million people. By 2006, there were nearly 400 cities that had populations over a million. Today that number has surpassed 500 and is expected to approach 700 by 2030. It's projected that by 2050, three out of every four humans on the planet will be living in cities, albeit choked, congested, and collapsing ones.

But it's in what Davis described as "megacities" that have populations of 10 million or more and "hypercities" like Mexico City where 20 million or more people live where the implosions will explode human blast radiuses that will threaten to swamp countries not already mired in chaos.

Kimmelman's story notes that by mid-century, the failed states and staggering birthrates of humankind will have pushed 700 million people around the globe into perpetual migratory status—or a population twice that of the United States today that will be running, walking, stumbling, swimming, floating, and being carried ever northward. As the writer Christian Parenti put it to Kimmelman: "No amount of walls, guns, barbed wire, armed aerial drones, or permanently deployed mercenaries will be able to save one half of the planet from the other."

In other words, think *World War Z*.

And it has already begun. The proverbial "tipping point" was reached and passed some time ago. Greenpeace co-founder and Sea Shepherd Conservation Society founder

Paul Watson told me a quarter century ago that a sustainable peak human population on the planet was around two billion people and yet we're cresting ever closer to double-digit billions.

The Rubicon has been crossed. Peak humanity is here.

From the Middle East and out of Africa tens of millions of refugees are already on the move, and across the vast swathes of poverty in Mexico, Central America, and South America the floodgates are creaking. In India, the populations of Mumbai and Calcutta have collectively surpassed 30 million people, or nearly the entire state of California between two cities. In Lagos, Nigeria, the sprawl of the "greater metro" area encompasses more than 21 million people jammed into shanties stretching as far as the eye can see.

And in Southern California, nearly 25 million people have poured into a densely populated coastal region that is naturally arid, creating a water-dependency system that has bled the central and northern regions of the state bone dry, and yet the only thing growing faster than drought restrictions or dead lawns are new multi-family housing developments.

One evening back in the mid-1980s I was at a small dinner party in Los Angeles with some academic and musician friends along with Gregg Turner, guitarist of the LA punk band Angry Samoans, who also wrote for the rock magazine *Creem.* He and I discussed the global population issue, and I recall Turner's wry observation that the invention of the combustion engine and the development of antibiotics were two of the greatest disasters to strike the planet.

Reflecting on Stanford biologist's Paul Ehrlich's earlier work, Turner had concluded that short of a global consensus and dramatic collective action, it would soon be too late to avoid collapse and then nature's ensuing correction of a population grown wildly disproportionate to the resources necessary to sustain it.

"If they don't start turning it around within the next decade," Turner said, "you can pretty much party up, because it will be over."

I told him that I had already gotten a jump on living like tomorrow was an iffy layaway plan, so I was prepared for the worst. Years later I would have the chance to talk with Paul Ehrlich in Washington, DC, who left me feeling that Turner and I had it right that night, with the only question now being how fast would the decline accelerate into a cascading collapse?

And that's an open question. But given the multipliers in play now, it seems likely that most of us will live to see the opening acts make way for the headliner event in the coming years.

So as Gregg Turner advised: you can pretty much party up, because it will be over—much sooner than later.

Cheers!

(And to T. Bobby Malthus, one of the very first cats to see it coming...)

STILL WATERS, FLOODED STATE

As the drought worsens and the state burns, California continues a policy of "growth-as-usual"

First published in 2009

Twenty-five million beleaguered Southern Californians can look forward to the arrival of autumn this year with the relief of knowing that while the worst is hardly over in the long-term, the region will cool down and stop burning—at least for a little while.

And it might even rain some.

But there isn't likely to be much rest for the weary.

The raging wildfires that ignited across foothills and mountains that were so dry they exploded like arsenals packed with gunpowder may be over for now, but as development chews deeper into the shrinking margins of wild areas, the human impacts of fast-moving infernos promise to grow only more costly—to say nothing of the price paid by the state's stunning biodiversity.

And while the drought that has turned some of the state's most prized cropland into dusty, dead fields may ease somewhat with the onset of fall, the state's long-dwindling water supplies will continue to disappear with the Sierra snowpack that feeds it.

Yet as California continues to face a series of existential threats to the quality of life it can still offer the nearly 40 million people who call it home, a coherent population policy or plan has yet to be heard from the state's overly partisan and dysfunctional leadership.

But what homeowners, renters, and business owners *are* hearing from state, county, and local agencies this fall is that they have got to cut back on their water consumption—now—or else.

In cities across Southern California, water companies have instituted mandatory reductions in water use and will enforce them with dramatic fee increases for those who surpass their allotted ration. Some cities are also encouraging residents to spy on each other, setting up "tip lines" so neighbors can report each other for violations such as washing their cars and hosing down their driveways.

It seems Sacramento wants Californians to cut back on everything except more people.

The leadership well in Sacramento (never too deep of late) has run so bone-dry, in fact, that both parties are still espousing renewed "growth" as the singular formula for reinvigorating California's moribund economy, which they apparently believe in turn will restore everything else that's broken in the state.

This explains why our state's brain trust in Sacramento was hell-bent last week on sneaking through a waiver of environmental impact reports for a 75,000-seat football stadium that billionaire real estate mogul Ed Roski wants to build in the City of Industry—amid one of the most congested stretches of freeways and roads in Southern California.

In a letter to his colleagues, State Senate President Pro-Tem Darrell Steinberg hailed the 18,000 jobs the project may create without so much as raising a single question as to the long-term contribution another massive entertainment venue would make in a region that's already in perpetual gridlock.

Like most of his cohorts, Steinberg can't envision a future for California that's based on concepts like a sustainable population, one that balances quality of life issues with economic stability. Instead, Steinberg & Friends look at California as a cancer cell, something that essentially has to keep metastasizing until it dies.

While even conservative projections of population growth place upward of 60 million people in California by mid-century, there has been virtually no public debate in Sacramento over whether the state even has the carrying capacity to sustain such a human presence at our consumption rates and what such a future population would mean for those living here.

Until the state's leadership is either forced to seriously address the fundamental issue of California's growing population—and a population summit would be a good start—or until they are replaced by leaders who will take up the most critical long-term issue that confronts our state, then Californians can only expect their quality of life to vanish along with the water every passing season.

WHITE TWILIGHT

The changing face of America poses real risks to the nation

First published in 2008

If Sen. Barack Obama's candidacy has indeed placed race in the spotlight again this election season, then the Census Bureau's new projections that White America is fading into minority status much faster than previously thought offers a glaring view of the fissures that continue to spider-web our republic.

The meteoric rise of Obama's fortunes and the potential success—or failure—of his run for the White House has provoked much soul-searching about whether America "is ready" for a Black president, the subtext of which is really whether a Black president might be somehow intrinsically different than a White commander-in-chief beyond extra helping of melanin.

But the increasingly rapid erosion of the Caucasian population in America raises the stakes considerably no matter who wins the White House. The question transcends what the occupant of the Oval Office looks like and becomes whether Whites are ready for the accelerating changes that will result in an *America* that no longer looks like them, sounds like them, or necessarily embraces their cultural tastes.

The answer, as it stands now, is almost certainly "no."

But not because the nation's White majority, which presently retains an overwhelming demographic dominance of two-thirds of the country's 305 million people, harbor some inner bigot that recoils at the prospect of becoming a minority in a land they've always subconsciously considered their own.

No, it's not the end result that most White Americans likely find troubling today, but rather the factors that are fueling those projections, namely unrestrained immigration and the increasingly bitter sense that they have had little to no say about this matter.

The Census Bureau's estimate that American Caucasians will no longer make up the majority of the country's population by 2042—nearly a decade sooner than previously anticipated—is indisputably driven by the epic migratory waves of people from Latin America into the United States during the past three decades. And the fact is, many of those people crossed the border illegally and many more are expected to continue doing so, absent a much larger and firmer commitment to enforcing the laws already in place.

The demographic impact of this lack of commitment continues to be wide and deep.

White populations have dropped significantly in more than half of the nation's more than 3,100 counties since 2000. In just over 300 of them, ethnic minorities are now the majority population.

The facts on the ground created by mass immigration have been clearly visible throughout the Southwest for years, perhaps nowhere more so than in California, where entire communities have seen their racial demographics upended in less than a generation's time. The effect has often been the real-world elimination of hard-won racial balances, with traditional working- and middle-class Black and White communities effectively disappearing.

In many places throughout Southern California, the White flight that marked the efforts at integration in the 1960s and early 1970s struck again in the 1990s, turning into a middle-class Anglo exodus from the state in the face of massive immigration from Mexico, helping create the first minority-majority state in the union. It's a dynamic that continues to this day, as virtually all of California's net population gain is directly attributable to immigration and births to immigrants, while the state's native middle and working class continues its outbound migration.

This demographic upheaval has spawned another phenomenon among the White middle class that has become iconic: the gated community. Advertising private patrols that will deliver an "armed response" to intruders and bristling with security cameras and pass codes, new home developments today often resemble something more akin to a stylish Israeli settlement on the West Bank than the open neighborhoods we grew up with in the 1970s.

Last year, Harvard political science professor Robert Putnam created a brief firestorm when he released the results of an exhaustive study that correlated increased ethnic and cultural diversity with declining civic engagement across the nation. In Southern California, that epochal transformation has been on display for years, from the Los Angeles Unified School District that has seen its White enrollment drop to single digits in a city that's still well over 30 percent White to public parks in White neighborhoods that have instituted "user fees" for "non-residents." Realtors highlight homes in "stable" neighborhoods to prospective White buyers.

Feeling besieged, Whites are withdrawing and the real story that underlies the equation that's presented in the Census data will be how the nation's leadership addresses the significant challenges and serious risks these demographic shifts pose. This is no time for empty rhetoric or platitudes about the enrichment that diversity brings the nation.

This is a dangerous hour and the stakes are high.

The leadership in both major political parties will proceed with immigration reform at their peril if a majority of Whites feel the political class is continuing to address them in either a condescending or patronizing fashion. A smart first step among Republicans and Democrats would be to begin any new round of negotiation on immigration reform with an understanding that any effort to legalize the status of millions of illegal immigrants will be matched with a commensurate reduction in legal immigration into the United States, spread out over years.

This would go far in ameliorating the pervasive sense among Whites that America is being overrun.

Obama's address on race in America, delivered in Philadelphia this March, was rightly hailed as a candid, intelligent, multi-dimensional assessment of the complexities surrounding the issue. But for the vast majority of working- and middle-class Whites, Obama's words resonated for the simple reason that he openly took into account their perspective and their fears; and he wasn't dismissive in doing so.

That address was a great opening for a sustained national dialogue on a changing America; and the vital nature of that conversation is now again underscored by the Census projections.

Failure to seize the opportunity to build a real national consensus—one that can only be obtained through what surely will be a hard-fought compromise—is to risk further alienating a White majority that will ultimately insist on having its voice heard on these issues, one way or the other.

MEG-A-DEATH

Whitman's slippery approach to immigration spells doom for the GOP

First published in 2010

With the fall campaign now in the home stretch and the Republicans seemingly riding the crest of a national wave that will deliver them to sweeping gains across the country and perhaps control of one or even both chambers of Congress, the last whimpering gasps of Meg Whitman's soulless gubernatorial run in California are now fading quietly into the night.

By almost every measure it's a stunning defeat—at least at first blush.

In a political season that has seen the electorate slip establishment Democrats the dreaded black spot from Boston to Las Vegas, Whitman's bid for the Sacramento statehouse appeared to be a race that could safely be called early.

After all, Whitman is a billionaire businesswoman with the moderate credentials that Californians typically look for in a Republican (think Pete Wilson or Ed Zschau but with a bottomless purse) and who at 52 years old faced this year's archetypal political villain: Jerry Brown—a liberal retread pushing into his 70s who has never been weaned from the Golden State's political tit.

Indeed, Brown was running for office in California when Whitman was still in middle school.

While Brown was able to preemptively brush aside any challenge in the Democratic primary from the flashy mannequin mayors Antonio Villaraigosa and Gavin Newsom, his general election showdown with Whitman initially looked like it might be as evenly matched as Richard Nixon and George McGovern's 1972 match up.

Yet with just days before the election, Brown now leads Whitman by anywhere from five to eight percentage points in most polls, a spread that falls outside the margin of error even at its closest. The *Los Angeles Times* published a poll Sunday that gave Brown a 13-point lead among likely voters, a portent of an unmitigated election night blowout of the Republican in a state that is flat broke and facing a real unemployment rate of 20 percent.

Though the curtain hasn't yet dropped—six percent of voters polled in the last Rasmussen survey declared themselves undecided and the *Times* has a long history of blending its liberal ideology into its news reporting—Brown's momentum is undeniable and, barring some unforeseen late-breaking development, Whitman will have to sweep virtually all the undecided voters and peel away some of Brown's soft support to eke out a come-from-behind victory.

So, let the postmortem begin: how did this happen?

How did a political ghost like Jerry Brown, who was once connected at the hip to perhaps the most widely despised liberal in the state's history—the late Chief Justice Rose Bird—emerge from the Bay area fog in this Summer of the Tea Party to trounce a Republican who had little baggage and mountains of cash on hand?

At its root essence, the fundamental answer is simple: *immigration.*

The death spiral of the GOP in California can be traced back a generation to 1986, when George Deukmejian was governor, Ronald Reagan was in the White House, and California was seen as the sun-dappled redoubt of conservative success known simply as "Reagan Country." No Democrat had carried the state in national elections between Lyndon Johnson and Bill Clinton—a literal generation of Democratic defeats. The polling booth defections of the White working and middle classes, the so-called "Reagan Democrats," appeared to be a terminal loss for the coalition first built by Franklin Roosevelt.

But who could have known then that it would be Reagan, with the stroke of his pen in 1986 on the Immigration Reform and Control Act, who would unwittingly place his signature on what effectively was the death warrant for the Republican Party in California?

Though it was sold to an ambivalent public as a necessity that would help integrate about 900,000 illegal immigrants into American society, the measure ultimately granted a blanket amnesty to more than three million people—half of them in California—and rang a cattle bell throughout Mexico that triggered the longest sustained wave of mass illegal immigration in history.

The human tsunami that poured across the southern border smashed into California with a staggering force, overwhelming schools, hospitals, housing, public safety, and social services. Working-class Blacks, Whites, and Latinos were driven from jobs they had long held in a wide range of industries just as Southern California was undergoing its post-Cold War makeover, shedding tens of thousands of skilled labor manufacturing jobs in defense-related sectors.

Far from securing the border, Uncle Sam was AWOL as desperate California residents were reduced to symbolic acts like parking their cars on the border with their headlights pointed toward Mexico—illuminating the mass night crossings and pleading for help.

Legal chain immigration and the policy of granting "birthright" citizenship served as potent accelerants in the rapid and radical remaking of California.

By 1994, a fed-up electorate in California passed Proposition 187 in a landslide. The measure targeted a range of social services that acted as pull factors for illegal immigrants. While nationally the GOP had virtually no interest in securing the border or enforcing immigration laws, the reelection campaign of Gov. Pete Wilson saw the grassroots rage in California as a movement he ignored at his peril.

Wilson embraced Prop. 187 and proceeded to annihilate Kathleen Brown (Jerry's younger sister) at the polls, rolling up a 1.25-million-vote (15-percent) margin in the election, carrying 51 of California's 58 counties, including the entire vote-rich southern counties.

But that triumph of the popular will was short-lived. Latino racialists intent on maintaining their demographic momentum litigated Prop. 187 to death while illegal immigration continued apace, as did the erosion of the middle-class tax base in California as families fled the state looking for economic security and a better quality of life.

Rather than mount a vigorous grassroots defense of Prop. 187 and rallying the multi-ethnic majority to the defense of their state, establishment Republicans equivocated, offering little more than tepid denials to the rabid charges of racism that the Democratic leadership and Latino activists cynically heaped upon supporters of the measure.

The GOP had won a strategic battle in California—and then promptly surrendered the field.

That exposed a bitter truth to the coalition of voters who passed Prop. 187: the heart of Republican elite has never been in the fight against illegal immigration. That the corporate suits of the GOP were merely along for the electoral ride shouldn't have been much of a shocker, given the business interests that profit handsomely from the illicit importation of exploitable cheap labor that drives wages down and reduces worksite rights. And for whatever passionless overtures they have occasionally made for securing the border and enforcing immigration laws, the Republican elite sugared them for business by demanding more legal immigration into the U.S., more replacement workers for citizens still clinging to jobs that couldn't be outsourced offshore.

In the vacuum produced by the GOP leadership's paralysis, a surreal narrative emerged from the hyper-politicized newsrooms around the state, a feverish storyline that held while Wilson's embrace of Prop. 187 may have delivered him a landslide, it also alienated and energized a previously lethargic Latino electorate. That voting bloc would arise as an ethnically-motivated monolith—the story goes—that would draw no distinction between the third-generation Chicano citizen and an illegal immigrant from Michoacan who arrived a week ago.

And so the fabled "Latino vote" in California was born.

Yet in the 16 years that have passed since an enraged majority brought forth Prop. 187, that chimerical narrative has gone from a counter-intuitive Democratic pipedream to a largely Republican propagated semi-reality in California. With each passing election cycle, the GOP candidates have indulged in a bizarre ritual of stridently decrying illegal immigration during the primary—and then pathetically hedging during the general election campaign.

Whitman is the epitome of the GOP's suicidal double-talk on immigration.

Since fending off a primary challenge from Insurance Commissioner Steve Poizner, who made illegal immigration a centerpiece of his campaign, Whitman has slipped into something more comfortable: the milquetoast vernacular of the GOP elite when it comes to immigration. Whitman maintains a straight face as she declares she is "100 percent opposed to any form of amnesty" while simultaneously stating that she supports a "comprehensive federal immigration solution"—which of course will include the largest mass amnesty in the history of nation states.

Whitman declared that "English is America's national language" and demanded that immigrants be required to learn it—all while spending millions of dollars on courting Latino voters (who are all presumably citizens who speak English) with Spanish language ads.

When asked point blank if she supported or opposed driver's licenses for illegal immigrants, Whitman launched into an obfuscating blather about jobs, a Stepford Wife smile fixed across her cherubic face, terrified of verbally acknowledging that she—like most other Californians—oppose giving illegal immigrants driver's licenses.

The cherry was placed on top of Whitman's long con game in late September, when illegal immigrant Nicandra Diaz Santillan played her own blatant scam by stepping in front of the microphones to declare that she had been used by Whitman for nearly a decade before being discarded like so much "trash."

On cue, Whitman feigned shock that Diaz Santillan had been in the country illegally.

While most working citizens in California believe that a pair of conniving frauds like Whitman and Diaz Santillan deserve each other, it's clear that the episode was yet another payment by a GOP establishment that has been on an installment plan of betrayal, diligently selling out Americans as they work to build a state they are increasingly unlikely to ever win again in statewide and national elections.

The political deed to the state is about to be handed to the Democrats.

If Ronald Reagan's pen stroke graced the political death warrant for the California GOP in 1986, then it was George W. Bush who carried out the execution, sabotaging what little enforcement was being done and pushing hard for another amnesty that fueled even greater waves of illegal immigration across the southern border.

In 1986, there were an estimated 1.5 million illegal immigrants in California. By 2008, there were an estimated two million illegal immigrants in Los Angeles County alone and perhaps more than triple that figure in the state altogether. Los Angeles County recently estimated that it's shelling out more than $52 million a month in welfare payments through the CalWorks program to the children of illegal immigrants, all while the beleaguered taxpayers in the teeming county fork over another billion dollars every year to jail and provide healthcare for illegal immigrants directly. These numbers are all going up, not down.

It's now so late in the game that the Democratic leadership in California rarely bothers trying to conceal the fact that they have secured their political hegemony in the state largely by sheer ethno-demographic warfare, gleefully at the expense of the at-risk and in-need Americans in their traditional base. The Democratic leadership hasn't just pushed working-class Blacks to the back of the bus again— they have thrown them under it, effectively stripping them of their hard-won political, economic, and educational gains across the state.

Meg Whitman's failed campaign in California should serve as a final wake-up call to Republicans across the rest of the nation, especially those who insist on parroting Karl Rove's delusion that comprehensive immigration reform will somehow benefit their party. It won't.

Amnesty is an epic disaster for America and a death sentence for the Republican Party.

And Meg Whitman is just the latest name chiseled onto their California tombstone.

WHAT WE HAVEN'T HEARD YET

Four debates and not a single question—or answer—on immigration

First published in 2008

The three presidential debates and single vice presidential debate are now behind us and yet after nearly eight cumulative hours of the candidates regurgitating the sound bites they've honed (or dulled) on the stump, the nation has heard nary a word on immigration or the challenges it poses to our nation's future.

As they enter the home stretch of campaigning, Senators Barack Obama and John McCain undoubtedly hope to escape any serious questions on immigration, anything that would force them to address it beyond soundbites geared to their audience of the moment.

Both men surely breathed a sigh of relief last week when the final debate ended and the elephant in America's living room had yet again gone unmentioned.

CBS News veteran Bob Schieffer followed the template set by PBS's Jim Lehrer and Gwen Ifill and NBC's Tom Brokaw and allowed the candidates to avoid even a single tough question about America's immigration policy, a subject that both senators are loathe to take on in front of 70 million viewers of all political and ethnic stripes.

It was a disgraceful journalistic failure that bodes ill for the nation.

Immigration permeates virtually every marquee domestic problem facing the country today: healthcare, education, jobs, and the environment; it also factors into issues of national security and foreign policy. Given the size of the foreign-born population in the United States today—more than 40 million—it's difficult to imagine any policy initiative being successful that doesn't first address the fundamentals of immigration.

The candidates have talked about the financial crisis, spending as much time attempting to affix blame as they have trying to convince voters they were the guy with the best plan to get the country back into solvency and renewed prosperity. They have talked about earmarks and deficit spending. They have talked about job losses and their plans to create new jobs.

And yet they have said nothing about the millions of foreign laborers illegally in the United States today who have driven millions of Americans out of a wide range of employment sectors while suppressing wages for citizens still working in those industries. They have said nothing about the billions of dollars in tax revenues lost to this mammoth scam of the underground economy, or of the billions of dollars citizens pay to subsidize it.

McCain and Obama have talked with ease about greedy corporate villains, such as the executives at Fannie Mae and Freddie Mac, Lehman Bros., and AIG; but they have kept mum on the conniving suits who ran Howard Industries in Mississippi or Micro Solutions Enterprises in California, hi-tech firms that were raided by the feds this year for employing nearly a thousand illegal immigrants between them in their manufacturing plants.

The candidates have talked about the dramatic decline in the quality of public education in America today and argued over charter schools, teacher accountability, and the merit of increasing funding for a failing system.

But they have said nothing about the catastrophic impact that mass illegal immigration has wrought across thousands of public schools in the American Southwest, where school districts have been forced to cope with violently overcrowded campuses and parents have watched as classrooms turn into bilingual education labs at the expense of their own children's learning.

Both senators have talked studiously about the critical challenges we face in the environment but have spoken not a word about America's surging population growth—fueled almost entirely by immigration and births to immigrants—and the impacts that growth has on our vital resources, particularly fresh water supplies.

For either candidate to claim now that they support reducing consumption without also voicing support for an end to our surging population growth shows they are simply being intellectually dishonest, like a doctor encouraging radiation therapy for a lung and liver cancer patient while declining to forcefully recommend that his patient stop smoking and quit drinking.

Some may claim that since there isn't much daylight between the two candidates on the issue of immigration a detailed discussion of this topic wouldn't amount to much, but I suspect the opposite is true.

McCain was the co-architect of the "comprehensive immigration reform" legislation that would have resulted in the single largest mass amnesty for illegal immigrants in the history of nations—and Obama supported it.

But the American people clearly and decisively rejected it in 2006 and 2007; and there is little indication that they are in the mood for it now.

So in this time of national crisis, when economic peril looms large, both candidates should be asked pointed questions on their intention to reshape America's immigration policy.

Just several months ago, Obama and McCain addressed the National Council of La Raza's annual conference in California, where both men vowed to make sweeping changes to United States policy that would *increase* the flow of immigration.

They should now be required to answer a key question: is that still their plan?

The issue that the two candidates were most reluctant to talk about is, in fact, the one they should be grilled on most aggressively. The question for every informed voter must now be: what are they afraid to tell us?

SILENCE OF THE GREENS

Why California's environmentalists are frightened of addressing overpopulation

First published in 2008

Environmentalists are fond of saying that the debate over global warming is over. The fundamental questions about its existence, its impacts, and the human contribution to it have been settled and time is of the essence as we consider local, regional, and global responses.

But when it comes to the issue of population growth, particularly in the United States and specifically in California, environmentalists are fond of saying as little as possible and, preferably, nothing at all.

It's an understandable silence, given that it's a matter of self-preservation. Environmentalists are increasingly silenced on the issue of population growth out of fear of being tarred as "racists."

That rigorously enforced self-censorship was on vivid display last week in Santa Monica, where some of California's most respected environmentalists joined several politicians to discuss the impact of the election on the environment.

Convened at the prestigious Milken Institute, environmental heavy hitters like David Allgood from the California League of Conservation Voters, Andy Lipkis from Tree People, and Jonathan Parfrey from Green Los Angeles held forth for the better part of two hours about the drubbing the ecosystem has taken under the Bush Administration and the silver lining the electoral sea shift may offer.

Allgood, Lipkis, and Parfrey rightly spoke enthusiastically about promising developments in alternative energy and imaginative methods to increase fresh water supplies. And the three commendably expressed the urgency that Californians must demonstrate as we confront perpetual drought and our precarious environmental health.

But for all the talk about sustainability, not one sentence about California's surging population growth was uttered among them; indeed, not a single word.

Before the evening drew to a close, I decided to take their encouragements to raise our voices to heart and shouted from the back of the room, "What about our population growth?"

The question produced a pregnant pause and some bemused stares from the panelists, before they slipped right back into their talking points and closed out the discussion without addressing it.

I asked Parfrey and Lipkis afterward how they could avoid the core issue of population growth that's so central to our carbon footprint, spiking greenhouse gases, and the increasing pressures on our shrinking water supplies.

Lipkis actually looked pained for a moment as he carefully considered his answer, then acknowledged that population growth was a key issue—but said it was better addressed by someone more versed on it than he was.

Parfrey, God bless him, didn't mince words. The issue was simply untouchable, he said, because White environmentalists "must demonstrate real racial sensitivity" to the cultural needs that are fulfilled for Latinos by having large families.

His candor was simultaneously both refreshing and stunning. Refreshing because it's rare to hear such a succinct admission of the politically correct strictures that govern many White environmentalists. Domestic population growth in particular is a subject they dread to venture into.

It was equally stunning to hear the eloquent voice of a progressive like Parfrey so willingly submit to self-censorship even as we face looming environmental catastrophe. Ironically, his admonishment that "racial sensitivity" trumped open discussion also smacked of the suggestion that Latinos are too emotional to engage in a reasoned discussion of a culturally-loaded issue.

And it presumes that Latinos must all think alike on this issue.

But it's past simply being intellectually dishonest by not addressing population growth when discussing the increasing pressures on the environment at this late hour—it's downright fraudulent. And it's dangerous.

Environmentalists like Parfrey, Lipkis, and Allgood know this very well, but they are also keenly aware of the consequences of speaking out on this issue, since to do so might mean a brief foray into the realm of population policy, which is linked inextricably to immigration policy—a definite No-Fly Zone.

The consequences of daring to broach the issue were recently highlighted when Californians for Population Stabilization (CAPS) launched a national ad campaign to raise awareness of the impact that population growth was having on the environment. The response from some Latino groups was fast and furious.

Zuraya Tapia-Alfaro, a lobbyist for the New Democrat Network in Washington, DC, blogged on the group's website that CAPS was part of "the hate network," shamelessly listing CAPS alongside the KKK, Neo-Nazis, and criminal skinhead street gangs that are monitored by the FBI.

In one despicably deft swoop, Tapia-Alfaro likened CAPS, with board members such as Ben Zuckerman, a professor of physics and astronomy at UCLA, or Stuart Hurlbert, the director of the Center for Inland Waters at San Diego State University, to Klansmen, Nazis, and hate-mongers who spread violent terror.

Working from Joe McCarthy's playbook, Tapia-Alfaro smeared CAPS not only to punish respected academics like Zuckerman and Hurlbert, as well as Dr. Henry Mayer, a clinical professor of medicine at Stanford University's Medical School also on the board at CAPS, but to remind environmentalists everywhere of the toxic wrath that awaits them if they get out of line and dare to speak up.

The resounding silence indulged by the panel on the issue of population growth at the Milken Institute last week was a powerful demonstration as to just how potent a smear campaign can be—and guys like Parfrey, Lipkis, and Allgood clearly got the memo.

While they steadfastly remain silent even as California remains on track to reach 60 million people by mid-century, let's hope that other environmentalists will find the courage to raise this critical issue and foster a respectful dialogue— one in which no threat to the environment is held hostage by politically correct etiquette.

That discussion needs to take place now. Californians deserve nothing less.

IN THROUGH THE OUT DOOR

Convicted felon and illegal immigrant Jose Vega-Zuniga's easy-come, easy-go traveling roadshow highlights the violently wide-open reality that remains America's southern border and the government's malfeasance that perpetuates it

First published in 2016

The story itself was hardly front-page news for anyone who has been paying even semi-attention to the cold facts on the hot ground along America's southern border: a convicted felon and illegal immigrant who had been deported numerous times had managed to dodge federal authorities once more and slip *out* of the United States and back into Mexico just ahead of a looming 20-year federal prison sentence.

But Jose Guadalupe Vega-Zuniga, whose crimes in the United States ranged from smuggling heroin to assault with a deadly weapon, didn't disappear into a shadowy underground railroad operated by the Mexican narco-cartels, hopscotching from one safe house to another until he could be shuttled through a tunnel back into his homeland.

Far from it, as the Department of Homeland Security knew exactly where Vega-Zuniga was up until early August: kicking back at home in Southern California with his wife, knocking back some tall cans and taking it easy as he waited for his sentencing date in federal court, which had been scheduled for October.

But intent on wintering in Mexico rather than a federal prison, Vega-Zuniga snipped off the tracking device that DHS had ordered him to wear and by August 18 was enjoying a smooth, air-conditioned ride in his wife's Ford F-150 back across the border to Mexico, where it was undoubtedly margaritas and mariachi time for the felon, though he did eventually send his old lady back north with a message for Uncle Sam: *"Adios, pendejo."*

When news of Vega-Zuniga's *ballet folklórico* across the southern border made the *Los Angeles Times* last week there were a few more laughs to be found, not the least of which was the Department of Justice expressing a cold sense of betrayal that the felon's wife—who's presumably an American citizen—helped her old man go on the lam. While federal marshals finally caught up with Elba Soto on September 14, arresting her back at home and charging her as an accessory to her husband's crime of fleeing, the United States Attorney's office seemed shocked that Soto would help her career criminal hubby bolt.

"The evidence in this case indicates the defendant knowingly transported her husband to Mexico while he was pending sentencing in the latest of his criminal cases," U.S. Attorney Eileen Decker stewed in a statement issued by her office. "If these allegations are proven, the defendant knowingly assisted a convicted felon avoid justice. As a result, the defendant now faces her own criminal case and a significant prison term."

Soto, in fact, now faces a decade behind bars if she's convicted and U.S. Magistrate Sheri Pym ordered her held without bond following her arraignment. But chances are better than even that Soto isn't exactly shaking in her boots at the prospect of facing a federal penitentiary's menu for 3,650 consecutive days, and that shouldn't come as a surprise either. Consider that Soto's *el esposo* walked in and out of custody and then back and forth across the border unimpeded for the better part of the past two decades and look where it landed him.

Probably at Hussong's in Ensenada with his feet up, savoring his footloose ways in the very birthplace of the margarita.

Soto has children, so how long will it be before her court-appointed counsel plays the "separated family" card on a motion to grant bail, with an electronic monitoring device, of course.

But while the American federal government's feigned concern that they had been taken for a ride once more by a violent convicted heroin-smuggling illegal immigrant—oh, and Vega-Zuniga had been released on a $100,000 *unsecured* bond prior to his "Baja or Bust" getaway—is worth a laugh or two, the real rib-splitter came from the pages of the *Los Angeles Times*.

As any reader of the newspaper of record here in the City of Angels can tell you, along with its sister brides *The Washington Post* and the *New York Times*, the *Los Angeles Times* long ago issued a fatwa on Donald Trump and has been waging a rabid journalistic jihad against him for well over the past year. While the ever-shrinking broadsheet's panic-fueled rage over Trump's enduring candidacy has yet to crescendo, no other single news topic has been more carefully subjected to the newspaper's rigorous editorial cleansing and purification process than mass immigration in general and illegal immigration specifically.

So it was surprising to see Vega-Zuniga's southbound soiree even make the pages of the *Los Angeles Times*, particularly in this election season, considering that the fundamentals of the story contradict the newspapers' most sacred homilies on the subject and in large degree support what Trump has been maintaining (however inarticulately) since he launched his campaign last summer: violent career criminals have no trouble crossing America's southern border at will and have long been the beneficiaries of intentional malfeasance by a corrupt federal government in America.

The newspaper did bury the story in its B-Section and, in some fine comedy writing, declared Vega-Zuniga's rally to Baja "a brazen escape," lest readers get the feeling that this is commonplace in the United States today, a place where hardened criminals with lengthy felony rap sheets filled with violent crimes are literally released on a promise to appear and in the meantime instructed to stay out of trouble.

Yet that is the day-to-day reality that Vega-Zuniga's story highlights to brutal tragic-comic effect.

The southern border remains a violent expanse of forbidding terrain that's honeycombed with smuggling routes which have been secured by the Mexican narco-cartels to ensure the unimpeded passage of its contraband, be it drugs or smuggled humans.

But it's in the American interior where the federal government's brazen complicity in aiding and abetting mass illegal immigration into the United States remains on vibrant display as tens of thousands of career criminals like Vega-Zuniga continue to waltz around content in the knowledge that there is little to worry about.

While Vega-Zuniga is cooling his heels back in his native Mexico, the true scope and depth of mass illegal immigration pouring into the United States was glimpsed again just recently when Edward Alden, a senior fellow at the Council on Foreign Relations—an elitist policy group that favors mass immigration—acknowledged that throughout the administration of George W. Bush as many as three million immigrants illegally crossed the southern border successfully *every year*. During the Obama administration, Alden claims that tidal wave has flattened to a tidal flow of merely 250,000 illegal immigrants successfully crossing annually as of last year.

But of course, Alden's playing with the numbers, as that figure, which is certainly an understated projection, doesn't include the hundreds of thousands more from Central America and elsewhere who cross illegally into America and then turn themselves in, relying on being released as Vega-Zuniga repeatedly was: with little more than a tracking bracelet and a promise to appear.

For all of the sensationalized "fear" of deportation that has been spun into platitudes holding that millions of peoples are hiding in the shadows and are now once more being played in high rotation this election year, the truth is that Jose Guadalupe Vega-Zuniga puts a face to the reality.

After a life of crime led in the United States and being deported repeatedly but never successfully, Vega-Zuniga has finally retired to Baja for now, but he may well grow bored of lobster and micheladas for breakfast and return to his American summer home and his old job in the distribution and franchising business.

But one thing's for sure: it's up to him. No one else seems to be watching the door or the floor.

They don't call America the Land of Opportunity for nothing.

MEMO TO THE GOP

Republican long-term survival will ultimately hinge on immigration policy

First published in 2010

In the wake of the dramatic Republican success in the midterm election there has been considerable celebration among Democrats of their precious few but critical victories, among them California, Nevada, and Colorado, where Latino voters provided the crucial bulwark that prevented the GOP from taking more state houses and Senate seats.

There's certainly no shortage of different prisms through which to view the results of this election. The Democratic elation at winning 64 percent of the Latino vote in House races must be cold comfort when they consider their party lost 60 percent of the White vote in the same contests.

So just how bad was the loss of White voters for Democrats this time around?

Republican Christine O'Donnell, the strange little candidate who will most assuredly be remembered for opening her general election campaign with a commercial in which she declared that she wasn't a witch, easily beat Democrat Chris Coons among White voters in Delaware, carrying 51 percent of the White vote across the state. Coons was only able to win the election by carrying 93 percent of the Black vote, a demographic which accounted for 22 percent of voters who went to the polls.

In California, which has been transformed into a virtual Democratic coastal fortress, GOP Senate and gubernatorial candidates Carly Fiorina and Meg Whitman both won a plurality of the White vote, which accounted for 62 percent of voters going to the polls in the financially battered Golden State. Fiorina carried 52 percent of White voters, beating Sen. Barbara Boxer among Caucasians by a nearly 10-point margin. Whitman scored 50 percent of the Anglo vote while former Gov. Jerry Brown trailed her by four points among White voters. And while California is now a minority-majority state, Whites are still the largest racial demographic.

But both Boxer and Brown were able to easily overcome their deficits among White voters by trouncing the Republican standard-bearers among Latinos. Both Boxer and Brown wrapped up about 65 percent of the Latino vote and carried upward of 80 percent of the Black vote. Considering that Latinos accounted for 22 percent of California voters this year (with Black voters at nine percent), it was more than enough to ensure comfortable victories for the Democrats.

It was much of the same across the country.

In Nevada, Senate Majority Leader Harry Reid lost White voters by a deep 12-percent margin, but he beat Sharron Angle by bagging 68 percent of the Latino vote, which had surged to 15 percent of the state's voters in this election.

In Illinois, Republican Mark Kirk managed to capture Barack Obama's old Senate seat by racking up 64 percent of the White vote, a demographic that accounted for nearly 70 percent of voters going to the polls. But Democrat Alexi Giannoulias was able to make it a squeaker by taking 94 percent of Black voters and 63 percent of Latino voters.

It's indisputable that rolling up massive victory margins among ethnic minorities—particularly now among Latinos—is how the Democrats have managed to survive their half-century bleed-out of White voters. No Democratic presidential contender has carried a majority of White American voters since LBJ in 1964.

The existential question now facing the Republican Party is: how much longer can it prevail by simply winning a sizable majority of White voters when that demographic is largely static or shrinking, while Latinos are growing dramatically as a result of mass immigration and birth to immigrants?

The conventional wisdom holds that the GOP must come to terms with a rapidly growing Latino population that is demographically reshaping America and its electorate. The theory is that Republicans must accommodate Latinos—and specifically on the issue of illegal immigration—or it will doom itself to a future of dwindling prospects at the polls as the party retracts into a political backwater of disgruntled Whites and business interests. The net conclusion is that by continuing to make illegal immigration an issue and supporting enforcement-based responses to it will ultimately prove suicidal for Republicans.

But in fact, just the opposite is true.

The GOP shouldn't fool itself in believing that the present dynamic will somehow shake out in its favor through assimilation or relentless pandering to Latinos. It won't. The Republicans are unlikely to capture much more than a third of the Latino vote in any given election for the foreseeable future.

California is the shining example of what Republicans can ultimately expect across the country if mass immigration continues: a failing state that has bankrupted itself even as the Democrats successfully groomed an ethnic demographic succored on public programs in a self-perpetuating culture of tax-supported entitlements. The Democrats successfully used the mass amnesty of 1986 and the ensuing waves of Latino immigration as essentially a voters-on-layaway plan that has delivered rich results. And it's a formula they now intend to use across the country. There is a reason that Harry Reid declared his early opposition to the policy of birthright citizenship was the biggest mistake of his political career: he recognizes now that mass immigration is perhaps the last, best hope for the Democratic Party.

If Republicans want to remain a viable party in national elections past the next 20 years, they must act decisively now to end illegal immigration and significantly reduce legal immigration. Instead of surrendering the issue in the vain hope of ultimately achieving a deeper reach among Latino voters, the Republicans must double down and get serious about developing an immigration policy that is in the best interest of the nation and its own survival as well.

This means the Republicans must finally confront and prevail against the powerful business interests within the party that profit from mass immigration and the cheap labor it provides. In effect, the GOP leadership will have to bite one of the hands that feed it, but it's a hand that must be bitten—and deserves to be. Continuing to do the bidding of such groups as the U.S. Chamber of Commerce on the issue of immigration makes hollow such campaign slogans as "Country First" and most voters can smell the hypocrisy.

If they get their own house in order on immigration, the Republicans will be in a much better position to call out the Democrats without looking like hypocrites pandering to the fears that unrestrained immigration has stoked across parts of the country where it has hit the hardest. To that end, the GOP must field candidates who can deliver inspired, articulate arguments that challenge the breezy platitudes which have become truisms in our culture, such as immigration is somehow inherently always good for the United States as long as it's legal immigration.

With more than a million legal immigrants—many of them foreign workers—pouring into the nation every year amid demands from some quarters that those numbers be increased, the Republicans have ample room to make an honest argument for dramatically reducing those numbers during this time of high unemployment and evaporating resources for American citizens. While calls for limiting legal immigration are certain to evoke even more hysterical attacks by Democrats and their surrogates, a reasoned appeal to reduce immigration and allow America to catch its breath will resonate with most citizens, but only if Republicans are able to rise to the occasion and make the case.

Yet given the party's spotty record on even making the case against illegal immigration, which should be a slam-dunk, one can't be too sanguine.

Sharron Angle in Nevada perhaps best demonstrated just how badly Republicans can fumble the issue as she offered a halting, hedging, and somewhat surreal explanation of the tone and context of her campaign's television ad that took aim at Reid's record on illegal immigration.

She had a golden opportunity to offer an unflinching, factual assessment of illegal immigration to members of the Hispanic Student Union she was addressing. Angle could have stated plainly that the vast majority of illegal immigrants in the U.S. are Latino and so that's what ads on the issue should reflect, that America's southern border has been overrun in many locations, making it a violent and dangerous place and that contrary to popular myth, not all of the immigrants crossing into the U.S. illegally are good, hardworking people.

She could have described how the rule of law in the United States is what sets it apart from a Mexico that's so hopelessly mired in a pervasive culture of corruption that millions of the failed nation's citizens flee north every year—and declared that those who abet illegal immigration are creating the same culture of corruption here.

Angle could have looked those students in the eye and calmly said that enforcing immigration law isn't by definition an attack on Latinos and that we can either enforce the law uniformly or surrender to chaos.

Whether or not they would have been swayed by her arguments, the students could at least have respected her candor and reason.

Instead, Angle offered a bizarre ramble about how she wasn't sure if her TV ad had featured Latinos or not, that it was difficult to tell, and by way of example she claimed that some of the students she was addressing appeared Asian-looking. Just as Whitman's meltdown on her illegal immigrant housekeeper defied all reason, Angle's incoherent babble about her own ad proved disastrous.

But even if the GOP begins fielding candidates who don't implode when called upon by Latino audiences to explain their position on immigration, the Republicans must face the reality that Latinos are essentially a bedrock Democratic vote and no amount of parsing or pandering is going to fundamentally alter that voting pattern.

Exhibit A is Sen. John McCain, whose very name became synonymous with a plan for the largest amnesty in the history of nation-states. Along with his Senate colleague Lindsey Graham and former president George W. Bush, no other Republican so relentlessly sought to barter an open-border policy into raw votes among Latinos. Yet the election results of 2008—in which two out of every three Latino voters cast their ballots for Obama—demonstrated the absolute failure of that formula. McCain essentially did no better than Angle or Fiorina among Latino voters.

Even infused as they now are with the zeal of a Tea Party movement that is intent on finally securing the border, it's unclear whether the Republican Party can bring itself to accept the true stakes that continued mass immigration poses for the nation's future as well as its own.

But one thing is certain: whether they accept it or not, time for the Republicans to act is indeed running out.

MOUNTAIN, MOLEHILL, OR MIRAGE?

In its relentless editorial narrative of Western White guilt, the *Los Angeles Times* scrubs some news stories while inventing others to serve its agenda

First published in 2015

The gunfire was still echoing in the streets of Paris when the *Los Angeles Times* published a story that compared the slaughter of the staff at the satirical magazine *Charlie Hebdo* by radical Islamic terrorists with the execution of Nazi war criminal Julius Streicher by the Allies following World War II.

Published on January 9 as part of its news package entitled "Attack in Paris," staff writer Nigel Duara's story cooly noted: "Western society expressed universal horror this week over the *extrajudicial killings* [emphasis added] of those involved in the publication and dissemination of an irreverent, left-leaning satirical weekly in Paris. The attack was denounced as barbarism, apparently perpetrated by a narrow subset of Islamist fanatics."

Duara's news story then deadpans: "But the largely forgotten execution of Streicher serves as a reminder that Western society has also set limits on what is deemed acceptable speech." Then, after clearly linking the wanton murders of journalists—which Duara describes as "extrajudicial killings"—with the death penalty imposed on Streicher by the Nuremberg tribunal, the *Los Angeles Times* reporter seeks to ameliorate the outrageousness of his relativism by acknowledging that "few would suggest that there is a moral equivalence..." Yet with that limp-wristed disclaimer out of the way, Duara proceeds to unleash another 600 words of an indictment of Western civilization and the alleged hypocrisy of its recoiling horror at Islamic terror even as the body count continued to climb in the City of Light.

Coming on the second day of the terrorist attacks in Paris, Duara's news story followed an initial group of stories the *LA Times* published on January 8 in the wake of the assault on the magazine, the front-page lead story of which suggested the journalists killed were accomplice in their own murder for "angering the Islamic faithful with [their] taunting push against the boundaries of free speech." In fact, that connection between the "Islamic faithful" and the vicious, vengeful bloodletting unfolding in one of the capitals of The Enlightenment, was one of the precious few linkages the *LA Times* has made between the religion and the terror since the attacks began.

That a scant 24 hours had passed before the newspaper of record for Southern California rushed a relativistic rewrite into print is sadly no longer surprising. That the newspaper didn't fabricate some of its reporting might be.

On April 19, 2013, just four days after the Islamic terror attack on the Boston Marathon route killed three people and wounded more than 260 others, the *LA Times* exploded its own indictment of the American people on its news pages, publishing a column in its print edition by veteran staff writer Robin Abcarian that alleged Muslims were under siege in the United States. As Exhibit A in her case, Abcarian opened her story in an unnamed town in northeast Ohio, where a woman named "Karen" lived with her Palestinian-born husband and their five kids. It's a forbidding landscape of Amish and Mennonites, where few Muslims dare to tread lest they face rude Americans who insult them for their customs.

Abcarian's column then debuts "Yusef," ostensibly Karen's 10-year-old son, whom readers are informed had been placed on detention and was sent home from school with a "punitive strike on his record" for allegedly telling his fellow fifth-graders that he was going to blow up the elementary school as news of the Boston bombings buzzed across campus. Abcarian details the dialogue that supposedly took place between the fifth-graders that led to this Muslim student being singled out for punishment.

According to Abcarian's column, it was actually another student who declared to his classmates that Yusef was going to blow up the school—apparently because he's Muslim—and when Yusef repeated the claim in shocked disbelief, the teacher heard him say it and asked students what happened. Framed by his fellow fifth-graders, Yusef was ordered out of the class and segregated from his fellow students in the library, where he was forced to eat lunch alone.

Abcarian reported that Yusef's mother Karen, who happened to be a teacher at an unnamed Islamic school, had decided to keep Yusef at home, apparently for his own safety, until she could "straighten things out" with the school. Abcarian dutifully reported that Karen was so terrified of America in the immediate aftermath of the attacks on September 11, 2001, that she "locked herself in" her home for a week straight.

But the interesting element that was pervasive throughout Abcarian's set-up wasn't the amount of detail she spent on the story that she chose to set the stage for the latest installment of the *LA Times*'s long-running serial that would best be entitled "Evil & White: Christian America," but rather the glaring lack of basic details Abcarian didn't seem to have to substantiate—not only the claims of the unnamed Muslim family, but actually as to whether the incident as described even took place at all.

Missing from Abcarian's column wasn't only the name of the family victimized by America's seemingly innate Islamophobia, but the name of the school and school district where this transgression allegedly occurred, the name of the teacher who allegedly took action against Yusef or the name of the principal who sanctioned the discriminatory discipline. Also absent from Abcarian's reporting was any evident effort to establish whether an alternate version of the incident existed; say, perhaps from the other students.

Deep in her reportage of this alleged xenophobic assault of a Muslim elementary school student came Abcarian's admission that she had first "heard" the story from Anum Hussain, who at the time was the Boston regional director of the Muslim Interscholastic Tournament. Abcarian quickly noted that Hussain herself was a victim of nativistic harassment in the wake of the 9/11 attacks, being told to "go back to your country" even though she's American by birth.

However, what Abcarian didn't mention about Hussain was that she had also been a reporter for *The Boston Globe*, ironically the same broadsheet where columnist Mike Barnicle was fired after editors determined that he had fabricated people and events in his columns about race relations.

Hussain apparently had heard the story of "Yusef" being accused of being a fifth-grade jihadist from his sister, whose name apparently is "Amanda." So, Yusef told Amanda who told Hussain who told Abcarian who told more than a million readers of the *Los Angeles Times.*

Now that's quite a game of Pass It On.

Abcarian claims in her column that she "briefly spoke" with Yusef over the telephone but had vowed to keep his identity a secret since his mother Karen "doesn't want to bring greater embarrassment to her son."

It seems rather odd that a mother who is herself a teacher would talk to a reporter for a major metro daily newspaper about her 10-year-old son being discriminated against because he's a Muslim, then suddenly want to wear the veil of anonymity to avoid "greater embarrassment." If the story as related was true, there was nothing for Yusef or his family to be embarrassed about.

If it was true.

So, on the day Abcarian's column was published, I sent her an email at the *LA Times* and asked her how it was that given she used the story of "Yusef" as a keystone example of Muslims in America who are shivering in fear, that it would be so devoid of any corroborating factual details?

Abcarian replied, "Thanks for writing. It seems like you didn't quite grasp the point of the column. The family did not wish to be identified for fear of further embarrassment, and because, as I wrote, they wanted to deal with the school in a non-confrontational manner. The story is about the fear of backlash that American Muslims are feeling. It's not about mediating a dispute between two 10-year-olds. It is possible at some point the family will be comfortable letting me identify them."

On April 22, 2013, I emailed four editors at the *LA Times*, informing them that I was researching a story on Abcarian's column and asked them a series of questions regarding their standards of attribution, the thresholds they employed for confidentiality of sourcing, whether they actually knew themselves the identity of "Yusef," as well as other specific details the newspaper didn't publish, such as the name of the school. I queried editors Ashley Dunn, Shelby Grad, Mary Meek, and Linda Rogers, all of whom would potentially have worked with Abcarian on the column.

Not one replied to multiple queries.

I also called and left multiple voicemail messages for Dunn, who himself had made media news when, in 2011, his memo to *LA Times* staffers was leaked in which he addressed looming newsroom layoffs with a surreal declaration of, "To those who are understandably feeling a bit down, I say: We don't get our asses whipped, we whip asses. We don't get ulcers, we give ulcers."

Whether he was swigging Pepto-Bismol or nursing a sore gluteus maximus, one thing Dunn and his fellow editors were definitely not doing in April 2013 was taking any questions about the veracity of Abcarian's story. As the crickets chirped at the *LA Times*, it was clear they weren't "kicking ass" so much as trying to cover their own. (That didn't stop the newspaper from calling out *Rolling Stone* this past Christmas Day, putting Jann Wenner's magazine on its "naughty" list for failing to adequately report the allegations of a gang rape at the University of Virginia.)

On May 28, 2013, I enquired with Anum Hussain, Abcarian's original source in Boston, as to whether she had any additional information that would corroborate the story as told by Abcarian. Hussain replied, "I do not—the family did not want to unveil all information at the time of the story for the sake of their son's privacy."

When I noted that as such it would be difficult if not impossible to verify the story, Hussain replied, "The story came from the source in both the BBC article and the *LA Times* article. Fortunately, both those media outlets chose privacy of the 10-year-old over a need to triply verify what is obviously not a made-up story."

Yet the BBC's story tracks back to the same origination point as Abcarian: Anum Hussain. Unlike Abcarian, however, the BBC's Lynsea Garrison regurgitated the narrative without ever explicitly stating whether she had even spoken with someone named "Yusef" or his family members. But Garrison did add the detail that school officials had searched a locker belonging to Yusef. Like Abcarian's column, Garrison's column names neither school, nor teacher, nor town, nor any other comment or perspective from any other individual who would normally be contacted while reporting a news story.

So, I called the Ohio Department of Education and spoke with Associate Director of Communication John Charlton, who told me at the time the state agency was aware of Abcarian's column but couldn't substantiate *any of the allegations* it contained. No one from the *LA Times* had called the department seeking to substantiate any alleged anti-Islamic incidents on Ohio school campuses in the wake of the Boston bombings, nor had the department received any alerts from campuses across the Buckeye State.

"We do a good job of keeping an eye on anything like that and we haven't seen anything to date from the districts," Charlton said. "The lack of confirmable detail in her column is pretty amazing."

I also called the Islamic Society of North East Ohio and left messages seeking comment on Abcarian's column and whether it was aware of the incident she wrote about, but those calls weren't returned.

It's worth noting that Hussain appears to be the original source of the story for both the *LA Times* and the BBC, and the story wasn't picked up or followed by any other news outlet. Even Abcarian never followed up on her column about this fearful Muslim family struggling to survive in the cold American heartland.

But as the *LA Times* demonstrated with Abcarian's column in the wake of the Boston Marathon bombing and again this week in its immediate recasting of the slaughter in Paris as an "extrajudicial killing" that is an outlier of radical Islam best viewed as a prism through which to judge the evils of Western civilization, the newspaper has long since jettisoned reporting actual news in feverish pursuit of validating a narrative truth it believes must be woven into its editorial fabric.

Abcarian wrote in her column: "Let me hasten to add for those worried about molehills becoming mountains, the family is not looking for publicity. No one is making a federal case of this, no one is screaming civil rights violations, no one is threatening lawsuits."

As fantastical as it is to claim a family that allegedly told a reporter from a national newspaper their tales of woe and oppression that served as the basis of a story which paints America as a land of violent nativism was, gulp, "not looking for publicity," it makes a little more sense when one comes to the conclusion that Abcarian's column was neither a molehill nor a mountain—but rather, simply a dark mirage all along.

GOP FINIS

The Republican Party's long funeral procession, led by its corporate pimps turned pallbearers, is now on the final approach to its electoral gravesite where it will be politically buried along with the country and culture it completely betrayed

"Western civilization is going down the tubes and we don't even need an earthquake to finish it. We're performing music for the final dance of death and... aw, you know what? Truth lies beyond the grave."

— Jim Morrison to Ian Whitcomb, summer 1967

First published in 2018

The old American warlord John McCain discovered last year whether or not Morrison's observation on the veritas of oblivion proved to be a cosmically cogent estimate of what we are all destined to find on "the other side," but Morrison's take on the self-immolation of Western civilization in the here and now of this world was and remains undeniably on the money.

The jazz funeral for the West that Morrison described during that gilded Summer of Love more than 52 years ago has continued its long parade, devolving as it has into a tech device-lit bloody spectacle replete with mass consumer gluttony that's self-administered as a morphine drip to numb the creeping sense of dread that has spread across America and its cultural cousins. But even the ever-escalating doses of dope and digital distractions aren't enough to quell the percolating sense of doom that now transcends mere partisan affiliation as the national prognosis becomes ever clearer that the jig is just about up.

But of course, as Morrison's observation to British one-hit wonder Whitcomb in a Sunset Boulevard diner back during the Johnson administration attests, this long funeral procession is marking the death of a culture—and the nation-states into which it once breathed life—that has been terminally ill for decades.

The unfolding collapse of the West has been an epic demolition on such a massive scale that it surely rivals the collapse of Imperial Rome in antiquity and surpasses it with the swiftness of its death. And like the fall of Rome, the death of the West is a massive re-landscaping that was made possible by the deep and expansive veins of greed-fed corruption that its ruling elites have woven throughout the power structures from which they govern, like deadly spiders spinning a powerful web of self-dealing and unjust enrichment at the expense of those who labor futilely under their profit centers presented as social policy initiatives.

In the mid-1980s, Jello Biafra of the seminal punk band Dead Kennedys remarked rather glibly to an audience of students (this writer was in the crowd that night) at SUNY Stony Brook: "If voting really worked, they'd never allow it." It was a throwaway line probably cribbed from some earlier figure in history that yet sounded at least somewhat clever in that era marked by the prevalence of Bolivian powder and passion for its jet-fueled excess. Biafra's smug utterance has oddly proved to be resilient enough to not only stand the test of time, but like a fine wine it has aged quite well. Today it's simply undeniable that the corrosion and rot infecting the eventual successor empire to ancient Rome has resulted in a vast if somewhat slow-motion sociopolitical implosion that has continued despite the electoral wailing and raging of the *vox populi* at the ballot box in protest. More than three years after voters in the United Kingdom cast their ballots to leave the European Union, the yoke of the globalist confederation remains firmly over the once proud island nation. The fate of Brexit spotlights not only the insidious subjugation of the British through bureaucratic obfuscation and delay, a very public murder of the popular will through process and protocol, but in its glare is also revealed the true motives of those who wield power and the hour of reckoning that now arrives for the Western world.

And that is but one of the many grim hallmarks of the total disconnect between the governing and the governed—more aptly described now as the ruling and the ruled—which punctuate a cultural disintegration as the geographic borders that once outlined and meaningfully defined the sovereign states of the West are simply erased amid the relentless stampede of the aided and abetted mass migrations across them.

From public gang rapes in Cologne to the beheading of a British soldier on the streets of London, the Death of the West is a very public affair. It can be seen in the explosion of cartel-related kidnappings in Phoenix to the teeming and violently chaotic No-Go Zones of Paris and Malmö, where France and Sweden have become dangerous places for ethnic French and Swedes—and, it turns out, a *60 Minutes* film crew dispatched there to "debunk" the myth of No-Go Zones, which was promptly attacked in the street by a migrant gang as the cameras rolled. It can be seen on the streets where it's ever more perilous for any who would dare wear a Yarmulke and at the former universities across the United States that have been repurposed as cloistered five-star ideological grooming spas which are now intellectual No-Go Zones for American citizens who believe in the nation as a nation and are even more dangerous for those who would risk the political fashion outrage of sporting a MAGA ball cap.

In Germany, that old and once proud nation which was brutally bifurcated by a grand alliance that had quickly soured after the shooting stopped into the post-war Mexican standoff of East versus West with the bristling guns of the Warsaw Pact and NATO pointed at each other as the world held its breath; well, today that reunified and semi-sovereign-on-paper "country" can't even meet basic recruitment rates to fill the ranks of its own military enough to adequately defend its reconstituted body. Understandably, headlines even now in late 2019 datelined Berlin and heralding "Germany Re-Arms!" might still trigger hurried evacuations in Paris and London and prompt Moscow to declare a state of emergency and mobilize to war-footing, but the fact is that the Kremlin need not worry about the Germany that rolled into Russia twice during the 20th century. It simply no longer exists—and not just as a darkly antagonistic state hell bent on mass murder in delusional pursuit of some ethnic-based *lebensraum*. It has vanished as a nation-state that's able to defend its own country's frontiers and the nation's interior from either perceived threats or very real ones. It relies instead on paperwork and the generous largess of the American people, quite content to live under a "security guarantee" provided by America's sons and daughters. The memo-waving moneyed bureaucratic worm that squirms west across the Vistula today makes the flaccid Weimar Republic look like Europa's dangerously roaring lion of old.

In Paris, President Emmanuel Macron—the French version of Robert Francis O'Rourke (better known by his nom de pop crush: "Beto!")—has remained steadfast in his commitment to the effective erasure of the nation that was revolutionary America's older sister-in-arms, with his administration merely the latest in a long bureaucratic shuffle that has collaborated with those seeking its dissolution, a betrayal of a vintage not seen since the dark days of Vichy, for the French appear to have again evacuated Paris without much of a fight. France, that beautiful beacon of fundamental human freedoms that she has evidenced in everything from her culinary menu to her talent for coitus, is being washed away in a treacherously ministerial manner filled with doublespeak and double dares that would surely have de Gaulle, to say nothing of Napoleon (who while remembered for the feats of his *Grande Armée* left an enduring legacy across France and much of Europe that includes a civil code, secular education, and the codification of French as the nation's official language), wondering what the hell has happened.

Liberté, Egalité, Fraternité? Well, as Camus once wrote: "Dream, *monsieur*, cheap dream. A trip to the Indies!"

And as for Britannia; well, London has indeed fallen.

Today Her Majesty's crown of a capital has seen its ethnic British population reduced to under three percent by a relentless immigration blitz that has forever remade it in the image of those whose eyes light up at the euphemism: "world city." It's a demographic carpet bombing that left The Who's legendary Union Jack-sporting frontman Roger Daltrey smoldering with rage as he considered it on the record in 2013, no longer stuttering when he's *talkin' 'bout his generation's* greatest betrayal, telling *The Sunday Times:* "I will never, ever forgive the Labour Party for allowing this mass immigration with no demands put on what people should be paid when they come to this country. I will never forgive them for destroying the jobs of my mates, because they allowed their jobs to be undercut with stupid thinking on Europe, letting them all in, so they can live 10 to a room, working for Polish wages."

Steven Morrissey, the former frontman for The Smiths who achieved an iconic rock status nearly equal to what Daltry managed with The Who, has weighed in repeatedly as well to the smoldering chagrin of the lockstep Left: "England is a memory now," Morrissey told the venerable *New Musical*

Express back in 2007. "The gates are flooded and anybody can have access to England and join in… Although I don't have anything against people from other countries, the higher the influx into England, the more the British identity disappears. So the price is enormous. Travel to England and you have no idea where you are. It matters because the British identity is very attractive."

As *the New York Times* recently reported, the United Kingdom's military has atrophied so much over the past two decades it has reached a point where analysts have determined it can no longer adequately protect the island nation from another hostile nation-state without resorting to its nuclear umbrella. Of the five permanent members of the UN Security Council—the über-exclusive World War II winners' club—Britain and France no longer possess militaries capable of carrying the fight to a foreign adversary of any note and wouldn't be able to long sustain a successful defense of their respective homelands. If Argentina wants to militarily reassert their historic claim to the Malvinas (or as Margaret Thatcher reminded the world in 1982, "the Falkland Islands," as the UK considers them), well, now would be the time.

And in America, the makeover that has rolled through Europe looks like little more than a touch-up when contrasted against the mass population renovation Washington kicked off with the Immigration and Naturalization Act of 1965 and subsequently supplemented two decades later with the Simpson-Mazzoli Act, a mass amnesty which triggered an earthquake across Mexico that produced a tsunami of mass illegal immigration that rolled across the southern frontier of the United States and has yet to subside more than three decades later.

Back in the day when Morrison caught a whiff of this funeral pyre when it was still quite early in the burn, he knew an inevitable three-alarm house fire when he saw one—and determined there was little to do but lyrically document it, put a score to it, and dance amid the firelight. In the United States, the political sabotage that has led to the passing of an American way of life has been largely orchestrated and managed by the business interests that effectively completed their takeover of the Republican Party during the Reagan era and has ever since carefully led it down a path of shedding national identity and interest in exchange for a world order that enshrines global markets offering a dividend of a glittering empire for its shareholders that make up the governing class.

But like a virus that infects and feeds off a host organism until it's dead, the looming electoral fate of the GOP now suggests the disease of unadulterated greed that defines the Republican Party's leadership is now entering its end stage.

***

The Republican Party's death ride into political irrelevance on the national stage and the subsequent consequences that will clearly befall American citizens of every stripe as the former republic dissolves into a polyglot, balkanized mess that's subject to one-party rule has stoked a bitter sense of betrayal throughout much of what constituted the foundation of the GOP since 1972: working-class and middle-class Whites. While the great exodus of White working-class voters from their century-old political roost in the Democratic Party started with a dribble in 1964 and then began in earnest in 1968—just enough so to reward Richard Nixon's appeals to them with a squeaker of a win over Vice President Hubert Humphrey while Southern firebrand George Wallace carried five states and swiped 10 million voters from the two parties—by 1980, Ronald Reagan was able to roll up staggering margins among the very voters who had been the Democrats' bedrock bloc since industrialization, trouncing President Jimmy Carter by a nearly 10-million-ballot margin in a 478-electoral-vote blowout.

Four years later, the political realignment of "the hard hats" (and rednecks) appeared complete and Reagan buried Walter Mondale by winning nearly 17 million more votes than the former vice president and reaching 525 electoral votes, leaving the Democratic standard-bearer with a single state win and 13 electoral votes—a political annihilation more stunning in its scope and depth than LBJ's obliteration of Barry Goldwater in 1964, an election when Johnson was still able to carry more of the states that had made up the Confederacy than Goldwater even while his administration expanded its commitment in legislative deed to the Civil Rights movement.

In 1988, the Republicans were able to score their third consecutive presidential victory and make George H. W. Bush the first incumbent vice president since Martin Van Buren in 1836 to win. But while the Democrats seemed on the brink of literally unraveling as a viable national political party following Massachusetts Governor Michael Dukakis's bloodless apparatchik campaign, underneath the sea of familiar red that was painted across the United States election map were some very telling numbers.

For starters, while Bush was largely able to run most of the electoral board from coast to coast, including rolling up wins in the big enchiladas of New Jersey, Pennsylvania, Illinois, Ohio, Florida, Texas, and California, the White working- and middle-class popular vote juggernaut that Reagan had commanded in 1980 and 1984 lost notable steam with Bush on the ballot. Dukakis was able to narrow the popular vote loss by more than half—to a mere crushing six million voters. But it proved to be, in fact, the very real silver lining the Democrats needed to see (as an activist Democrat at the time, this writer was one of them), as illusory as it may have appeared in that dark winter of January 1989.

In the coming decade, after the Republican Party has been buried as a relevant player nationally, political historians may well look back at the period between the swearing in of Bush as the 1980s came to a close and the dawn of 1992 as something of an emergency protocol period for the Democrats, a pivot in which the national party's heavyweights decided that the demographic complexion of the electorate had yet to be sufficiently altered enough to abandon White working- and middle-class voters altogether.

And in that moment of the Democrats' existential panic lay the live birth of William Jefferson Clinton's presidency.

The advent of Bill Clinton's improbable 1992 campaign and its repeated resurrections on the road to victory that November was and remains nothing short of a pilot able to pull a jetliner out of a death spiral and not only safely land the plane but pull up to the gate on time and with a courtesy round on the captain. And all of that happened—*indeed it only happened*—because Clinton and Gore navigated the party back to a political agenda that appealed to working-class and middle-class Whites as almost as candidly as Nixon's 1968 and '72 runs did. Thus, the Boston-to-Austin axis of the party's 1988 ticket was jettisoned for two Southern "everymen" who could speak effectively with—not just down to—White Americans. Make no mistake about it: that was the very core of the Democrats' so-called "Third Way" and it worked, saving the life of the Democratic Party and its national viability while the mass immigration that was by then reshaping much of America well outside the Southwest continued to run its course. In essence, the Democrats' ticket of Clinton/Gore in 1992 and again in 1996 and all the policy measures and social signaling it entailed were designed to buy desperately needed time for the Democrats with White voters while the remaking of America continued apace.

This was critical because America in 1990 was a much different place than it is now, three decades down the road, having still more in common in several vital respects to the America of 1970 than it does with an approaching 2020 in the United States. Thirty years ago, America's population had reached 248 million people, of which nearly 76 percent were classified by the U.S. Census Bureau as "White, non-Hispanic." More than three out of every four Americans identified as ethnically White when Clinton hit the campaign trail—a fact that was never lost on him—and his good 'ole boy sensibilities were summoned on demand and to impressive effect. In contrast, Bush seemed to drift about the hustings at times bewildered but more often just bored, having already taken a series of unexpectedly powerful punches throughout the primaries by the renegade candidacy of Patrick J. Buchanan, who had the cast-iron stones to take on a sitting president whose approval ratings had pierced 90 percent in the aftermath of Desert Storm. While Bush's road to the nomination was never really in doubt, Buchanan's populist plank proved devastatingly effective at painting Bush & Co. as hopelessly detached from the common American, finishing the detail on the composite sketch of the Kennebunkport yachtsman that Texas Governor Ann Richards had started back in '88 when she drawled that Bush had been born with a silver foot in his mouth.

Buchanan drew blood as he railed against a "King George" who was comfortably out of touch in Imperial Washington and surrounded by a congressional cohort that was equally dismissive of the average American citizen.

At its fundamental essence, Buchanan's fire-breathing run in 1992 drafted much of what would become the basic blueprint for Trump's 2016 campaign, a campaign that unapologetically made naked appeals to White working- and middle-class voters based on their cultural values and laced them with dire warnings of what the future held if the elites in Washington were allowed to continue plotting the course of the nation with no real regard for the fate of the American people. It was a message that earned Buchanan nearly 25 percent of the total GOP primary voters that year (clocking more than 35 percent in some key states) and by the time the campaign arrived at the convention, Bush had clearly been gored. Enraged by Buchanan's costly challenge but deathly afraid of the consequences that would ensue if they were to deny him entrée at the convention, Bush and the GOP establishment swallowed hard and offered Buchanan a prized opening night speech at the Republican National Convention in Houston. Already despised by the Bush clan and its East Coast power structure for the gleefully unvarnished mockery Buchanan had leveled while on the stump at the blue-blooded "country club crowd" that Bush epitomized, the GOP establishment's blood ran arctic cold as Buchanan made it clear there was no love lost, unleashing a primetime stem-winder that would be instantly immortalized as the "Culture War Speech" for its clarion call to the battlements over what he declared was a war for more than just America's future, but for the very soul of the nation itself.

"My friends, this election is about much more than who gets what. It is about who we are. It is about what we believe. It is about what we stand for as Americans," Buchanan told a packed Astrodome. "There is a religious war going on in our country for the soul of America. It is a cultural war, as critical to the kind of nation we will one day be as was the Cold War itself. And in that struggle for the soul of America, Clinton and Clinton are on the other side, and George Bush is on our side. And so, we have to come home, and stand beside him."

The appeal to the White working- and middle-class voters that Buchanan had keenly sensed were increasingly feeling dismissively ignored by Bush and the establishment to "come home" was the required boilerplate Buchanan had to offer, but if it seemed incongruous that was because it was undeniably clear as to what animated Buchanan's passion as he recounted the America and the Americans he encountered while out on the stump.

"There were the workers at the James River Paper Mill, in the frozen north country of New Hampshire—hard, tough men, one of whom was silent, until I shook his hand. Then he looked up in my eyes and said, 'Save our jobs!' There was the legal secretary at the Manchester airport on Christmas Day who told me she was going to vote for me, then broke down crying, saying, 'I've lost my job, I don't have any money; they've going to take away my daughter. What am I going to do?'

"My friends, even in tough times, these people are with us. They don't read Adam Smith or Edmund Burke, but they come from the same schoolyards and playgrounds and towns as we did. They share our beliefs and convictions, our hopes and our dreams. They are the conservatives of the heart."

It was Buchanan's clear warning offered as an appeal to the Bush cronies who glared down at him from their skyboxes in the stadium that if the party continued down the path of supporting not just a *business-first* agenda but a *business-only* agenda, surrendering the sovereignty of the nation as well as retreating utterly from the cultural battlefields of academia, the popular media, the entertainment industry, and other critical fronts, then the collapse of the party would inevitably precede the disintegration of the American nation. Buchanan knew that Clinton was connecting on a very basic, human level with White working-class and middle-class voters, and that his numerous peccadillos were insignificant to a critical bloc of voters who were beginning to slide into a sense of embittered abandonment. He may have pegged Clinton as something of a charlatan, but he knew that simply dismissing Clinton as "Slick Willie" was a recipe for disaster. Buchanan knew that Clinton was actually campaigning where and with whom it still counted, and he was talking their talk and listening to White voters—not just lecturing or ignoring them.

"They are our people. And we need to reconnect with them," Buchanan told the crowd. "We need to let them know we know they're hurting. They don't expect miracles, but they need to know we care."

***

It was a seminal moment in American political history and it proved to be a prescient foretelling of what lay ahead for the nation. It also marked the last time that a true believer of America as a nation state and as a democratic republic founded on Western ideals and values would be allowed to speak at either of the major parties' national conventions. Senator Zell Miller's blazing keynote speech at the Republican National convention in 2004 has been compared with Buchanan's 1992 barnburner, but the old Georgia Democrat bolted his party in 2004 not to raise the general alarm on the home front but rather to endorse continued American intervention abroad. When Miller stood at the dais in Madison Square Garden to deliver his scathing rebuke of Sen. John Kerry and the national Democratic Party, he spoke relentlessly of who could be trusted to wage a global war against terrorism. At a moment in history when hundreds of thousands of American combat troops were locked in the bloody morasses of Afghanistan and Iraq even as millions of illegal immigrants were successfully crossing the United States' southern frontier each year and exploding communities under the sheer weight of the migration, nary a word about mass immigration or border security was uttered by Miller. The words "immigration," "border," "sovereignty," and "culture" do not appear at all in Miller's speech and the word "nation" appears only once.

Pat Buchanan's 1992 appeal was focused on saving a nation and its dominant culture, but by 2004 Zell Miller's speech was a stark cry for continued American military intervention across the globe. It was a telling evolution and one that reflected just who controlled the Republican Party and, indeed, to what end.

The Democratic Party's Hail Mary pass with Clinton in 1992 paid off and the GOP didn't see red so much as they did blue in critical states that Clinton/Gore managed not only to recapture, but in fact drop a heavy enough anchor in that it would see the Republicans driven from them in national contests to come. Clinton was able to mount electoral-rich trophies like New Jersey, Pennsylvania, Illinois, Ohio, Michigan, and California on the walls of the Democrats' War Room, alongside the spiffy desk decorations of Georgia, Louisiana, Arizona, Colorado, Montana, and Nevada. It was a major conquest and a dizzying reversal of fortune that was rooted in appeals to the White working voter that delivered a margin of victory for Clinton/Gore of more than 100 Electoral College votes along with five million more popular vote ballots than Bush/Quayle.

While a narrative has emerged in certain circles in the aftermath of the 1992 election that it was the independent campaign of billionaire H. Ross Perot which cost Bush his reelection, that's little more than pure speculation dressed up as a conclusion and one that unsurprisingly seemed to comfort the Republican power players. A plainspoken Texan with a Texas-sized wallet, Perot shocked the political duopoly by managing to do something in 1992 that hadn't been done since 1968: run a viable "third-party" candidacy nationally. Perot's entry into the general election race shook Washington because his message—not unlike George Wallace's in 1968 and to a somewhat lesser degree John Anderson's in 1980—was a populist appeal (Perot was a billionaire but he spoke the language of the common man and organized labor) but unlike his fellow Son of the

South's campaign in 1968, Perot's campaign was matched with a checkbook that made him a viable national player out of the gate. And anyone who was there and paying attention remembers the sea of "United We Stand" lawn signs that suddenly sprang up across the nation like California wildflowers after an unusual rainy season.

Veteran political observers at the time comforted themselves amid this unexpected turn of events by noting Perot was drawing support from polar opposites of the established political spectrum, drawing prospective voters from the camps of liberal Democrat Sen. Howard Metzenbaum to conservative Republican Sen. Jesse Helms, and they surmised that such a wildly divergent appeal couldn't possibly last come that November. But they were likely wrong, as they calculated Perot's ultimate election day appeal through the only prism they were familiar with: a label-laden affair of "conservative Republicans" and "liberal Democrats" and the so-called "moderate" middle that would break to one party or another on election day.

Maybe it would have, but perhaps Perot would have pulled off Trump's astounding feat a quarter century before the Manhattan apparent billionaire managed it.

But we'll never know what Perot might have managed to do come election day had he not self-sabotaged his campaign along the way, first by falling asleep at the wheel and selecting Admiral James Stockdale as his placeholder running mate who then became his permanent running mate after Perot suffered some sort of mid-campaign nervous breakdown and withdrew from the race while bizarrely accusing the Republicans of attempting to ruin his daughter's wedding. Yes, that actually happened. Returning to sanity or maybe sobering up, at least for a while, Perot jumped back into the race in time to make the debates where he clearly provided Clinton cover and unloaded effectively on Bush, who during one of them made the fatal but revealing mistake of looking at his watch as an everyday American

Black woman posed a poignant question that working White America was also wondering about the national debt.

Bush actually responded with more than a hint of grinning disgust as he sarcastically suggested that maybe she should be in the White House and read the mail that he got from citizens who were worried about it. After Bush's snarky answer it's quite likely that millions of working- and middle-class Americans of every racial and ethnic stripe thought the Black woman asking the question might be a better selection to occupy the Oval Office as well, particularly when it came to reading their letters and understanding the challenges they confronted and what endless debt ultimately meant for their future.

An indignant Bush also slipped up and gave the nation a glimpse of the Republicans' policy of "engaging China"— rather than isolating it diplomatically and economically— following the wanton slaughter in the summer of 1989 that Beijing unleashed in Tiananmen Square on peaceful demonstrators who had dared to display models of the Statue of Liberty during their collective cry for freedom. Bush was quite ill-advisedly to the point: "But you isolate China, and turn them inward, and then we've made a tremendous mistake and I am not going to do it and I have had to fight a lot of people that were saying 'human rights'… We are the ones who put sanctions on and stood for it. And [Clinton] can insult General Scowcroft if he wants to, they didn't go over to coddle, he went over to say they must make the changes they are making now."

Perhaps not surprisingly, while Clinton took what was then seen as a more hawkish stance toward China and its brutal totalitarian regime, Bush's business-first agenda was a policy that both parties have come follow with near religious fervor since. Clinton wasn't in the White House for even two years before he reversed his campaign pledge to deny China a return to the coveted Most Favored Nation trading status (first granted to China in 1980 and reviewed for renewal annually) that had been suspended following the massacre of pro-democracy demonstrators and a massive wave of arrests and executions.

But in the fall of 1992, Clinton could at least play tough on China and appear sincere, for who could know any better? Bush was ultimately relegated to the role of an irritated and not particularly interested incumbent and Perot, following his own head-spinning stumbles, ended up cast as the spoiler who netted nearly 20 million votes and yet didn't win a single state in the process. After conceding on election night, Perot was nonetheless all smiles as he took his wife for a spin around the dance floor to the tune of Patsy Cline's "Crazy" while Clinton emerged jubilant as Fleetwood Mac's "Don't Stop (Thinking About Tomorrow)" blared away onstage as both a celebration and a battle plan—one the GOP either didn't seem to grasp or chose not to care to.

***

If 1992 was the epic and exhilarating election when Clinton rescued the Democrats as they dangled from the edge of political oblivion, the 1996 race would be something of a pro forma affair with the GOP looking oddly like the Democrats had in 1984, uncertain what to do save nominate Sen. Bob Dole as the next old establishment player in line to serve as the sacrificial goat on the altar of Clinton's reelection. It was a strange campaign, coming across at times like a weak Hollywood reboot of 1992, complete with a returning cast of players. Buchanan once more dashed through the primaries, coming within an eyelash of victory in the opening Iowa caucuses. He then scored an early victory in New Hampshire and again sent waves of panic and rage through the Republican establishment, prompting Dole to grimly declare the primaries would be a clash pitting "the mainstream against the extreme"—a straw man storyline the GOP elites have never really retired since.

But the early primary field among the Republicans in 1996 was more crowded than four years earlier and Buchanan found himself running against not just the Midwesterner Dole but also scion Malcolm Stevenson Forbes Jr.—an epitome of East Coast Old Money—as well as former Gov. Lamar Alexander of Tennessee, Sen. Richard Lugar of Indiana, and a garden variety of other regional vanity candidates who sprouted across the ballot. Despite his early win in the Granite State and clocking more than 30 percent of the votes across other key states—including beating Alexander in the former governor's home state of Tennessee—Buchanan was again an inspired insurgent facing an establishment horse whose victory was never really in doubt after March of that year. When the GOP landed at the San Diego Convention Center in August 1996, the blood between Buchanan and the Republican establishment had putrefied to the point of no return, with the happy renegade refusing to endorse Dole and the cigar lounge leaders of the party—along with California Governor Pete Wilson—banishing him from the convention hall.

Buchanan didn't miss much of a party in 1996, and he knew it.

Meanwhile, amid the balloon drop in San Diego, Dole also realized he didn't have much of a victory lap to savor that hot August. Sensing that he was likely to be seen as something more of a reanimated political cadaver than a viable candidate on the campaign trail against a virile Clinton that fall, Dole tapped native Californian turned former New York Congressman Jack Kemp as his running mate, who at 61 years old at the time appeared like a spring chicken alongside a 73-year-old wounded Dole. Cast from a GI Joe mold, but unlike Dole's very real and courageous battlefield bona fides that he earned during the closing weeks of World War II in Italy, Kemp had understudied in

America's professional football leagues as a quarterback for both the San Diego Chargers and the Buffalo Bills before making his way into Congress in 1971, where he embraced and evangelically espoused a religious faith in the radical theology of so-called free market economics; a belief system that subverts the nation-state and its people to economic considerations alone and declares its Holy Trinity as: Open Markets, Open Borders, and Open Loopholes in the Tax Codes for the seven-digit annual income and higher crowd. While the rationale for Dole to run the play with Kemp was obvious, what was evidently missed in the decision to put the former pro quarterback on the field is the fact that the joyful fanaticism with which he proselytized for the privatization of everything from the U.S. Post Office to AmTrak to Social Security and the Gospel of the Global Marketplace that he preached along with the power of private enterprise as the miracle water that could cure the entrenched and multi-generational poverty that gripped America's Great Cities had never really, well, actually *worked.* Relentless academic war games and prototypes of his beloved "Enterprise Zones" to establish proof of concept aside, Kemp was something of a Republican Jerry Brown—a cheerfully earnest enough fella who was a fount of ideas that never produced anything that could be described as a breakthrough success.

On the other hand, the Dole/Kemp ticket was an academic enterprise itself, a doomed march to election day that saw the Republicans even acknowledge the futility of their national duo by running ad buys in key markets asking voters to split their tickets and vote GOP down ballot so as to "not write Clinton and the Democrats a blank check in November."

While the election of 1996 might not have seemed much of a surprise or even such a disaster for the Republicans at face value—even if its outcome wasn't much in question despite the 1994 mid-term trouncing the Democrats had taken—looking a little closer at the map revealed the continued amazing return from the brink for the Democrats and hinted at a remaking of the American body politic which, left unchecked, would ultimately portend the politically fatal event the Republicans have marched steadily toward ever since. Though Clinton only added a net gain of nine electoral votes to his roster in 1996, up to 379 from 370, he turned his five-million-ballot margin in the popular vote tally in 1992 to a 7.7-million-vote spread in 1996—with Perot again in the race. Perot's nearly 20 million votes in 1992 had withered to a still respectable eight million ballots in 1996. The outcome offers some evidence that Perot's 1992 campaign didn't cost Bush his reelection after all but rather, limited the extent of Clinton's first national triumph. While Clinton lost Georgia, Colorado, and Montana in 1996—all states he carried in 1992—he flipped Florida and Arizona into his column, which more than made up for them. And underneath an electoral map that looked relatively static there were some profoundly disturbing takeaways for the GOP to consider; chief among them was the cold fact that Clinton could have lost Georgia, Colorado, and Montana *and not* picked up Florida or Arizona *and then* even lost Illinois, Ohio, Pennsylvania, and Kentucky and still gone to bed on election night with 270 electoral votes in his pocket.

Such was the electoral depth of the Democrats' national resurgence in a nation where just two decades earlier the GOP had managed to paint virtually the entire country crimson red.

***

The great Republican floodwaters of the 1980s that had appeared so biblical in their sheer scale were now receding and as the party's leadership continued to morph into a Wall Street-driven global market annex it seemed precious little attention was being paid to how much vast electoral territory the Republicans had so quickly squandered. The first atomic blast of Richard Nixon's 1972 re-election that had been built entirely on his successful appeal to White working- and middle-class voters might have been a fond but somewhat distant memory, but the successive Reagan tidal waves of 1980 and 1984 had to have been so fresh that even the hangover of Bush's less enthusiastic win in 1988 couldn't mask how much they had so recently won and how much had slipped through their grasp once more.

And as it turned out, vital states had become lost to the GOP forever: California, New York, Illinois, and New Jersey.

Reagan won all four in 1980 and again in 1984, and he did so in a walk. Bush Sr. carried California, Illinois, and New Jersey in 1988 without too much trouble, but New York fell from the GOP's grasp. Yet since 1992, all four of those critical voter-rich states and their combined 118 electoral votes—approaching nearly *half* of the 270 electoral votes needed to win the White House—have gone for the Democrats and it's difficult to imagine a realistic political circumstance in this era that would put them in play for the Republicans once again.

Those states are gone for the Republicans and unless the Democrats nominate Congresswoman Ilhan Omar as their standard-bearer in 2020 or 2024, they aren't coming back. And by 2028, Omar could well be able to carry not only those states but numerous others as well, but that's making the assumption the United States as even now constructed and sputtering on is still in actual existence as a functional First World nation-state by the end of the next decade. On the other hand, if the Democrats were to run the already three-letter acronym-worthy Alexandria Ocasio-Cortez in 2020, good money could be placed on her picking up California and New York, and possibly run the board in Illinois and New Jersey as well. And that cold fact speaks volumes of not only how psychotically unspooled the Democrats have become, but it paints in high relief the grim fate now fast approaching the GOP. In several respects, Ocasio-Cortez is the progressive Left's current political "It Girl" who by today's metric for a growing strain of the voting public checks more than a few critical boxes: she can dance a rooftop like nobody's business, brazen hypocrisy and faux outrage are second nature to her, she possesses a command of method acting that is Tony Award caliber, she's fluent in progressive psycho-babble, English, and Spanish, and, oh yeah, she's hot. Librarian hot. (Cue the outrage…)

The dawn of the millennium saw the Republicans recover the Chief Executive's office that November by the whisper of a margin of victory in which the GOP carried just enough states to prevail over Vice President Al Gore and his running mate Connecticut Senator Joe Lieberman, snatching an Electoral College victory made possible not by Ralph Nader running on the Green Party ticket in Florida or by Pat Buchanan's purportedly confusing placement on the Sunshine State's ballot, but rather clearly by Gore's inept campaign that saw him lose his own home state of Tennessee. And that's to say nothing of the Gore/Lieberman campaign's inability to win a single state in the former Confederacy—unlike LBJ, Carter, and Clinton before them. For all the hysterics about Florida in the 2000 election, had Gore/Lieberman been able to pluck just a single state south of the Mason-Dixon Line, the election—and history—would have been changed.

***

Victory granted by your opponent's incompetence is worthy of a sigh of relief, but it's certainly nothing to cheer about or gloat over. Yet the suits running the GOP hardly seemed to notice that Bush ultimately prevailed via litigation. He was handed the keys to the White House effectively by court order. Had they studied the map with an eye to long-term strategic prospects as filtered through continued mass immigration rates and declining assimilation standards, the Republicans would have seen they had, in fact, very little to comfort them as the new century fell over the land. They had won the election but actually lost the popular vote by a margin of several hundred thousand ballots. And that wasn't even the bleakest indicator by a stretch; far from it. While the high-altitude view of the national map in 2000 looked comfortably red and the GOP carried once again the bedrock of the South, the five-electoral-vote margin by which Bush/Cheney managed to win despite the popular vote was a grim forecast indeed.

Whether one supported or opposed Bush, the first year of his presidency wasn't something one would wish upon a political opponent, let alone the nation he led. Bush was in office hardly two months before an American Navy spy plane collided with a Chinese fighter plane over the South China Sea, killing the Chinese fighter pilot and forcing the badly damaged American spy plane to land on China's Hainan Island. And thus began a tense standoff not really seen since the days when Moscow and Washington would tango on the global dance floor as the world nervously looked on while a diplomatic solution was brokered. While not carrying the world to the brink of the nuclear abyss, the situation tested the mettle and instincts of the new president right out of the gate and shortly before true catastrophe struck.

A little over four months later came September 11, and the world shuddered as the World Trade Center's iconic twin towers collapsed and the reverberations of its carnage that day was destined to change the world along with America's place in it.

Or perhaps it *cemented* America's place in it.

***

In the rubble of south Manhattan came what would be widely seen as George W. Bush's finest moment. Clad in little more than a windbreaker and wielding nothing more than a bullhorn, the new president stood amid the wreckage with his arm draped around New York City Firefighter Bob Beckwith and declared, "I can hear you. The rest of the world hears you and the people... the people who knocked these buildings down will hear all of us soon." And the crowd of first responders roared, as perhaps well they should have. Yet hindsight must bear witness: just what were they roaring for? Vengeance, of course—and understandably—but harnessed and aimed where and to what ultimate end? If there was ever a moment since World War II that called for an American president and Congress to fulfill their constitutional duties and formally declare a state of war, the September 11 attacks were surely it. It was true that America faced a mercurial enemy it hadn't yet encountered on such a scale: a transnational guerilla force that was able to infiltrate the nation and inflict more casualties and chaos on the American homeland than Nazi Germany, Imperial Japan, Fascist Italy, and any single nation-state enemy or adversary combined since WWII had been able to. And yet Afghanistan was clearly the home base of Al-Qaeda, a Taliban-sanctioned operational headquarters for the global jihadist network.

So it's hard to imagine that roar of cheers from the emergency personnel gathered around Bush and literally standing among the still scattered and smoldering remains of their fellow Americans wasn't in part emerging from a full-throated belief that America was heading into an old school righteous war of the variety that had the destruction of the enemy's ability to carry out further attacks as its primary objective and with more mass devastation administered to

Afghanistan as a punitive measure that would be duly noted around the world as an unmistakable message: "This is what happens when you let Al-Qaeda open up shop in your country."

But when Bush stood before Congress on September 20, 2001, it wasn't to seek a declaration of war to avenge a gravely wounded nation, to launch a massive campaign to punish its attackers, and to protect American citizens and ensure American sovereignty. He didn't rise in the well of the Capitol to speak of such things. Rather, Bush spoke of a global imperative brought to life as a result of the attacks against America. He thanked Congress for singing *"God Bless America"* on the steps of the Capitol and thanked the congressional leadership for their "friendship." He spoke of the world's sympathetic reaction to the carnage on America's shores—from Europe to Asia to Latin America— and of the loss of life in Lower Manhattan that extended well beyond that of Americans alone. He spoke of the importance of understanding Islam and implored Americans to not confuse the mass terror attacks as a product of true Islam or a reflection of American Muslims.

And he did speak briefly of war. Bush declared that the "enemies of freedom committed an act of war against our country." Yet he remarkably sought no declaration of one in return. Instead, he issued what sounded like a court order.

"Tonight, the United States of America makes the following demands on the Taliban," Bush declared, after noting there was indeed little discernable difference between the government of Afghanistan and the terror organization it housed. "Deliver to United States authorities all the leaders of Al-Qaeda who hide in your land. Release all foreign nationals, including American citizens, you have unjustly imprisoned. Protect foreign journalists, diplomats, and aid workers in your country. Close immediately and permanently every terrorist training camp in Afghanistan, and hand over every terrorist, and every person in their support structure, to appropriate authorities. Give the United States full access to terrorist training camps, so we can make sure they are no longer operating. These demands are not open to negotiation or discussion. The Taliban must act, and act immediately. They will hand over the terrorists, or they will share in their fate."

And then after making such a "you better or else" demand even as the Taliban and Al-Qaeda were hurriedly evacuating their leadership structures through Tora Bora and into the decidedly safer environs of Pakistan and then regions around the globe, Bush informed the American people that while a true war wasn't about to start, an era of what would prove to be endless combat around the world with no end in sight was about to begin, even if he did finesse the perpetual nature of it a tad.

"Now this war will not be like the war against Iraq a decade ago, with a decisive liberation of territory and a swift conclusion," Bush said. "It will not look like the air war above Kosovo two years ago, where no ground troops were used and not a single American was lost in combat. Our response involves far more than instant retaliation and isolated strikes. Americans should not expect one battle, but a lengthy campaign, unlike any other we have ever seen. It may include dramatic strikes, visible on TV, and covert operations, secret even in success. We will starve terrorists of funding, turn them one against another, drive them from place to place, until there is no refuge or no rest. And we will pursue nations that provide aid or safe haven to terrorism. Every nation, in every region, now has a decision to make. Either you are with us, or you are with the terrorists. From this day forward, any nation that continues to harbor or support terrorism will be regarded by the United States as a hostile regime."

And Bush posed a rhetorical question to his fellow Americans: "Americans are asking 'what is expected of us?'" His answer to his own question proved quite telling.

In summation, he told them to hug their children, go back to work, and keep spending money. He told Americans to be resolute and calm, to have faith in American principles, and then told them to remain confident in prosperity and the *economy*—a word he used three times in his national address before Congress that night.

Bush didn't use the word *sovereignty* even once.

Eighteen months later, with American combat troops deeply embroiled in a so-called "nation building" exercise that had swallowed them ever deeper into Afghanistan, Bush ordered the invasion of Iraq and thus plunged the nation's soldiers and its people's bullion into a bloody quagmire from which it has yet to emerge and now perhaps never will. When the invasion of Iraq began, more than 13,000 U.S. troops were in combat in Afghanistan. By 2009, American troops in Afghanistan topped 100,000 soldiers—not exactly a sign of success.

***

A decade ago, there was no end in sight in either Afghanistan or Iraq and a decade later there still isn't. Whether one believes this was a terrible miscalculation by the Bush administration that was compounded by its total incompetence or rather just sheer calculation of imperial realpolitik, Bush's decision to not seek a declaration of war and wage one but to instead launch a police action-meets-social experiment while seeking franchise rights in two ancient death traps would have profound effects on the eventual fate of the political fortunes and lifespan of the Republican Party while exacerbating the already deteriorating prospects for the United States as a nation and the West as a coherent culture writ large.

With America locked in dual major military conflicts overseas, the outcome of the election of 2004 certainly appeared at the outset as anyone's guess, with the national sensibility of sticking with the commander-in-chief during a time of even pseudo-war competing with what was by then an equally undeniable pervasive sense among the American public that Bush & Co. had reached a level of malfeasance so grim it had become darkly comedic, complete with a Made For Hollywood scene of Bush arriving on the flight deck of super carrier USS *Abraham Lincoln* in a Navy S-3B Viking to declare "mission accomplished" on May 1, 2003. May Day.

Or as Americans were looking at it by the campaign of 2004: *Mayday.*

And so the Democratic Party's leadership saw an opportunity to avenge what they felt was at least a semi-stolen election four years earlier and once more melded a New England-meets-Dixie ticket that must have seemed more out of central casting than Dukakis/Benson or Gore/Lieberman combined. Senator John Forbes Kerry, the stoic-looking statesman who had seen combat in Vietnam was paired with slick Southern trial lawyer John Edwards, a man who possessed none of the authentic charm and little of the intellectual depth and dexterity of Bill Clinton and yet all of his sexual proclivities and ethical deformities.

The election of 2004 was clearly going to be a referendum on the wars in Iraq and Afghanistan and the GOP was clearly nervous that the Texas Air National Guard pilot topping their ticket was facing an actual combat veteran who had returned from Vietnam scarred by not only the horrific nature of war but also deeply troubled by the policies of multiple administrations in Washington that led America into such a nightmare and had kept it there. And Dick Cheney's record-breaking five draft deferments that he arranged to avoid the war in Vietnam naturally didn't help ease the Republicans' fears.

Unable to compete with Kerry's combat service record, Karl Rove, the Republican's chief political strategist who himself used multiple deferments throughout the height of the Vietnam War to avoid serving in it even as he supported its continued prosecution, decided the GOP should instead sully Kerry's military record and accuse him of turning on the very troops he had fought alongside. And thus was launched a smear campaign that would be effective enough in 2004 to become a verb in political parlance ever since: "swift-boating."

Yet such dirty political trolling wasn't what carried the day for the GOP in 2004, though it surely helped contaminate enough of the atmosphere surrounding Kerry that it effectively blunted Kerry's chief appeal to voters that he could extricate America from another foreign adventure-turned-disaster, but rather Bush was returned to office by holding almost his entire map of 2000—save New Hampshire—and adding New Mexico and Iowa to it. When the dust settled as the sun rose on November 3, Bush had collected 286 electoral votes, hardly a resounding margin of victory by any historical measure. But Bush had the oh-so-sweet pleasure of racking up a three-million-popular vote margin that stunned Democrats, who believed they had the election safely in hand.

Following Bush's second round of inaugural balls, the real festivities started for the corporate elites who by then had assumed virtually total control of the Republican Party's national apparatus, kicking off a nearly four-year blowout marked by wild spending sprees, Wall Street's meth-like subprime mortgage addiction, and the delusions of wealth it fostered. Wide open borders saw millions of immigrants successfully crossing illegally into the United States with ease, dislocating millions of working-class Americans from their jobs, disrupting the affordable housing stocks available to them and seriously compromising—and in some regions just outright destroying—the public education system their kids relied upon. Trampled underfoot were other key signatures of the American social compact, such as a healthcare system accessible to virtually every American and some semblance of a safety net for the less fortunate that ideally helps people recover economically and emotionally from hardship.

***

While the disaster of mass immigration had been building for more than two decades before he took office, for eight long years after George W. Bush placed his hand upon the Bible and swore to defend the nation, the Republican Party flooded the zone with cheap labor for its corporate owners that would quite literally be subsidized by the American taxpayers they were replacing all while the GOP went about proselytizing their religion of consumption without end.

This orgy of dysfunctional consumption raged on even while American soldiers sank ever deeper into the gore-filled quagmires of Iraq and Afghanistan, their open-ended engagement with misery an afterthought to America's political masters and apparently forgotten by the American people. The populace increasingly contented themselves by "Remembering the Troops" for three minutes at a time amid vast sporting spectacles staged in corporate stadiums and arenas where they lined up like a well-tended herd for the privilege to buy $12 hot dogs and $15 beers and a chance to gaze up at the luxury boxes they dreamed of one day occupying. All this while obscenely compensated "athletes" danced their little shuffles and jigs in the end zones and raced across the courts and fields mouths agape and faces fixed in mock rage-meets-ecstasy as if their touchdown, goal, or dunk had liberated humankind from some pox or plague.

And so the band played on all the way through the mortgage crisis, when the house lights were turned back up at least momentarily during the Great Recession just for a quick glimpse of the wreckage scattered across the

American homeland, before dimming again for the opening of this third and final act. The successive elections of freshman Senator Barack Obama and the old salt tapped to be his reassuring running mate, Senator Joe Biden, in both 2008 and 2012 demonstrated the truly precarious state the GOP had stumbled into and how—no matter how dire conditions become—the perfect storm of continued mass migration, the total occupation of the academy, and the perverse corruption of what now might be best described as the media-entertainment complex will most assuredly advance the Democratic Party to a political pantheon of one-party national rule within the next three national election cycles—and quite possibly sooner.

***

By the dawn of 2008, the Republicans' quandary was coming into focus. While the markets hadn't yet collapsed under the weight of the vast mortgage schemes that like the dark art of some lost medieval alchemy was able to cook home values into real gold for a few and fool's gold for the rest, the floodgates were creaking and the bulkheads had begun to ominously groan as the national debt approached $11 trillion and America's imperial wars dragged on.

After eight years of Republican rule in the White House and violently storming seas ahead, it might have seemed that whatever remained of the party's top-tier contenders would have taken a momentary powder and intentionally let the Democrats captain the ship into the maelstrom and then blame them for it.

But power always beckons those who seek it.

Thus as the curtain opened on the 2008 campaign, a field of relatively A-List candidates emerged from within the Republican Party's establishment to succeed Bush, not the least of whom was Rudy Giuliani, the former federal prosecutor who managed to become a Republican mayor of New York City and win reelection despite the Democrats' overwhelming advantage among Gotham's registered voters. Along with Giuliani was former Sen. Fred Thompson from Tennessee, who had first been introduced to the television-viewing public in 1974 when he served as counsel to the Senate Watergate Committee but by 2008 had become much better known for his role as Manhattan District Attorney Arthur Branch on NBC's *Law & Order*. Thompson's well-established political bona fides, his Southern charm, and his career as an accomplished actor on both a television hit series like the *Law & Order* franchise and big screen blockbusters like *The Hunt for Red October* made him a formidable contender.

Joining Giuliani and Thompson among the GOP's starting bench in 2008 was Mitt Romney, the coiffed private equity player who had proudly funded Staples Inc.'s drive to wipe out the smaller, service-friendly office supply stores on Main Street, USA, and replace them with effectively self-service warehouses stocked deep with cheap foreign-sourced products that were frequently defective in the box or quickly broken during assembly. Romney was fresh from a surprise term as governor of Massachusetts—the hunger for power is more prevalent in Romney's genes than Beto O'Rourke's; his father George Romney was the governor of Michigan who ran unsuccessfully for president while his mother ran unsuccessfully for a Senate seat in Michigan—and his time in the Massachusetts statehouse solidified his image as a deft and dapperly dressed carpetbagger, considering Romney didn't actually live in Massachusetts when he decided that he needed to run the state.

Three other undercard players seemed to have at least a potentially plausible long shot that year: Senator Sam Brownback of Kansas, Governor Tommy Thompson of Wisconsin, and Governor Mike Huckabee of Arkansas, with the oddity and amusement factor being offered by the likes of Alan Keyes (of whom Tim Meadows did a terrific send-up on *Saturday Night Live*), Rand Paul, Duncan Hunter, and Tom Tancredo.

And then of course there was the Senator from Arizona, John McCain, who still seemed to carry an angry grudge from his defeat in the 2000 GOP primary at the hands of Bush. Eight years after that stinging loss which was crafted in no small measure by another carefully orchestrated smear designed by Karl Rove and unleashed in the critical South Carolina primary, McCain was in his 70s and looked at the outset like political roadkill on a retreaded tire. But McCain was undoubtedly the globalists' globalist, proudly standing shoulder to shoulder with Sen. Ted Kennedy to sponsor the disastrous Kennedy-McCain mass immigration amnesty bill just a couple of years earlier. McCain teamed with Teddy early in Bush's second term to introduce what would have been the largest mass amnesty ever recorded in the history of nation-states, dubiously entitled the Secure America and Orderly Immigration Act, ultimately giving citizenship to as many as 30-plus million immigrants illegally in the country and kicking off the final phase of swamping and then sinking America as a recognizably Western nation.

Perhaps believing at the time that his shot at the presidency had come and gone in 2000, McCain had gone all in with Kennedy and the so-called "Gang of Eight" plan in 2005 to not just ensure the borders remained wide open, but rather forever eliminate them in any meaningful sense whatsoever. In the process, McCain had taken to taunting working Americans with the old libel that they won't and don't work the jobs that immigrants work, an overtly antagonistic stance that might not have seemed terribly prudent for someone who then decided to hit the campaign trail once more for a second swipe at the Oval Office.

But as previously noted: *power always beckons those who seek it.*

While McCain's boosters have long portrayed his support for mass immigration as a virtue of his character, a sign of his placing principle above what's popular among the citizenry, in actual fact McCain's position on mass immigration was merely in keeping with what had by then become orthodox doctrine among the Republican Party's leadership. Sustained mass immigration was foundational to the profit centers of the corporate and business interests that the GOP by then existed exclusively to serve. Therefore whatever action—or inaction—that elevated and ensured the primacy of continued mass immigration into the United States was always paramount, and securing the border from illegal crossings was merely one element amid a significant range of responsibilities that the Republican Party either abandoned or sabotaged in order to achieve their goals of eliminating American labor and ushering in a replacement population, from workplace enforcement of laws to ensure a legal labor force to laws that ensured housing and healthcare were prioritized to the benefit of American citizens. The fate of the nation and its White working- and middle-class people were completely inconsequential in the end game but they mattered in the meantime only to the extent that they could still be harnessed like an electoral mule and used until the date arrived when they were simply no longer necessary and could be put to pasture, or otherwise disposed.

To that end, as McCain entered a surprisingly populated primary season he reverted back to performing his little Vaudeville routine of pretending to offer the bedrock of the GOP voter base "some straight talk" that was salted by his writers with the required folksy asides, the faux humility and the transparently false assurances that he was just like them—even as he was actually dismissively lecturing them yet again on how their "concerns" about what was happening to the country were neither legitimate nor rational. Only "the crazies" were worried that America was dangerously overextended abroad and literally overwhelmed at home.

But it's hard to say whether McCain was running at least initially in 2008 with the thought that he might actually win the very nomination he had been denied eight years earlier, or rather whether he merely hoped to increase his national profile (which is why even sure losers run for president) and further elevate his stature among the GOP's elite and perhaps gather enough delegates along the way to become a kingmaker at the convention if no one rolled into St. Paul, Minnesota with enough steam to seal the nomination on the first ballot.

Across the aisle, the Democrats were also seeing a number of old warhorses file into the starting gate, including five sitting senators and one sitting governor who were all very plausible presidents. Among them were Sen. Joe Biden of Delaware, Sen. Chris Dodd of Connecticut, Sen. John Edwards of South Carolina, Sen. Barack Obama of Illinois, and Gov. Bill Richardson of New Mexico. And joining that Boys' Club was the Madame herself, Sen. Hillary Rodham Clinton, who like Romney had moved to another state, New York, to run safely for a Senate seat in order to position herself for a run for the White House. Clinton brought one of the few true distinctions to the table on either of the parties' racing form: biological sex and gender—a very real distinction that was transcended by the pure lust for power that bound them all.

***

As surprising as the Democratic primary race turned out to be, with Hillary Clinton outmaneuvered and then overturned by the implausible rise and triumph of Barack Obama's lean and nimble campaign that delivered a historic stunner of an upset which would be overshadowed only by her encore of destruction at the polls delivered at the hands of Donald Trump eight years later, McCain's ability to stumble into the nomination was a head-turner as well. Despite months of building anticipation throughout 2007, Fred Thompson seemed to lose interest in his own campaign almost immediately after he formerly announced his candidacy during an appearance on *The Tonight Show* in September. By January 2008, following performances throughout the frontloaded primaries that ranged from lackluster to piss poor, Thompson pulled the plug.

Fellow heavyweight turned dud, Rudy Giuliani also expired on the launch pad, with the self-declared "America's Mayor" reduced to a meandering campaign that saw him performing a cheap stump shtick in which he pretended to take a cell phone call from his wife during campaign stops, a gimmick that proved about as effective as he was as a candidate. Apparently believing that he wouldn't have much of a shot in either Iowa or New Hampshire, Giuliani decided to bet everything on Florida's winner-take-all primary that had been bumped into January that year. He tanked, trailing McCain and Romney by hundreds of thousands of ballots and was nearly beaten by Huckabee. Like Thompson a week earlier, Giuliani euthanized his campaign before February 2008 had even dawned.

There were some interesting moments to follow, with the Iowa caucuses again proving it's a strange process long-succored in that heartland state (as well as still practiced in some others) that few other Americans really understand and a place where Huckabee pulled out a win and the media pretended, along with seven more states after his surprise Iowa victory, that a governor from Arkansas who wasn't named Bill Clinton was somehow going to be president.

But what was more telling was that Romney, Huckabee, and Rep. Ron Paul from Texas between them won as many votes throughout the primary as McCain, meaning McCain was crowned the nominee after winning less than 47 percent of primary voters. For those listening carefully to McCain, the ghosts of the Mondale and Dole campaigns could be heard rustling.

Obama facing McCain in the general election was a rout in the making, and it wasn't one of simply a vibrant and young Black senator from Illinois overtaking an old and wounded White man in the imagination of voters, though that surely played a significant role in the ultimate outcome. Running as a war hero might have had a nice ring to it during the focus groups, but the fact was McCain had run as a war hero eight years earlier—when he still had at least some residual vim and vigor—and he lost to a decidedly non-war hero (well, all about war, just no hero), so it's unclear why the corporate brain trust running McCain 2008 really thought that was going to work nearly a decade later. Of course, they tried to dress the war hero in the cloak of an elder statesman who would be just the captain for the rough seas into which the ship of state was clearly sailing. It was from that desperate script McCain was reading when he "suspended" his campaign and flew back to Washington to consult with President Bush along with Obama to discuss the nuclear meltdown of the financial markets, but Obama along with the rest of the nation recognized pathetic political stagecraft as performed by McCain and the campaign wound down whether McCain was looking to pause it or not.

And with good reason.

If the country held an election in 1944 as World War II raged across the globe and American soldiers were being killed by the thousands every week, with the electorate ill-advisedly returning a clearly ailing FDR to the White House for his fourth consecutive term, as grim as the financial crisis proved to be in the fall of 2008 the election wasn't going to wait nor should it. McCain's late-hour stunt merely demonstrated how doomed he clearly understood his campaign to actually be.

***

The only glimmer of hope that ever flashed across the radar screen tracking McCain's flaccid general election campaign came in the beautiful form of Sarah Palin, that American Girl (cue Tom Petty) and governor of Alaska who appeared at the convention that summer to jolt the GOP faithful like a double dose of Viagra, stirring to life however briefly an otherwise impotent campaign. Palin's genuine appeal was recognized immediately by the national press corps, which properly identified it as the only viable threat McCain's otherwise limp presence posed to the newly christened Democratic standard-bearer Barack Obama. The establishment media responded accordingly, launching a frenetic and visceral multi-front attack on Palin and her family (which *Washington Post* writer Dana Milbank eventually took to a stalker-grade pathology) while simultaneously pretending to maintain an honest respect for McCain, a tenuous charade that they were prepared to play as long as Obama seemed poised to win.

While McCain may have hoped to bottle Palin's lightning at the convention, it wasn't long before she had stolen the campaign's thunder along with the hearts of many more people than the senator and his staff could ever abide, and McCain's rage and fury quickly mounted as he watched Palin draw thousands of energized and cheering supporters out on the stump while he more often than not drew merely hundreds of people during his solo appearances that were noted for the scattered and awkward applause that would later become a hallmark of the Jeb Bush 2016 campaign.

And so America was treated to the surreal spectacle of the GOP's machine turning on its own vice presidential candidate in 2008 during the election for the offense of being far more genuinely popular than its ailing and stumbling presidential candidate and in doing so, self-immolating literally the only real thing their campaign had going for it. Sarah had "gone rogue," the Republican suits fumed, disgusted at her brazen nationalist appeals against "crony capitalism" and her commitment to secure America's borders. In a sense, she certainly had gone rogue, and in doing so foreshadowed a campaign yet to come, but Palin's bucking a traditional role of tuchus-smoocher for McCain's ambulance ride into November is what made her, well, *Sarah*. Yet while the pure pettiness of McCain's intermural political envy was suddenly on vivid display, Palin's sheer appeal—and who found her appealing—once more demonstrated the Republican Party's reliance on the White working and working middle class as the only voting bloc that could deliver them November.

Despite her plain-spoken intellectual depth which so rabidly infuriated her establishment critics, as most memorably evidenced by ABC's Charles deWolf Gibson and CBS's Katherine Anne Couric's cold sweat of contempt for Palin's actual working-class existence that was caught on camera, to Sarah's unflinching anchor in and her candid commitment to core American values and her unvarnished holistic beauty that by all accounts triggered screaming fits of jealous rage in McCain's second corporate wife Cindy McCain, the medicinal brew of Americana roots that Palin provided to McCain's campaign was simply not enough to save the cadaver from its fate with the senator at the helm.

Simply put, the Republican machine unsurprisingly got it backward, as the only chance the GOP probably really had at all in 2008 would have been with a Palin/McCain ticket emerging from the convention—and that's assuming McCain had to be on the ticket at all.

By the time the voters left the polling booths the reality of McCain's electoral erection dysfunction finally struck the GOP hard, so to speak, as Obama ran the board. While McCain managed to hold onto a near identical popular vote that Bush garnered in his 2004 reelection, meaning nearly 60 million votes, Obama trumped that by an almost 10-million-popular vote margin and in the process rolled up 365 electoral votes to McCain's stagnant 173 electoral votes. Despite Palin's best efforts on a doomed ticket headed by a doddering candidate and sabotaged by the old man's corrupt cabal, the national map confronting the Republicans in 2008 reflected the erosion the party had suffered among its base.

Obama's win echoed the success of Clinton before him as he recaptured Virginia, Florida, and North Carolina in the Old South and rolled through Ohio and Indiana in the Rust Belt, Iowa in the Midwest, and Colorado, Nevada, and New Mexico in the Sunbelt, all states that had fallen to Bush only four years earlier. McCain performed only slightly better than John Kerry had in 2004, but he managed to lose those nine states because he couldn't make an effective case to working White Americans that they should stick with the Republicans—or just turn out for them even if they weren't going to vote for Obama. He simply didn't have any credibility throughout much of a voting bloc that he had spent years dismissively denouncing and lecturing and the one element of his campaign that did resonate with such voters, Sarah Palin, was accordingly scuttled.

Thus came the inglorious end to McCain's lifelong endeavor to wield power from the Oval Office, a warlord vaunted by the Beltway Establishment for his total commitment to a global empire completely obliterated at the ballot box by a community organizer from Chicago who had been a Senate backbencher only a couple years earlier.

And while it was ultimately a predictable defeat it was still nonetheless crushing to McCain and his family, a personal humiliation that only filled the McCain clan with an even greater reservoir of bitter hatred for the American nation-state and the White working class that had forged so much of it. Glowing with that radioactive animus, McCain himself slunk back to his Senate seat where he would dedicate the rest of his life to ensuring America wouldn't long survive him.

***

Despite the GOP's hemorrhaging voters and states in 2008, the first midterms that followed Obama's election delivered a stunning rebuke to the Democrats at the hands of a White working- and middle-class electorate that began to better understand the party of FDR, JFK, and LBJ wasn't really how they remembered it, that it had changed considerably since even Clinton had saved it, and they unleashed a grassroots rejoinder that resulted in the largest congressional realignment in more than 60 years. It was a comeuppance that momentarily terrified the Democratic Party's power players and its media assets, who descended into a frenzied meltdown that would serve as a teaser of attacks against White voters yet to come, but the ballot blowback of 2010 was ultimately harnessed by Establishment Republicans who spent it to further their own corporate agenda—a profiteers' to-do list that had nothing of merit to offer all those angry voters who were tired of watching their quality of life, indeed their *way of life*, continue to erode by the week if not the day.

By the time the card was being drawn up for the 2012 election, the GOP's leadership thought they had arrived at a workable plan for victory: run a younger version of McCain. And so, Willard Mitt Romney's moment had finally arrived. After galloping through an uninspired primary season in which he rolled up wins in 37 states but tellingly only claimed 52 percent of the primary votes, Romney tapped former Jack Kemp acolyte Paul Ryan as his running mate in the misguided belief that White working- and middle-class voters would be drawn back to the Republican fold if two visually White and supposedly moderate males were on the ticket—no matter what they really represented. Romney had managed to sew up the primaries amid an uninspired collection of opponents that was most notable for who wasn't among them: Sarah Palin. While the former governor of Alaska admirably decided that slogging through another national campaign wasn't worth it for her family—her youngest son Trig, who was born during the 2008 primary season, was just four years old—professional political glutton and former Speaker of the House Newt Gingrich just couldn't resist making a last run at the Washington trough he had fed so long at, presenting himself to voters as a professorial statesman and leading intellect in the GOP who was ready to return the party to presidential power.

Unfortunately for his campaign, as a career congressman from Georgia dating back to the Carter administration, Gingrich had spent two decades diligently working round the clock for the corporate interests that have profited mightily from the Republican Party as they've ridden it to its death and the disintegration of the nation. Gingrich was a trusted foot soldier for Wall Street to ensure the borders remained wide open while immigration enforcement at worksites in the interior of the country remained unenforced. Gingrich was the legislative point man to protect the vast flow of mass immigration of cheap replacement workers that was pouring in to what business defined merely as "labor markets" while decimating working-class jobs in construction, installation, manufacturing, assembly, auto works, hospitality, and across numerous other industries that once paid living wages to American citizens. Gingrich's attempted makeover and his revisionist historical take that he had attempted to staunch illegal immigration didn't pass the laugh test with voters and the former Speaker of the House tanked early and took his talent for error-prone prognosticating to Fox News.

There's no question that as summer faded into fall in 2012, the GOP could look past the deep corrosion of credibility it had suffered among the American people and reasonably convince itself that it had an even shot at overtaking Obama on election day. The metrics for the incumbent were troubling, to say the least. The Great Recession remained a black hole which consumed the jobs, homes, and, in a more figurative respect, the lives of millions of Americans. Many Americans remained in financial anguish while tens of millions more confronted economic uncertainty every day. The launch of the Affordable Care Act, so-called "Obamacare," proved fitful at best and demonstrated the president's assurance that Americans who liked their doctors and their health plans could keep them was a lie. Mass migration into America continued at a brisk clip even as the nation struggled to help its own citizens.

Overseas the news wasn't much better. With American combat troops still mired in Afghanistan, Obama had decided on a "surge" of reinforcements to keep the Taliban on the defensive, but the 30,000 troops who were ultimately deployed were nowhere near enough to defeat the enemy or accomplish really anything other than to maintain the status quo. It would later be revealed that Gen. Stanley McChrystal provided a classified briefing to the then new president in September 2009 informing Obama that a successful campaign against the Taliban would take 500,000 combat troops and a relentless all-out-for-victory approach expected to last about five years. Obama blanched, then took a pass, but in the fine tradition of wanting to seem to be doing something (versus getting the hell out of there), he agreed to put a fractional amount of more boots on the ground in Afghanistan.

If that weren't problematic enough, while the landmass formerly known as the nation of Iraq continued its dissolution into tribal fiefdoms and terrorist redoubts with a corrupt make-believe central government succored on American dollars and supported by American troops, Obama decided to run a regime change play that echoed the Bush administration's brilliant calculations, first by throwing

Hosni Mubarak under the bus in Cairo despite the Egyptian strongman's three decades of supporting the West and then, with John McCain at his side, ordering the air campaign that would eventually knock out Libya's Muammar Gaddafi. Despite Secretary of State Hillary Clinton's gleeful boast of, "We saw. We came. He died!" the reality was the homicidally eccentric Gaddafi had held the country together much in the same manner Saddam Hussein indisputably had in Iraq. With Gaddafi gone, what was once Libya completely disappeared into a violent churn of competing governments that ran little more than neighborhoods in cities with more than 300 militias spread across the former nation-state. Just as Bush had effectively erased Iraq as a functioning nation, Obama managed to make Libya vanish and in doing so offered fresh territories ripe for ISIS and Al-Qaeda's career development centers.

This was the record Romney got to run against, and there's no question that Obama was nervous about some of his weaknesses (he didn't mention the "victory" in Libya much during that campaign), but an interesting thing happened on the way to election day.

Romney didn't seem to know much of what to do beyond run a lifeless campaign based on what by then had become the Republican Mass: tax cuts, deregulation, and privatization. Oh, yeah, and about that whole illegal immigration thing: um, well, people who broke into the country and then broke into jobs often using stolen Social Security numbers can just "self-deport."

It probably didn't help that he came out of the gate believing he had no shot whatsoever with nearly half the country. During comments made at a Boca Raton fundraiser that September that was leaked to *Mother Jones,* Romney declared to wealthy donors, "There are 47 percent of the people who will vote for the president no matter what. All right, there are 47 percent of the people who are with him, who are dependent upon government, who believe that they are victims, who believe the government has a responsibility to care for them, who believe they are entitled to healthcare, to food, to housing, to you name it—that's an entitlement. And the government should give it to them. And they will vote for this president no matter what," Romney said. "I mean the president starts out with 48 or 49 percent... He starts off with a huge number. These people pay no income tax. Forty-seven percent of Americans pay no income tax, so our message of low taxes doesn't connect. So, [Obama] will be out there talking about tax cuts for the rich. I mean that's what they sell every four years. And so my job is not to worry about those people. I'll never convince them that they should take personal responsibility and care for their lives."

While he sought to quickly recover the pseudo-gaffe by expressing regret for the comments—and it's not clear at all that they did any lasting damage to an otherwise bland campaign—it was actually a profound observation that revealed the GOP's elite and their corporate owners understand that the electoral tipping point into their oblivion draws near. Equally profound was what Romney left unsaid: just how did the Republican Party find itself in a country which by their own description was now no less than half-populated by "people" who in lieu of not paying taxes want a cradle-to-grave system of handouts? Just who are these "people" and where did they come from?

While denounced by the usual suspects as a racial dog whistle, the cold arithmetic doesn't support that as Whites in 2012 were by far the dominant voting bloc and there's no way half of the American voting populace is comprised of anything less than tens of millions of White Americans of every economic strata and cultural caste. In January of this year, the Pew Research Center projected that in 2020 the so-called "Boomers" (of which this writer is a member) of the post-war "Baby Boomer" generation, which is overwhelmingly Anglo, will still comprise the single largest generational bloc of eligible voters who may—or may not—amble over to the polling place on election day next fall. And even among Gen Z (appropriately entitled to signal The End) voters who may cast ballots in 2020, the Pew Center notes, more than 55 percent of these potential voters will be White. Yet in the most generic of assessments it's Gen Z that embodies the most privileged and pampered generation in American history.

So Romney's caught-on-candid-camera kiss-off to half the electorate wasn't so much a farewell to, in the parlance of today, "voters of color" (but them too) as much as it surely was a recognition of the GOP's precarious position among a broader range of White Americans who don't see Social Security as a giveaway or FHA home loan guarantees as a socialist plot, may dread the DMV but are rather fond of their local U.S. Post Office (don't think so, just try to close one) and don't believe in privatization as a religious cure for every bureaucratic ill. And they are even less enthused about academic theorems that advance the hypothetical glories of free trade, open labor markets, and the mass immigration that fuel vast profits for so few while "displacing" so many.

In any case, while Romney and tag along Paul Ryan may have appeared to be the best shot the GOP had at unseating Obama and his understudy Joe Biden, the Republicans' refusal—and by this time perhaps their politically genetic inability—to run candidates and a campaign that spoke directly to the concerns of the single largest voting demographic in the nation likely doomed the effort from the start.

Like McCain just four years before him, no one was excited about a Romney presidency, least of all the people he needed to be the most.

***

And so it was that while Obama shed about four million votes in November 2012, he still cruised to reelection, picking up a comfortable 332 electoral vote spread and ceding only North Carolina and Indiana from his 2008 roster. The Republicans' cerebral hemorrhaging was evident in Karl Rove's state of denial on Fox News as he insisted Ohio was still in play and the election was still up for grabs even as Obama was perusing the invite list for his second inaugural. Obama had beaten Romney by more than 100 electoral votes and by five million popular votes. It wasn't even close.

And like John McCain before him, post-defeat Romney too would make plans to slip into the Senate from a safe state like Utah where, filled with an icy rage for the White working and middle classes that rejected him, he has diligently pursued his plans to wreak terrible vengeance upon them. Like McCain before him, Romney has always believed that he was born to be president, and the denial of his perceived destiny by a motley rabble that shares little more with him than also being Caucasian has stirred in Romney—just as it did in McCain—a jihadist zeal to see America as a sovereign nation-state utterly erased into a borderless mass consumer market. That was the endgame intent all along, of course, but in defeat Romney has found an even greater sense of imperative purpose.

In an amazingly comical display of dark humor, the GOP's establishment as led by Republican National Committee Chairman Reince Priebus drafted a "postmortem" on just what went wrong for the party in November 2012. It was and remains a manuscript of grotesque beauty presented as a map to the future with the word "DOOM!" crossed out and "future" scrawled above it. According to the GOP management team, the only way the Republican Party had a workable future as a national political force following the 2012 debacle was, well, more of the same. The media had a field day cavorting through the GOP's letter to itself, which *Talking Points Memo* summarized in six key points, the first of which said everything: Pass Immigration Reform *Yesterday*. That's right. The Republicans have lost multiple elections as its base of a working- and middle-class White voting bloc abandons it—in no small measure due to mass immigration and particularly illegal immigration—and priority one is to grant another sweeping amnesty to illegal immigrants and expand the legal avenues in which millions of migrants can arrive in the United States in vast numbers irrespective of the impact on American citizens, including the struggling Black and Chicano Americans who, like their White American brethren, desperately need a hand from Uncle Sam.

After losing in 2012, the Republican Party's leadership, as directed by Wall Street and associated business-first entities, determined that the problem with Romney was he didn't push open borders and mass amnesty strongly enough. The underlying message of the so-called postmortem was that the GOP had to plunge even deeper and faster into the playbook that the California Republican Party had been running its ground game from since well before the millennium: jettison any cultural connection to White working America and offer snappy econo-sops to Black and Latino voters in the fever-dream that they may somehow wheel around into the GOP's corner.

And this actually passed as a plan for a political party's future, when it really was the playbill for its funeral.

Well, that free market, open border prescription was once more dutifully swallowed inside the Beltway by the bulk of the GOP's congressional cohort and the media establishment that cheers it all the way over the cliff, but the sweep of working White America didn't need to reject it as they didn't really bother to pay attention long enough to read it following Romney's implosion.

Despite the second consecutive loss of the White House, the Republicans could take some significant solace in the

2014 midterm elections, where they saw net gains in the Senate, the House, and in gubernatorial races across the country, albeit gains that had virtually nothing to do with the Priebus-penned postmortem. House Majority Leader Eric Cantor's loss in the Virginia primaries to an unknown professor who effectively ran a one-issue campaign—taking a hard line on mass immigration—demonstrated once more how out of touch the GOP's leadership had become to the will of their constituents. Yet their nine-seat Senate pickups were the spear-point in an advance that heralded yet another moment that should have given the Democrats a chilling pause, as while Obama remained securely in the Oval Office the map nearly everywhere outside the District of Columbia looked somewhere between ugly and downright grim. In short, by 2014, the GOP's electoral holdings outside of the presidency—judging by any map—appeared overwhelming.

***

But while maps provide useful charts of topography, they aren't the geological survey that studies what's actually happening underneath the surface. As journalist-turned-historian William Shirer chronicled with meticulous detail in his seminal tome *The Rise and Fall of The Third Reich*, when 1942 came to a close the scope of Germany's conquest seemed almost terrifyingly unimaginable when evaluated from a map, encompassing a portfolio of real estate surpassing the height of the Roman Empire and stretching from the English Channel to the Volga River, from the Norwegian Sea to the southern shoreline of the Mediterranean and deep into the Caucasus. And yet as history would reveal in its own epic postmortem, the Germans were already toast by the dawn of 1943. The map said one thing but the fundamentals underneath it spoke to something else altogether and as that fateful year of 1943 got underway, much of the German High Command sensed it. The Germans were sitting on this vast bounty of conquered soil and were meticulously looting its spoils yet with every passing day, the creeping feeling that they had reached high tide and shot their last real effective bolt couldn't be shaken and by the late summer of 1943 it couldn't be denied, if still not spoken so openly. The Germans slogged on for two more carnage-filled years but by September 1943, the outcome was never really in doubt.

It's not too much to say that 2014-16 was quite likely the GOP's electoral 1942-43, a high tide that preceded its total collapse.

Like the Germans of WWII before them, they will attempt to trade some real estate for time, writing off some states and shifting resources to others that they hope to put or keep in play, but soon enough they will no longer be able to deny they are increasingly in short supply of both—and precious little in the way of reliable voters to make it up with—much like the rest of the Western world today. It's worth noting that in the cold winter of January 1942, even a brooding Adolf Hitler, who weeks earlier had pounded another nail into his nation's coffin by declaring war on the United States, pondered America's future when considering its construct and rhetorically asked his generals, "It's a decayed country… How can one expect a state like that to hold together—a country where everything is built on the dollar?" The answer turned out to be "long enough to wipe Nazi Germany and the Axis powers off the map," but his observation that an all-consuming adherence to a currency versus a culture to define a country cannot allow a coherent nation-state to long survive seems more relevant for the United States today than when Hitler stewed on it in the gathering gloom of his own murderous regime's doom.

The meteoric ascendance of Trump fueled a firestorm of hysterical yet obscenely inaccurate (and intentionally so) comparisons of the duly elected 45th President of the

United States to the rise of Hitler and Germany's subsequent descent into its twelve-year nightmare of Nazi Party rule as the horrors of it unfolded across Europe and much of the globe. The analogies tying Trump's stated policy objectives (as empty as they ultimately proved to be) to Hitler and the Nazis weren't a particularly new tactic from the progressive playbook nor was the regurgitation of it across the nightly news cycles, but the vehemence and volume of the smear in this iteration were jolting, as were the "legs" it picked up in anchor seats and the class of punditry that affords various networks and shows prepaid positions on particular issues. Finding someone to muse aloud whether Trump's election was a prelude to migrant round-ups, media shutdowns, and, inevitably, concentration camps for illegal immigrants, hasn't been terribly difficult since about mid-2016 after it became apparent Trump was going to be the Republican nominee and even easier following his election that November.

But for all the outrageous mischaracterizations of Trump and the brazen manipulation of historical facts in an effort to make Trump and the GOP's base seem at least something akin to a close relative of the Nazis—carriers of a bad gene in their political DNA that should make them suspect at all times—there is of course no meaningful comparison for anyone even tenuously tethered to historical reality. Naturally, that caveat places an increasing swath of the emerging generation of Democratic Party activists in play as they not only routinely make the comparison but actually believe there is an ethically honest correlation between the Republican Party and the National Socialists who seized power in Germany and brought genocide into the Industrial Age by committing it with all the bloodlust of antiquity but with a conveyor belt efficiency that heralded the arrival of the 20th century.

While there is no sane equivalence between the GOP and the Nazis in their philosophy or practice, nor in their motives or methods, if there is a similarity to be glimpsed anywhere between the Nazis and the GOP it can be found amid the reactions of both parties' true believers as the roof is caving in on them.

Richard J. Evans, a professor of modern history at Cambridge University whose exhaustive account of wartime Germany, *The Third Reich at War,* was published in 2008 to become a *New York Times* bestseller includes an account from a young woman who toiled away in Berlin at a frenetic pace even as the downfall of the Nazi regime grew ever closer.

"Every one of us worked with hectic energy. Countless projects were started up, knocked out by the effects of the war, abandoned, taken up again, cancelled, altered, rejected once again, and so on," wrote Melita Maschmann. "During the last months of this, the feeling crept over us that all this feverish activity… was hardly producing the slightest response in the country. Our office was like a termites' nest, gradually pervaded by the sense of the coming collapse without a single person daring to breathe a syllable about it… Our brains gave birth to plans and still more plans, lest we should have a moment to stop and think and then to have to recognize that all this bustle was already beginning to resemble the convulsions of a dance of death."

The sort of frenetic, hive-like mentality Maschmann recalled as the young automatons busied themselves in end-stage delusions can be found throughout the GOP today, with its college outreach initiatives that aren't just dead on arrival but are actually met with frenzied mob violence on campus and its dead-end ethnic minority outreach efforts—which at times still seem to be little more than appearances by the duo Diamond & Silk on Fox News and Candace Owens's Twitter account—and ever more bizarre declarations from the Republican leadership that Americans are a people united in their values and beliefs and priorities when, in fact, the country is dissolving into Babylon on the Balkans all around them.

***

When the respective primaries got underway for the presidential election of 2016, America was faced at the outset with the very unsavory prospect that dynasty—just another word for entrenched corruption—was going to deal its hand in a rematch of another iteration of Clinton v. Bush, with former Secretary of State Hillary Clinton poised to make the title bout and square off with former Florida Governor Jeb Bush (pronounced "Yeb Boosh" among his detractors) and for a few months in late 2015 it appeared that America was destined to be led for the sixth time by a member of one of two families who had held power in the White House for twenty consecutive years since January 1989. If that were the case and either Hillary or Jeb were then reelected, it would mean two families ran the executive branch of the United States for twenty-eight of the past thirty-six years.

And this is the reality from a nation whose elites routinely rail against the Russian oligarchy without the slightest whiff of irony.

But as fate would have it, Bush v.3 proved to be more amazingly feeble than even McCain's general election run eight years earlier. Despite having amassed a deep $200 million-plus war chest and having built/inherited a national campaign structure populated by career establishment figures with ties stretching back to his dad's CIA days, Jeb managed to do little more than burp, cry, and fart on the stump until his family begged him to abort his campaign in the first trimester, which he did in late February 2016. The patriarch George H. W. Bush is said to have sobbed in his wheelchair at his family's total humiliation at watching his son Jeb plead to an audience, "Please clap."

As for the hundreds of millions of dollars that were funneled into Bush's stillbirth of a campaign, it's doubtful the donors saw a dime of it back, and one must wonder how that went over when all that cold cash bought the players was approximately 286,000 votes for Bush while Ben "Who?" Carson running on shoestring, wax paper, and a jar of paste racked up nearly a million votes. Senators Ted Cruz and Marco Rubio, along with Governor John Kasich, pulled together more than 14 million ballots between them and carried a considerable number of states, but it was the odd man out from the beginning, Donald J. Trump, who would go on to garner more than 14 million votes alone and had the nomination in hand by May 2016, a precursor political upset that begat the most profound political upset in the history of American presidential elections.

Enough has been written and more still will be as to just how this happened, but it's worth revisiting for a moment in this late hour of what remains of the Republican Party's life and the in-progress collapse of America and the Western world itself, particularly to provide context to the debacle that would soon follow Trump's inauguration. Oceans of ink, both real and digital, have been expended since Trump descended on that now legendary escalator on June 16, 2015, to announce his candidacy. And almost all of it focused on what journalists understood, innately it seems, to be his *punch line*: mass immigration, particularly of the illegal variety, essentially because no one else was talking about it in the terms that he used, save perhaps more than 200 million actual everyday Americans. And he got right down to it, in his manner of speaking, which between his vocabulary, syntax, and linear coherency seemed even at that early date to peg him at possessing between a sixth- or seventh-grade intellect. His announcement was a sure sign that Trump either freestyles his own "speeches" or veers wildly off whatever was actually written for him.

"When Mexico sends its people, they are not sending their best," Trump declared. "They are not sending you. They are not sending you. They are sending people that have lots of problems, and they are bringing those problems with us. They are bringing drugs. They are bringing crime. They are rapists. And some, I assume, are good people. But I speak to the border guards and they tell us what we are getting. And it only makes common sense. It only makes common sense. They are sending us not the right people."

Amid his opening ramble were two sentences that would take on greater importance later: "When was the last time anybody saw us beating, let's say China in a trade deal? I beat China all the time. All the time," and "Islamic terrorism is eating up large portions of the Middle East. They've become rich. I'm in competition all the time."

China? *"I beat China all the time."*

ISIS? *"I'm in competition with them."*

While it was an oddity for many reasons—and thus laughed off by most people in news and punditry as a momentary sideshow to the main event—the emergence of Trump's campaign from its Manhattan womb was immediately notable primarily for two things: Trump spoke much in the manner of a developmentally disabled student trying to recite memorized CliffsNotes on his keynote issues; and the challenges facing America always came back to him personally. America is losing to China—*but he beats them all the time.* ISIS is getting rich—*but not as rich as he is.* It's unlikely that any president from George Washington through Barack Obama ever spoke in a manner even remotely akin to such self-serving word gruel, but that apparently was the rub, or more specifically, beside the point. A dominant swath of the American body politic had by 2015 unraveled to the point of desperation where they were willing to listen to a brazen braggart hold forth in bizarre cycles of conversational repetition that would try the patience of even the most experienced parent simply because he was actually *talking about* the key issues that mattered to them most and in a manner they considered at least forthright if not exactly couth.

Trump's supporters back then, and those who remain, were and still are routinely fond of referring to his amazing "instincts," his deft skill at playing something they call "3D Chess" (as if the guy who struggles to speak in complete sentences is suddenly transformed into a Garry Kasparov when confronted with a foggy American landscape populated with the political pawns, rooks, bishops, knights, queens, and kings of his opponents in every direction) and even those who will acknowledge his obvious difficulty in maintaining an attention span past that of an infant surrounded by colored lights and blown bubbles still insist he's some sort of a card-counting savant à la Raymond from *Rain Man* or Alan in *The Hangover*.

Trump is neither a political grand master nor an insurgent savant who is beating the house at its own game, but he did manage to grasp something in the summer of 2015 that the other candidates in either major party didn't: what the majority of White working Americans—as well as significant numbers of Blacks, Chicanos, and virtually every other racial and ethnic stratum of American there is—wanted in terms of immigration. He also was able to demonstrate a layman's understanding of their weariness of foreign wars without end and their escalating contempt for a globalist construct that had in every real sense left them behind.

This didn't make Trump a genius. Nor did it mean he was a mad scientist or a crypto-Fascist in a developer's garb. Ann Coulter likely summed it up best when she observed that Trump was simply the guy who looked down and picked up the $1,000 bill on the ground that everyone else had walked by.

After fending off fantastical efforts to deny him the nomination by the GOP establishment and emerging from the convention as the nominee, he hit the ground running against Clinton, who had survived her own much-too-close-for-comfort brush with another backbench challenger who nearly denied her the Democratic nomination a second time—and arguably would have had she not ginned the DNC deck with enough cards planted in her favor.

***

Throughout the general election campaign of 2016, Trump, for the most part, clung to that $1,000 bill that Coulter noted he had picked up and waved it around from the podium as he framed the election as the last chance to save the United States of America as the country had been primarily constituted in broad strokes for generations. And for the first time since Reagan and in a candid manner not really seen since Nixon, Trump appealed directly to the White working Americans and at least appeared to understand that they were really the only chance he—and his party of choice—had at landing back in the White House. He became the first candidate since Nixon and Reagan who didn't get drawn into the Democratic Party's game of trying to make the Republicans apologize for speaking directly to a majority of Americans in almost the same fashion the Democrats appeal to their own ethnic base of Black and Latino voters, just less stridently and not nearly as venomously framing the opposition's voting bloc.

The difference, of course, was still clearly evident on the campaign trail as Clinton could and did speak directly to what she would deliver for Blacks and Latinos—by name—while Trump still never said something along the lines of, "This is my plan to help ease the disastrous impacts that open borders have brought working-class and lower-income *White* Americans," but everyone knew he was speaking to the racial category that was and still remains a solid majority in the nation. Instead of saying the term "White America," the Trump campaign settled on "rural America," but his audience was clear.

Naturally, the Democrats defecated on themselves in outrage, or at least pretended to, as they had grown accustomed to a GOP leadership (Bush, Dole, Bush II, McCain, Romney, et al) that would mostly ignore White Americans even as they fed off them and even when they did make appeals that appeared to be directed at White voters, they were generally understood to be transparently half-hearted and of no particular value.

Yet by 2016, the Democratic Party considered its demographic realignment nearly complete and the Clinton who ran in 2016 didn't need to have, let alone want to have anything much to do with the essential bloc that her husband harnessed enough of when he ran in 1992—the working White voters Bill Clinton had tapped to save it back then. By the fall of 2016, the Democrats had come to believe the transformation of America was close enough to "finished" that its coalition of Blacks, Latinos, and millennial Whites of the college-educated variety were enough to carry them not only to victory, but to the first landslide in what they believed would be a perpetual series of electoral tidal waves. So carried away, in fact, had the hubris swept so many Democrats, including old pols among them who should have known better, that veteran political observers in California were projecting Clinton victories in Texas, Georgia, Florida, Arizona, and North Carolina—all states she would have been hard-pressed to confidently expect to carry on election night—and they never dreamed that their fabled "Blue Wall" of overwhelmingly working-class White states anchored in Ohio, Pennsylvania, Indiana, Michigan, and Wisconsin would fall to Trump.

Not only did their Blue Wall crumble, but Trump also picked up Florida and Iowa and held onto North Carolina as well. The tidal surge of White voters in the polling stations also brought Trump to near victories in Minnesota and New Hampshire. According to a Pew Research Center analysis of the 2016 election complexion, Trump rolled up insurmountable margins among the White working class, drawing 64 percent of their vote to Clinton's 28 percent. And according to Pew, working-class Whites accounted for more than 44 percent of all ballots cast in 2016. That Trump trounced Clinton among all White male voters in 2016 wasn't a surprise (though the 30-point spread turned the Democrat's stomach), the fact that Trump also won the majority of ballots cast by White women voters— particularly considering Madeleine Albright's dire warning of that "special place in hell" allotted for female voters who would dare not vote for Hillary—is likely what prompted Clinton's election night psychotic break that left her unable to appear and graciously thank her stunned supporters (the campaign tasked John Podesta for that classless act) and explains her enduring public bitterness.

While the Democrats were expecting a "blue wave" in 2016, what showed up at the polls was in fact a red-faced White wave. Or as author and cable commentator Van Jones framed it, "a whitelash."

No matter how it's phrased, one thing is clear: that's how utterly wrong the Democrats got it in November 2016. But that doesn't mean they were wrong in the long game. In fact, they were likely just a tad premature, off the mark by only an election cycle or two if the demographic and cultural trend lines that have clearly emerged since the dawn of the 1990s continue unabated.

Which is what makes Trump's transition and first 100 days such a fantastic fumble in the penultimate clutch moment so amazing, a bizarre act of pure political malfeasance of such magnitude that it's akin to watching a quarterback at the Super Bowl in scoring position on fourth down with 10 seconds left on the clock take possession of the ball at the snap and then start hurtling the wrong way down the field while his "teammates" cheer him on. There were, of course, some immediate signs of what was coming from a Trump presidency, such as Trump's obsession with the crowd size at his inaugural address and other random, petty fixations with what were really meaningless distractions that seemed like the soulless babble of a reality television show. The starring roles doled out to Ivanka Trump and Jared Kushner also premiered the nepotistic rot that had taken root in the White House on day one of Trump's arrival. But nothing was more of a dead giveaway that Trump either really didn't know what he was doing or he never actually intended to act decisively to bring mass immigration under heel, restore lawful order to America's immigration laws, and secure the sovereign borders of the nation than when he effectively handed the critical opening act of his administration over to Senate Majority Leader Mitch McConnell and Speaker of the House Paul Ryan—two men who epitomized the status quo of the GOP's business class leadership who are committed to strip-mining everything possible from the country as they oversee its death. That and his nearly as fast distancing from and then his disgraceful long-running denouncement of the honorable gentleman from Alabama, Attorney General Jefferson Beauregard Sessions III. His dispatching of Steve Bannon in August 2017 was another clue as to the authenticity of Trump v. 2015-2016.

In the most fundamental of senses, and by no hand but his own, the Trump presidency, at least as advertised, was dead on arrival.

***

Trump didn't drain the swamp at all; rather, he slipped into it on a floating chaise lounge, told Paul and Mitch he was happy to let them keep running the national agenda, and promptly started Tweeting about his unfolding legacy as the greatest president in the history of the United States of America.

The Trump Show, and that's exactly what it has proved to be, has seen him zigzag all over the proverbial map, posing in front of prototypes of a wall that would never be built and issuing proclamations that would never be carried out, all while embarking on an arena U.S. concert tour in celebration of himself—a roadshow that has yet to end. As the 2020 election draws closer, in lieu of governing in a coherent and effective manner, Trump instead has attempted to continually rattle his political opponents by riffing wide-eyed boastful taunts much in the vein that Muhammad Ali would hurl at opponents back in the day when truly towering adversaries like Smokin' Joe Frazier stood stoically ready to dance when the bell rang—and the Democrats would be smart to channel a little of Frazier's calm demeanor that betrayed none of his deadly power in the ring (Frazier could take brutal punishment for eight rounds and then come out raining nuclear bombs on the boxer in front of him)—but while they were both fond of declaring, "I'm the Greatest!" it's clear that Trump is no Ali.

The Champ often talked vividly poetic smack and then, with a few epic exceptions (see Smokin' Joe Frazier and George Foreman for further details), he delivered and often dazzlingly so in the ring. He could float like a butterfly and sting like a bee. In contrast, since January 21, 2017, Trump has stumbled around tragically sober but looking increasingly punch-drunk as he has rambled a raft of low-rent smack-talk while delivering absolutely *nothing* in terms of his core campaign promises. *Nothing.*

Not one single mile of the real wall he vowed to build has been funded let alone actually built—and that includes the two solid years when the Republicans held the House, the Senate, and the Oval Office. Not one mile. Not. One. Mile.

Trump's rampant vows of issuing "Day One" instructions to the GOP leadership—which again at the time held the entire legislative and executive branches and all while there was a so-called "conservative" majority on the Supreme Court—died the very day he set foot in the Oval Office.

And perhaps none expired more glaringly than the prospect of ensuring that workers who had no legal right to be on the job, or even in the country, would be identified and administratively removed through E-Verify. Even more than Trump's mythical wall, the refusal of the American president and his cronies in the Republican leadership to institute a mandatory comprehensive verification system for employers to ensure that workers employed in America actually have a legal right to compete with American citizens for *any* job whatsoever is the benchmark sign of the GOP's total and irreversible corruption. When the easiest, most common-sense legislative step to protect American workers languishes in Congress and Trump does absolutely *nothing* to secure its passage but rather whines on Twitter at 3:00 a.m. (again, sober, which in and of itself is revealing) then it was undeniably clear even well within his first critical 100 days that the jig was up.

For all the weeping and wailing from the Left, one thing had to be clear come Christmas 2017: Trump was actually a splendidly wrapped early gift to the Democratic Party—as well as to the GOP establishment that had so desperately sought to kill his candidacy once it became clear its core messaging was resonating with a huge bloc of the American people that fateful summer of 2015. Trump hasn't been transformational in the slightest—he has been the status quo on steroids. He has been a bad goof. A loud-mouthed gag. A face-melting fart in a full elevator. While the Left insisted he was a Kluxster suited up in Brooks Brothers instead of a hood and robe courtesy of a repurposed Walmart bedsheet, in actuality Trump has proven to be little more than a carnival huckster who conned more than 63 million voters into buying his miracle water as he regaled them with his tales of extraordinary feats and accomplishments.

Faced with such brazen political domestic abuse by the head of the national household, many of the working- and middle-class White voters who cast their ballots for Trump appear to have retreated into a deep state of denial that borders on comatose; a virtual shutdown of their intellectual capacity to process and accept the horrifying depth of their betrayal at Trump's hands. A common refrain now heard and read across social media maintains that Trump "is doing everything he can" and "he's just one man against a horde of swamp-dwellers" and, even more hallucinatory, "He's winning!" It's a delusional estimation that's something akin to members of Custer's 7th Calvary Regiment telling each other it's not as bad as it looks as they faced complete annihilation at Little Big Horn.

**

In order to restore the nation's sovereignty by restoring sanity to its immigration policies, Trump could have summoned Ryan and McConnell to the White House on January 22, 2017, and informed them of the following: That without immediate congressional approval for $100 billion-plus in funding for a 60-foot concrete blast barrier that would traverse the entire southern border, an immediate passage of E-Verify, an immediate quadrupling of the DHS/ICE/CBP budget, and an immediate legislative fix to the bad policy of so-called "birthright citizenship" (one that would "grandfather" in all who have been granted citizenship under it but decisively ending the practice from a set date going forward), then *any* action on the GOP leadership's ongoing agenda of corporate tax breaks, ending the Affordable Care Act, deregulation, etc., etc., etc., was simply dead on arrival in the Oval Office.

Trump could have made it clear that the single greatest political upset in the history of American presidential elections was indeed going to have massive legislative consequences. He could have made it abundantly clear that failure by Ryan, McConnell, and the GOP caucus to get in line and pass the clear-cut immigration agenda he ran on would not only mean he would veto every single piece of legislation that Congress did deliver but that he would also immediately denounce the GOP leadership— and the members who supported their obfuscation on immigration—as betraying the American people in favor of their corporately delivered thirty pieces of silver. Trump could have told them that unless they moved and moved quickly on a dramatic and restrictive overhaul of mass immigration into the United States, he would begin holding his political rock shows in their districts—no matter what size the venue—where he would denounce them as craven traitors beholden to nothing more than the glint of bullion as the country disintegrates around them.

Trump *could have* done all of that and much, much more. He wielded *immense power* that the voters invested him with and in the earliest weeks of his administration that political capital was at its zenith. Ryan and McConnell would have had to deliver up what Trump demanded on behalf of the American people or face total political annihilation at the hands of the president within months of him taking office.

Instead, Trump did nothing of the sort; rather, he surrendered his leadership in favor of a Twitter show and signed a blindingly massive budget "deal" that explicitly enshrined the policy of open borders and explosive mass immigration rates. Ryan and McConnell must have shared a chuckle as they so easily rolled him during his first year in office.

With virtually every single one of his mass immigration-related policy vows either abandoned, punted, killed, or altered to the point of irrelevance, Trump has spent much of his presidency on the links—147 days as of August 31, 2019, according to the detailed tee-time log maintained at TrumpGolfCount.com—and online. On August 31, 2019, Trump had already posted 11 Tweets by midday alone, all part of a 44,000 Tweet tsunami that he has unleashed since March 2009. Even if spread over the past decade that Trump has been on the platform, he has averaged 4,400 Tweets per annum or nearly a dozen Tweets every single day of the year. But it's far more likely that most of Trump's Twitter storm actually broke and has poured forth unabated since June 2015. And unlike some other public figures or corporate execs who employ social media marketing teams to produce their brand content, Trump is clearly solely responsible for his Twitter feed. And in that respect, it resembles just another one of his gaudy and garish properties—a mirrored world that feeds his ego while white-glove catering to his extremely limited vocabulary.

Trump and Twitter, togetha 4 eva! #TrueLove.

With Paul Ryan and Mitch McConnell and their respective business-class caucuses left completely in charge of the Republicans' national agenda, the GOP returned to its business-as-usual practices, which is to say the facilitation of the accelerating mass looting of the country. The ongoing firework displays of events like Brett Kavanaugh's confirmation hearings or the gun control "debate" that's rolled out in the wake of every mass casualty shooting (yet rarely if ever in relation to mass casualty cities where under one-party progressive governance, Democrats have long instituted European-grade gun controls to no effect whatsoever on the annual body count), while instructive in that they reaffirm the undeniable reality that the end of America's days is now at hand, ultimately are merely Polaroids from the larger grim picture. The Democrats have plunged into an absolute psychosis that has turned them against working- and middle-class White Americans on a breathtaking scale and with a vehemence that increasingly is approaching something close to the dark days that were precursors to some of the 20th century's mass murder movements, all while the Republican Party's leadership remains laser-focused on monetizing every element of the country that can be harnessed for profit while letting the rest of it burn down to the foundations.

If America is in the midst of a raging cultural and political riot—and it is—then the Democratic Party's leadership are the wild-eyed arsonists who are setting fire to every building they can and the Republican Party's leadership are the determined looters who trail behind them and race from building to building, leaping over the flames and dashing through them not to extinguish the fires but to haul off everything of value they can grab, right down to the old fixtures that they might be able to get something for on the global bazaar.

And like looters exhausted from running amok for so long as the town burns down around them, the GOP's corporate leadership now appears to at least suspect that the hour grows late for them and that soon they will have to make a break for it, an epic getaway that will be assisted by helipads and fortified yacht clubs where Jordan Belfort-worthy Naomi-class superyachts wait dockside with engines idling as the Wolves of Wall Street plan to split for parts unknown.

Even Trump's reelection in 2020, assuming he survives the Democrats' impeachment effort, is immaterial to the fate that now looms large for the Republican Party.

The die indeed is cast.

***

If he survives the effort to remove him from office which with every passing day appears to take on momentum that could carry it from an impeachment vote in the House to a Senate trial where the outcome is far less certain than it was during the Mueller investigation, Trump's reelection bid will remain clearly predicated on—unsurprisingly—simple math and a simple assumption. The basic arithmetic is that Trump merely has to hold the states he won in 2016 and if possible pick up a couple of spares he came close to last time around, namely Minnesota, where Trump lost by less than two percent of the vote and New Hampshire, where he lost by less than one percent. That formula is underpinned by the rudimentary assumption that the White working- and middle-class voters who handed him victory in 2016—including the simultaneously vaunted and reviled independent White women voters—will survey the group psychosis that's currently in progress among the Democratic field of candidates and conclude that four more years of a belligerent, nauseatingly boastful, Attention-deficit Disorder-suffering, Twitter-addicted Trump is tragically more desirable than the Jonestown progressive paradise the Democrats are currently stirring up in their ideological Kool-Aid vats.

Trump is counting on the oldest and coldest of pure cynical political calculation: "They have nowhere else to go."

Yet it remains a roll of the dice for Trump in 2020, particularly given his translucently thin margins across critical Rust Belt and Midwestern states the last time around, since it wouldn't take that many working White voters at all to decide on another equally old election day adage—to go fishin' instead of voting—to set the GOP's last blimp ablaze and signal the end of the Republicans as a national party.

Whether the polls rolling in through the autumn of 2019 are any more of an accurate bellwether than the polling data that filled the air throughout the fall of 2016 proved to be isn't yet known, but even assuming there is a greater pool of Trump voters awaiting election day to emerge from the shadows and into the voting booth to make their presence felt once more, the political landscape continues to shift and shake around the GOP as the demographic floodwaters from foreign shores continue to rise and the cultural institutions long ago surrendered *en total* by the Republicans continue to narratively program the waves of "students" that emerge each spring from an academia also equally abandoned to the radical progressive Left. Not that long ago, the Republican leadership and their handmaidens in the media could still be heard chortling about the college students who had majored in what they presumed to be useless or at least politically harmless ethnocentric studies and other, more bizarre curricula that they assumed assured them a future of nothing more threatening than a lifetime of living in their parents' spa in between shifts at Starbucks.

What the GOP either didn't count on or, more likely, care about was the reality that while some broke students happily returned to the home spa where they could be more conveniently catered to by their parent-servants, legions of others were quickly recycled back into academia while many more did, in fact, fan out across virtually every industry and market imaginable and set up their ideological shop inside established corporations and start-ups of every variety. There's a reason that more companies each year publish and promote so-called "value statements" that often read as if they were cribbed near verbatim from the cultural Maoist talking points that are now standard issue in academia. There is a reason that more CEOs and other corporate executives are politicizing and indeed weaponizing their brands in alignment and alliance with progressive Left virtue signaling (or what used to be called "marching orders") on issues ranging from the Second Amendment to abortion to gender identity to race relations—unsurprisingly in lockstep uniformity. The GOP's leadership, on camera at any rate, professes to be shocked, confused, and occasionally even "concerned" about the brazen and accelerating elimination from digital platforms of not just what are described as conservative voices but indeed increasingly really *any voice* that doesn't present an adequate adherence to the progressive Left orthodox dogma—and yet as with the legacy media, the nation's universities, its K-12 public education system, its entertainment industry, and so many other critical venues for public discourse, the Republican Party's leadership has been an idle spectator to its own demise on this front as well.

All of the trend lines marking the demographic shifts and cultural programming that will doom the GOP and destroy the nation as it existed have escalated since Trump was elected nearly three years ago, and their pace has only accelerated.

***

By 2017, while America had surged to more than 325 million people—a rising population tide driven by mass immigration and births to immigrants—the U.S. Census Bureau reported the classification of the "White, non-Hispanic" demographic had dropped by more than 15 percent to "just" 60.7 percent of the population share. That is still a dominant ethnic majority by any measure and far too White of a country in any respect for the progressive Left to ever accept and thus they continue their round-the-clock efforts to pummel it into silent submission. But while Trump and the GOP are still hoping that there are enough working- and middle-class Whites in the country pissed off enough and frightened enough to turn out in numbers that will carry the day once more—and they just might—they lose sight of the fact that for many of those voters Trump's election in 2016 was the last ballot cast for what once again proved to be a total betrayal, if this time a significantly more freakish one.

It's not that there aren't enough working- and middle-class White voters left in America to keep Trump and the GOP politically breathing for four more years. There certainly are; it's just whether there are enough left who decide it's worth it.

Trump's prospects of holding Michigan, Pennsylvania, Wisconsin, and even Ohio are probably an even bet at best—he prevailed in Michigan, Wisconsin, and Pennsylvania by razor-thin margins and he can't afford to lose even one of them—though he may hold onto Iowa, where he trounced Clinton by nearly double digits and will almost certainly score again in Indiana, where he blew Clinton out by a nearly 20-percent margin. All six of those states range from preponderantly White to overwhelmingly White and all have varying degrees of significant manufacturing footprints and deep reservoirs of rural culture—critical ingredients to keeping Trump in office and delaying however briefly the GOP's entry into political hospice care.

The states where Trump is clearly in trouble in 2020 are North Carolina, Georgia, Florida, and Arizona, four states he carried in 2016 that accounted for 71 electoral votes and four states he might well wave goodbye to, along with his reelection, in 2020. The demographics in all four of these states have continued to shift and the only real question come next November will be whether Trump and the GOP are able to not only return *all* of their 2016 voters for a repeat performance at the ballot box—including the considerable number of White Democrats that Trump managed to flip in key states—but to *expand* overall White voter turnout and further enlarge their share of it. In Florida, non-Hispanic Whites now account for 53 percent of the population. In Georgia that number is now 52 percent of the populace and in Arizona the number of non-Hispanic Whites account for about 54 percent of the state's population. In North Carolina, ethnic Whites still account for approximately 63 percent of the state population, but Trump's four-percent margin of victory there in 2016 reflected the shrinking fortunes of the Republicans from even 2004, when Bush beat Kerry like a bongo drum, running up a 13-percent margin of victory in the Tar Heel State.

If Trump were to lose any one of those four states, a combination of them, or all of them, it's hard to see where he could make it up across the electoral map in 2020. Virginia, a state that the Republicans could reliably count on for more than a generation—the GOP won the Commonwealth in seven consecutive presidential elections from 1980 through 2004—has been denied them since 2008 and is almost certainly gone for good, yet another Appomattox on the Republicans' trail of retreat having surrendered the nation's borders and its public school systems. Southwestern states like Nevada, Colorado, and New Mexico that had long been competitive for the GOP—Bush carried all of them in 2004—fell like Virginia in 2008 and haven't swung red since, and given the demographically-driven political genetics now dominant in those states it's likely they too are gone for good.

***

The halcyon days when the Republicans were power players up and down the western and eastern seaboards are but a faded memory, for 40 years after Ronald Reagan's triumph had once more heralded the depth and sweep of the White working- and middle-class vote from California to New York the GOP has long since completed its mass political suicide in those electoral rich anchors that once propelled it to 500-electoral vote, mushroom cloud bombings of Democratic contenders. The extinction-level event of the Republicans in California, which has seen the GOP completely annihilated as a relevant political force in the state and reduced to relic status that fields candidates as sideshow curiosities, has offered powerful portents of what one-party rule under a radical progressive Left will look like for the rest of the country by the end of the coming decade.

Gavin Newsom, the San Francisco pretty boy and social scene-maker who was treated to his own *Harper's Bazaar* photo spread that highlighted the carcinogenic amalgamation of politics and celebrity that is now ubiquitous in twilight America, decimated the GOP's sacrificial goat in November 2018 by a three-million-vote, 23-percent margin of victory. While 4.7 million Californians cast their ballots for a Republican named John H. Cox, their election day would have been better spent out on the beach drinking a long chain of Mai Tais in remembrance of a Golden State that is long, long gone, sleeping off the hangover, and then booking the U-Haul for their escape. While Newsom's victory was never in question—California hasn't had a Republican governor in a decade, hasn't had a Republican senator in nearly three decades, and the party has been eliminated from virtually all statewide offices—the absolute impunity with which Democrats now lord over the collapsing state was exemplified not by his election but by Newsom's nearly immediate and brazen reversal of the will of Californians by his decreeing a moratorium on all executions. Newsom's imperial decree came hardly a year after California's voters had once again convincingly affirmed their support for the death penalty and, with but a stroke of his pen, it radiated the cold contempt he harbors for the plebs.

Less than a generation ago, such a move on the death penalty would have been politically fatal—and quickly so—for Newsom in California, a state where three California Supreme Court justices were removed from office by a popular uprising at the ballot box for their obstinate refusal to allow capital punishment for the most heinous of convicted killers housed on San Quentin's death row. Yet in

2019, Newsom can defy the will of the people of California without any perceptible sense of foreboding whatsoever. The GOP has been politically exterminated, the media is in the bag, Hollywood is onboard, the campuses have transitioned into ideological grooming centers, and most of what remains of the once mighty middle class in California is plotting their departure.

Faced with a staggering homeless crisis, crumbling infrastructure from Yreka to San Ysidro, exploding rents and home prices, permanent gridlock on the traffic arterials that connect residents with their work, failed schools, and a chronic water shortage in the face of surging populations even as the most violent breed of criminal prowls the streets of California today fearless of official reprisal, Newsom has unveiled a radically different set of progressive priorities since taking office in January: he has ordered a halt to the death penalty, declared California a sanctuary state, granted clemency to illegal immigrants convicted of crimes in order to prevent their deportation, and targeted legal gun owners with an escalating plethora of restrictions designed to disarm them while unleashing developers to launch a massive campaign of high-density developments even as he retires for the weekends to his comfortable spread in rural Marin County.

This is the face and the fact of what one-party rule in California looks like today and it is indeed what is about to finish falling across the nation by no later than the end of this decade.

Gavin Newsom's view of California leading the nation into the abyss of dissolution and violent chaos has been slow cooking inside the beltway for nearly two generations. And at the heart of this stunning makeover has always been mass immigration. A quarter-century ago, veteran financial writer Peter Brimelow described in his 1995 groundbreaking work on mass immigration, *Alien Nation,* this so very telling exchange between Sam Donaldson of ABC News and NPR's

Cokie Roberts on the July 25, 1993, broadcast of *This Week With David Brinkley*:

"[Native-born Americans] don't have any more right to this country, in my view, than people who came here yesterday," Donaldson breezily opined. Roberts didn't miss a beat: "That's right!"

***

Eight years after Brimelow's cogent deconstruction of what mass immigration at the behest of the markets meant for the American people, Sen. Zell Miller's 2003 book *A National Party No More: The Conscience of a Conservative Democrat* hit bookstores and heralded what he saw as the end of the Democratic Party. Its dust jacket peppered with glowing plugs from the likes of GOP open-border stalwarts Jack Kemp, Larry Kudlow, and Newt Gingrich, as well as their nightly man-servant Sean Hannity, Zell's eulogy for the Democrats was, unsurprisingly, not just premature but completely wrong. While Miller mourned the transition of his political party from a home that he recognized and felt welcome into a progressive cult compound that would ultimately come to despise his very existence—he started out in a Democratic Party that reminded him of Tara but shuffled off this planet last year gazing upon a party that resembles Jonestown—Miller missed the mark about the Democrats' fortunes, apparently unable to grasp that the open border and mass immigration policies to which he himself was accomplice in actual fact guaranteed that a rabidly balkanized Democratic Party would be *the only party* left standing to wield power unchecked from Imperial Washington. While Miller finally bestirred himself to offer some canned commentary in his book about how he's opposed to illegal immigration and belatedly bemoans some of the more notable havoc it has wreaked across the country, he still refused to come to grips with the staggering weight that mass immigration *en total* had delivered the nation.

"Legal immigration? Certainly," Miller writes. "It's what helped make this country great. There are immigrants waiting in line to come into this country and they are obeying the law. Give them a chance to become American citizens, instead of illegals who have made a mockery of the American Dream." Actually, what made America work as well as it did across much of the 20th century was a profound reduction in all immigration to the nation, a moratorium that allowed for a great period of assimilation into a largely shared American ideal and national values conveyed and expressed in the English language. By the mid-1960s, the American nation was probably more culturally cohesive in the broader sense than at any time since its inception.

And virtually all of that has since been steadily eroded as men like Miller looked on, said one thing, and did nothing. A year after his book was published, Miller delivered the keynote address at the Republican National Convention and didn't mention the word "immigration" of any variety even once—in the middle of a Bush administration that was allowing more than three million immigrants to illegally cross the southern border annually. Miller instead hit all the cues that Bush Inc. demanded, calling for American soldiers to be flung into countries all across the globe but to never stand a watch on our own nation's frontier.

The Democrats were certainly by then not at any real risk of being wiped off the national stage but even as Miller spoke in 2004, the Republican Party was indisputably flying directly into its turbulent date with destiny.

***

The cancer that had been lustily gorging on McCain's brain for quite some time may have finally laid him six feet under in August of 2018, but even Stage IV glioblastoma couldn't knock him out of his Senate seat while he still had a detectable pulse. And that's because McCain & Co. were damned sure determined that deadly malignancy or no, America had better understand that McCain had a Senate seat *for life*.

And so it is for the American aristocracy that continues to rise and rule amid the rubble. As cities collapse and the heartland overdoses, the imperial elites flaunt a tenure they consider irrevocable.

But what, you may ask, of McCain's capably serving the seven million-plus people of Arizona, of reflecting their values and advancing their voice in the upper chamber of Congress and making sure their interests are skillfully represented? Surely the needs of the citizens whom he was charged with representing—and paid a handsome $174,000 base salary of tax dollars annually to carry out—would mandate that a terminally ill old man accept that his long run was at an end and prompt him to gracefully step down from the Senate to allow the governor to appoint a healthy replacement who could immediately focus full-time on Arizona and the nation—as opposed to hastily getting their affairs in order, making personal farewells, and settling some old political scores.

After all, considering that McCain was quite willing to surrender to an enemy on the battlefield in Vietnam for an extended engagement at the notorious Hanoi Hilton, surely giving up power in Washington was something that would come so much easier. No?

Ahhh, well, in the summer of 2018 the cold retort from McCain's ranch outside of Sedona to any suggestion that he and his family not cling to power to the truly bitter end was unmistakably clear and summed up rather simply: "Let them not eat cake, but rather let the pathetic proletariat rabble that dare call themselves *Americans* with any sense of national meaning gaze with hungry eyes at the glory of True Power and the sweet indulgences it affords. Let them behold the majesty of Imperial Washington and in their dumbstruck awe let them then understand their lot in life."

Thus the weeklong parade of Deep State pseudo-grief flowed forth from the Grand Canyon State to Washington in a tide of garish pomp and grim frills for the fallen imperial warlord amid choreographed proceedings that were filled with black Cadillac SUV motorcades complete with the Secret Service "war wagons," military honor guards, surreal on-air eulogies delivered by MDMA-dosed media players throughout the Beltway grid and, of course, that now most ubiquitous calling card of the governing-elite: the stone-faced security teams sporting ear-pieces and designer shades who serve as another silent but potent reminder to working Americans everywhere of just who possesses power—and who doesn't.

The ultimate measure of real power in America today is the presence of the Praetorian Guard, armored-up and packing immense firepower even as Jane & Joe Public's right to legally hold just enough heat to protect what little is theirs is eroding daily.

John McCain's state funeral was a watershed event in 21st-century America, as it highlighted in the starkest of terms the vast gulf that now divides the infinitesimal ruling class, the Romanesque global empire they have spun and woven, and the common American citizens whose labor, blood, and treasure they have spent so lavishly—indeed so wantonly—to assemble it.

And nothing was left to chance, nothing was left unscripted, in the cortege that Americans were reminded over and over again that McCain himself had spent the last year of his life meticulously planning (versus, say, going to work). Thus, with the nuclei of America's self-declared political royalty assembled in the National Cathedral in what they surely believed was an awe-inspiring congregation of raw power, the first order of business was to demonstrate the true meaning of power by not only highlighting who was on the guest list and visible in the pecking order of pews, but by underscoring who was *not invited* as well—and making a show of it.

That Trump wasn't invited as the sitting president was hardly a surprise but still poor form on behalf of the McCains, and some may argue that it was a classless move that sank to a petty depth that was simply, well, Trumpian. Yet it was McCain's decision to not only besmirch his former running mate Sarah Palin in his near-posthumous book *The Restless Wave* by letting ghostwriters spell out his regret at choosing Palin instead of Sen. Joe Lieberman for his vice president (his fellow "let's go to war bro" Sen. Lindsey Graham was assuredly McCain's instinctive choice as veep, but Graham's personal life wouldn't have survived the scrutiny a national ticket draws), but to then also 86 her from the invited guest list at his funeral once more revealed the sheer hatred of working White Americans that boiled inside of McCain even on his death bed. Sarah Palin provided the McCain campaign its shot of adrenaline to the heart of the American White working class and in doing so offered its only if fleeting chance to turn the corner on Obama in 2008, and in return of that service McCain—along with his wife Cindy and daughter Meghan—enraged that Palin stole McCain's lackluster show, repaid her by erasing her from the imperial rites that would mark his passage to eternity. It was meant as a cold slap in the face of Sarah to be sure, but even more so to the tens of millions of working White voters she politically embodied.

McCain simply no longer had any use for Palin or Americans like her and his death bed was his last chance to take another dump on them.

To say there was no love lost between the McCain clan in the immediate aftermath of his death and the White working-class Americans McCain and his family so despised would be an understatement. Even as McCain's corpse lay cold in the National Cathedral while his daughter Meghan weaponized her weepy eulogy in honor of her father, across the spectrum of digital media that ran from right wing to independent to the avowedly populist left, McCain was excoriated in real time for his fundamental roles in the wars without end, the rotten corruption of the Keating Five and his membership in it and, of course, his hellbent commitment to keep America's borders wide open to ensure the ongoing mass migration that is building a vast and foreign-supplied underclass in America will continue unabated.

In a blizzard of toxicity, McCain's name was gleefully dragged through the mud and sewers by millions of Americans who were clearly sickened by his royal send-off and the untethered and completely tone-deaf pomp that accompanied it all. While the networks were glued to McCain's long procession, much of the rest of America could be found on the "comments" sections on digital platforms across the political spectrum, yet mostly authored by working-class Whites on sites that would be classified as on the right side of aisle.

Even as Meghan McCain was tearfully spitting her fantastical homage to her father—to whom she does literally owe everything, not the least of which is her paycheck and alleged relevance (Hunter Biden, anyone?)—the web was on fire with jubilant denunciations of her as "Porker McCain" and recommending mourners send the McCain estate a baker's dozen of Krispy Kreme doughnuts in lieu of flowers. The McCain family's icy contempt for working White Americans was openly repaid during the funeral with unvarnished disrespect conveyed in a vast blast of popular disparagement, unlikely as it was to be paid any mind by the legacy media, let alone the elites who sound-proofed themselves from the masses long ago.

***

As America's descent into one-party rule now fast approaches, what the post-Republican era must be considered, at least briefly, for the Democrats' ability to hold the nation together isn't in doubt: they can't, nor actually do they intend to, but it's worth noting that as mass migration from all corners of the globe continues and accelerates into the fatally gored and badly listing United States of America, it's likely that the ruling elites who accomplished this epic scuttling of a ship of state will begin to feel their own sense of dread as the human tide begins to reach and breach their captain's quarters.

The correlation between the pursuit of empire and its inevitable exploitation of mass immigration to the benefit of the imperial ruling class is well established throughout history, from Rome to Napoleon's French Empire that *Monsieur* Bonaparte and his *Grande Armée* established across Europe in a breathtakingly short time as the 19th century dawned. Acclaimed biographer Frank McLynn's 700-page exploration of the watershed French statesman-turned-emperor, first published in the United States in 2002 and succinctly entitled *Napoleon*, paints a portrait of the Frenchman that reveals Bonaparte's dazzling achievements as he led France to its continental apogee and the destructive ends it ultimately wrought. The Paris of the opening decade of the 1800s, McLynn points out, was a thriving economic center which was fed by 14 "thoroughfares" that snaked throughout the continent and its 80 million inhabitants who fell under its imperial rule.

As the French army flowed out of France—like the American interstate highway system, Napoleon's road network was designed to facilitate the rapid deployment of troops—more than just "goods" flowed into the bustling City of Light as the empire swelled.

"Particular beneficiaries where the cotton, chemical, and mechanical industries, where the impact of war stimulated new technologies," McLynn writes. "The influx of foreigners to Paris in this period encouraged the manufacturing of luxury goods. Another, less welcome, influx was the annual immigration of 40,000 seasonal workers, many of whom stayed on in the city in the dead season to form the kernel of the 'dangerous classes' that are such a feature of 19th-century French literature. This aspect of the economic boom worried employers and the authorities, who did not want a concentration of workers in the capital, fearing overcrowding, famine, disease, unemployment, and riots."

Overcrowding, famine, disease, unemployment, and riots. Sound familiar? As the underlying overpopulation and population density issues drive those factors abroad on virtually every continent, they act as a massive push factor for the masses toward America, where they are already manifesting here and will increase in scope and frequency, eventually reaching a degree that even its architects cannot escape.

As for the fate of Europe, Turkish President Recep Tayyip Erdogan's recent public declaration that if the EU were to even describe Turkey's offensive into Kurdish-held areas of Syria as an "occupation," he would unleash more than three million refugees toward Europe's southern frontiers lays bare the reality that mass immigration is indeed an atomic-grade weapon—something political scientists in Mexico discovered long ago. Whether it's sooner or later, with millions of refugees now planted in Turkey, Syria, the former nation-state of Libya, Morocco, or any number of other states and regions, that trigger will be pulled. That button will be pushed. The day of Europe's own reckoning as a result of its policies is effectively at hand.

In America, the death throes of the Republican Party aren't without their comic relief, as Fox News programs reflect with a fascinatingly reliable frequency these days with the network putting Karl Rove—the GOP's "architect" turned undertaker—in high rotation across virtually all of its news and opinion shows alongside the congressional

Republican caucus's aptly-named minority leader, Kevin McCarthy from California. Or as they are frequently referred to by millions of Americans prowling the web and venting their political spleens: "Pig-Man & The Cuck." The reference to Rove as "Pig-Man" seems an amalgamation of the infamous if only briefly glimpsed character from *Seinfeld* that Kramer rescued from a government experiment and Rove's actual real-life passing resemblance of Porky Pig. The ridicule of McCarthy, a plain-spoken congressman from Bakersfield, seems to be anchored in the sense that he's a caretaker tapped by former Speaker of the House Paul Ryan to settle into a compliant role of clean-up duty in the oozie aftermath of the Ryan-led final gang-bang of the American working class.

These two men, along with various walk-on appearances from the GOP's veteran All-Star lineup that led the party to this moment of political obliteration, are featured as soothsayers of what should be done next. The fact that the Republicans elected McCarthy as their leader at all speaks volumes: the California congressional delegation numbers 52 seats in the lower House in 2019—45 of which are held by Democrats, just *seven* by the Republicans. Clearly the GOP leadership knows success when they see it. It seems likely that by 2028 at the latest, the last lingering Republican remnants of its congressional footprint will be washed away forever, a permanent erasure the GOP signed on for with its embrace of mass immigration.

California's one-party state fate, such as it foreshadows what awaits the nation, remains on full display in the nightly news cycle as the autumn of 2019 proceeds, with much of the state literally ablaze and the rest of it smoldering on the brink of explosion, calls to mind a passing glance of the Golden State's precarious national perch that author Scott Spencer reflected on in 2017 in his brilliant novel *River Under The Road*, which captures the devolving cultural zeitgeist through the eyes of two couples across a series of garden parties and city soirees that unfold from the 1970s through the 1980s, carrying the reader from New York to Los Angeles. Spencer, who hit big when he penned *Endless Love* in 1979, delivers a delicious estimation of LA's eventual certain doom through the eyes of a screenwriter who would soon detonate his career at a party gone awry in the Hollywood Hills:

"Put that hole in the ozone on hold, put those geological squeaks and twitters along the shit-eating grin of the San Andreas on hold. Put those wildfires in the hills of Santa Monica on hold... And by all means, put on hold the sense of impending doom that seized Thaddeus the moment his plane touched the runway at LAX, the sense that here was the place that one day was going to blow up or burn down or be swallowed whole, and when it happened no one in all the world would be terribly surprised—sad, yes, horrified, naturally, but there would not be the slightest element of surprise. The city would become a vast screaming ward of suffering survivors and the great unanswerable would follow them to their mass grave: What did they expect? How could they have built those multi-million-dollar houses where they could not stand? The city was like a display of Fabergé eggs set up on an escalator."

Thirty-eight years after *Endless Love* and Spencer is still offering deadly live fire on the pages: *How could they have built those multi-million-dollar houses where they could not stand? The city was like a display of Fabergé eggs set up on an escalator.*

***

The apocalyptic "Big One" that has long been forecasted to explode the Richter scale and lay Los Angeles to waste while sending California careening into the sea as America's Madagascar hasn't yet struck, but the high tide of mass immigration will indeed eventually rise to swallow all those fine Fabergé eggs at the top of the escalator to drown them in the violent chaos of dysfunction and corruption that had consumed the quality of life for everyone else below them. And on that note, the political extermination of the Republican Party and the ensuing self-inflicted death of the West brings to mind once more another moment when Jim Morrison offered his casually delivered yet eviscerating perspective on the changing landscape around him, though this time not uttered in a Hollywood cafe to a British one-and-done pop prop like Ian Whitcomb, but rather a flash caught on film a couple years later in his never commercially released *HWY: An American Pastoral.*(Note: This writer obtained a bootleg copy of the film decades ago.) Shot in mid-to-late 1969, the meandering amateur art film's story arc, if one could call it that, would go on to serve as the outline for The Doors' song *"Riders on the Storm"* that was featured on their final 1971 album *LA Woman.* But a brief scene toward the end of the film that had carried a hitchhiking Morrison from the Mojave Desert into Los Angeles finds Jim in front of what looks like a Skid Row bar at night, briefly bartering with the doorman over an apparent cover charge and pondering aloud, "Do they have girls in there?" Then as he looks around the street, he offers almost in dejected passing, "Is this LA or TJ? Some days it's getting kind of hard to tell." It was a casually dismissive comment tinged with the low-octane racism that was itself a product of the era, yet one imbued with irony given that Los Angeles in 1970 had one of the largest White populations among the Great Cities in America. Yet his caustic balking at Chicanos on the street captured an outlier of the racial divisions to come.

Less than two years later Morrison would make his way over to Paris for his own farewell, a Paris he surely wouldn't recognize today any more than he would his adopted hometown of Los Angeles.

But his long-form observations transcribed on vinyl nonetheless captured the heartbeats of the Western world as it danced along the cliff of its own demise still ring true today, and when it comes to America in late 2019, Mojo's taunt to the crowd on The Doors' *Roadhouse Blues* tour one night in 1970, possibly at The Felt Forum in Madison Square Garden, probably best sums up the end game of the West now in progress:

"But I tell you this, man, I tell you this, I don't know what's gonna happen, man, but I wanna have my kicks before the whole shithouse goes up in flames. All right!"

With the GOP leadership now voluntarily standing at their political gallows as America disintegrates and as Europe's bureaucrats put Western civilization's final affairs pleasantly in order, it seems like ol' Jimbo may have been right on the money once again on the way out of his own door all those years ago.

SMEAR & LOATHING ON THE CAMPAIGN TRAIL, 2008

Candidates Obama and McCain pay tribute to and sell their political souls for the National Council of La Raza

"A nation can survive its fools and even the ambitious. But it cannot survive treason from within. An enemy at the gates is less formidable, for he is known and he carries his banners openly against the city. But the traitor moves among those within the gates freely, his sly whispers rustling through all alleys, heard in the very halls of government itself."

From novelist Taylor Caldwell's 1965 *A Pillar of Iron*, which has been widely—and incorrectly—attributed to the Roman philosopher Marcus Tullius Cicero.

First published in 2008

The long days of high summer had settled across Southern California like a sticky veil that sapped the strength to do much beyond wait for the relief of an evening breeze to come rustling off the coast. Throughout the vast swath of stucco and concrete which is the hyper-developed suburbia that radiates southward and eastward from downtown Los Angeles, the heat had the upper hand. Air conditioners rattled and hummed and dogs stayed low in whatever shade they could find.

Just over 120 miles to the south, in the second largest city in the state, presidential contender Barack Obama was raising the mercury in a different way. The junior senator from Illinois took the stage in front of an exuberant crowd of thousands jammed into the San Diego Convention Center. But this was no ordinary stump speech Obama stepped up to offer his star-struck wing of Democrats. No, Obama took the stage at the annual conference of the National Council of La Raza. The organization bills itself as one of the "preeminent civil rights groups in the country" and is funded with an annual budget of millions of dollars which it has used to wage a relentless war against efforts to enforce the nation's immigration laws.

Obama came to town to give the La Raza leadership what they wanted and he didn't disappoint.

Indeed, the candidate that the media has alternately declared both "post-racial" and the epitome of America's racial conundrum, who himself has decried the "divisiveness" of ethnic tribalism, vowed fidelity to one of the most strident racialist groups in the modern United States. Obama was candid about his intentions and his sympathies.

In repeating La Raza's mantra that America's immigration system is "broken" and thus by extension blaming America's immigration system for illegal immigration, Obama declared the federal government's Immigration & Customs Enforcement agency is terrorizing Latino neighborhoods with raids that capture illegal immigrants. Obama hit all the bases La Raza expected him to, denouncing "hateful rhetoric" and "demagoguery," and again pressed the case for a mass amnesty that will bring tens of millions of illegal immigrants "out of hiding" and onto a fast-track path for citizenship with virtually no significant sanction for their crimes.

Not surprisingly, the Latino activists ate it up. Whatever deficit the young senator had with Latinos in his race against Senator Hillary Clinton for the Democratic nomination had seemingly vanished.

But Obama is only one half of the equation and La Raza intends to cover its bets in the race for the Oval Office.

The next day, Sen. John McCain, ostensibly the maverick warhorse of the Republican Party who suffered a political near-death experience only the summer before as a result of his angry championing of the most sweeping mass amnesty ever proposed in the history of nation-states, followed Obama's address with his own appearance in front of the La Raza gathering. The dark days of 2007 must have seemed a distant memory as McCain proudly recounted his frenzied effort to force the "McCain-Kennedy" bill through the Senate.

In an effort to add some empathy to his address, McCain ticked off a few names of illegal immigrants who died trying to cross the border.

Following a bland, perfunctory recitation of the obvious need to "secure the border"—an aside he served up *sans* any sense of passion and without a lick of detail—McCain then got down to sealing the deal with La Raza and again vowed to implement an immigration reform that was "practical, fair, and necessary" and took into account "economic and humanitarian responsibilities as well."

McCain wasn't speaking English or Spanish in that passage of his address; he was speaking code. While anything but "straight talk," this cipher is easily decrypted and his message is clear: If Latinos help put him in the White House, he will again attempt to force the passage of La Raza's agenda, the core of which is a mass amnesty that will effectively back-date entry visas for as many as 35 million illegal immigrants who broke into the country.

But if McCain thought his promise of another round of amnesty would at least shore up some support among

Latinos, his ethnic pandering resulted in a high moment of low comedy that brilliantly captures the demographic suicide the Republican hierarchy has been doggedly committing for a generation at the behest of their corporate benefactors. Just before McCain could leave the stage, a microphone in the audience was handed to Enrique Morones, one of the most strident Latino racialists active in California. While it's no surprise that McCain didn't know who Morones was, the La Raza throng burst into wild applause when they saw who had the microphone and a question for McCain.

"We have an organization that puts water in the desert to try to save peoples' lives," Morones said in introducing himself, offering a tidy, sanitized description of his group Border Angels for the candidate and his media entourage. Of course, Morones neglected to mention that he and his group are also fond of calling Republicans "Nazis" and had recently threatened to destroy a statue in San Diego of former California Governor Pete Wilson—who rose to political prominence in the U.S. Senate from his successful mayoral stewardship of the city. Morones also declined to acknowledge that when asked on national television if he would like to see Whites forced out of the United States, he declined to answer.

That a fanatical ethno-racialist like Morones was at La Raza's annual conference is hardly a surprise, but the roar of approval he received from the audience as he prepared to ask McCain a question was ominously revealing. McCain didn't know that Morones carries around signs depicting various Republicans as Adolf Hitler and Josef Goebbels— *but the crowd did.* They knew just where Morones was coming from, and they supported him.

Of course, Morones had a statement to deliver before he asked his question.

McCain listened intently as Morones blasted America for not providing poor Mexicans with a legal way to immigrate into the United States, and sarcastically noted that McCain's forefathers (read "White people") had no problem coming to an America where all were welcomed at Ellis Island. He then attacked McCain for supporting "the militarization of the border that has killed more than 10,000 people." With the crowd still cheering, Morones asked McCain if he would sign an executive order immediately upon assuming office that halted "the inhumane raids."

Morones's question put McCain on the spot and in a bit of a bind. If the senator took on Morones for declaring that it's America's immigration policies—the most liberal in the world, allowing more than one million legal immigrants into the nation annually—that are to blame for the deaths of thousands of immigrants as they try to sneak into the nation, and not the corruption-riddled regime in Mexico City and Mexico's outlying states, he would surely further alienate a group which already regarded his fidelity to their agenda with some suspicion. But keenly aware that his comments were being recorded, McCain could also not risk openly making such a pledge since it would have hit the blogs and talk radio and further eroded his weak standing with the GOP's voter base; though he most certainly would have been happy to do it privately.

So, the straight talker tried to split the difference. In a stern but calm tone he reminded Morones that he was very aware of the illegal immigrant deaths on America's southern border but insisted that America had to secure its borders in order to ensure enough support for another amnesty. In a crumb to the immigration enforcement movement, McCain actually referenced the fact that the narco-cartels use illegal immigrants and human smuggling routes to mule their deadly cargo into the United States, which results in the deaths of Americans. But he quickly repeated his pledge to champion another mass amnesty and said it would be his priority once the border was secure. At the end of his response to Morones, McCain said he respected Morones's point of view.

For Republicans (and I have never been one), this is a moment of such sheer irony that it borders on absurdist theater. To watch the party's presidential standard-bearer being reduced to assuring a race-baiting Latino zealot like Morones—a thug who gleefully promotes his brazen hatred for White Republicans—that he *respects* his point of view. But since the encounter lasted only a minute or so, McCain might be excused for not knowing just who Morones is or what he stands for at that very moment. But once the exchange made the newspapers and lit up the blogs the very next day, it was apparent to McCain's campaign that a radically ethnocentric Latino who espouses an end to United States sovereignty had sandbagged them.

McCain had a golden opportunity to respond quickly and decisively: he should have read a prepared statement denouncing Morones and his ethno-racialist agenda as the absolute antithesis of what his campaign stands for and, further, McCain should have taken the opportunity to warn the National Council of La Raza that the thunderous applause Morones received from its membership was alarming—and then he should have called upon the NCLR to publicly renounce Morones's toxic smear tactics.

But McCain did none of those things. He simply walked away from the encounter and let it go, feeling perhaps that he came off looking like a reasonable and pragmatic leader in contrast with a low-brow street urchin like Morones. Yet no matter what short-term dividends McCain's tactics may have yielded for his campaign, at the root of his inaction and reluctance to confront Latino racialists and smear merchants is a peculiar phenomenon that has spread among the Republican elite for more than 20 years.

Conventional wisdom in media circles throughout California holds that the once rock-ribbed Republican state slid irreversibly into the Democratic column as a result of Gov. Pete Wilson's strong support in 1994 for the wildly popular Prop. 187—which would have ended most public benefits for illegal immigrants—that stirred awake a sleeping giant in the Latino electorate.

Conventional wisdom in the media, however, frequently has little basis in reality.

And the reality of Prop. 187 is this: It passed with nearly 60 percent of the vote, including significant support in the Black, Latino, and Asian communities. When all the ballots were counted, more than five million Californians of every racial, ethnic, and religious stripe voted to end the taxpayer subsidies to illegal immigrants. Far from harnessing crass demagoguery, Wilson smartly tapped into a righteous backlash of voter disgust over a tidal wave of illegal immigration that was corroding their quality of life and a government that was doing nothing about it.

That groups like the National Council of La Raza had launched hysterical campaigns of invective both before and after the vote that labeled the initiative's supporters as Klan members is hardly surprising, as such tactics have become their stock in trade. But what is stunning is how this media-embraced narrative has slowly wormed its way into the top echelons of the Republican Party over the years, a bizarre development perhaps best exemplified by Karl Rove's steadfast insistence that the GOP reject immigration enforcement measures and embrace groups like La Raza. Rove and such McCain supporters as Sen. Lindsay Graham—who himself declared that opponents of McCain's amnesty plan were "bigots"—offered dire warnings that failure to placate Latinos with an amnesty is tantamount to electoral suicide, and they pointed to the fate of California's GOP as Exhibit A.

Yet that flawed conclusion conveniently disregards several critical factors that led to the GOP's present moribund condition in California, the most fundamental of which was the 1986 general amnesty that was signed into law by President Reagan. That sweeping pardon not only immediately legalized and put on a path to citizenship more than a million illegal immigrants in California, but it also triggered a massive wave of both legal and illegal immigration from Mexico into the state which by 1994 had reached critical mass, prompting the voters' backlash of Prop. 187. At the time, then State Senator Art Torres declared Prop. 187 to be the "last gasp of White America in California." In some respects, that prognostication wasn't that far off the mark.

It may not have been the last gasp of Whites in California—despite Torres's fervent wishes that it was so—but it was the beginning of the Republicans' death rattle in the state.

To almost anyone living in Southern California at the time, a fairly clear chain-reaction occurred within a decade of the 1986 amnesty: as the growing influx of immigrants began to stress and strain schools, hospitals, and other social services and community resources, including parks and libraries, the middle-class Anglos who had been critical to the GOP's hold on the state saw their quality of life spiraling down.

And they began to move.

Anecdotally, the dramatic shift in the state's racial demographics was visible everywhere in Southern California. My parents' middle-class neighborhood in Pomona, which had been primarily White and middle class since it was built during the Eisenhower administration, still maintained that characteristic in the mid-1980s. But within a decade following the amnesty, the neighborhood had become virtually unrecognizable as Latino immigrants poured into the city and Whites and Blacks moved out, often leaving the state all together. Neighborhood schools that had achieved a hard-fought ethnic balance by the late 1970s and early 1980s were swamped with the influx of immigrants, which effectively erased integration and turned the Pomona Unified School District, among dozens of other large public districts throughout Southern California, into what essentially is an ethnically homogenous entity. By 2007, Pomona Unified School District was more than 80 percent Latino.

The mythology Latino activists like to peddle through their ideological bedfellows in the media is that Governor Wilson appealed to White (and to a lesser extent, Black) resentment and fear over their rapidly changing neighborhoods and used Prop. 187 to demagogue his way into Sacramento, turning illegal immigrants into an army of Willie Hortons—the infamous furloughed Black rapist whom George Bush Sr. featured in an attack ad in 1988 that was largely perceived as a brazen racial appeal to frighten White voters. The problem with the comparison, though it continues to be dutifully regurgitated in news pages without critique, is that it misses the fact that Wilson came late into the game against illegal immigration, latching onto an already massive groundswell of anger against the sustained waves of illegal immigration that was destroying their neighborhoods and communities. Proposition 187 would have happened and been passed with or without Pete Wilson. In contrast, there was little if any direct connection between widespread voter concerns nationally in 1988 and Bush's Willie Horton attack ad—America's neighborhoods weren't being overrun with furloughed rapists of any color, but Bush's hatchet man Lee Atwater was able to craft an ad that stirred racial fears and painted Democrat Michael Dukakis as a weak liberal who was soft on crime. The bottom line is: Wilson was responding to a massive backlash against a real and immediate crisis that voters demanded action on. Bush Sr. was not.

Yet as the years went by after the passage of Prop. 187 and its eventual annulment at the hands of Gov. Gray Davis (who would be disgraced and driven from office by a voter recall election in 2003), the relentless campaign by Latino activists to paint the initiative and its supporters (all five million of them) as racist xenophobes began to gain traction in GOP leadership circles, partly because the Republicans establishment never seemed to muster the courage to confront and counter-attack their accusers.

They won the battle and then promptly surrendered the field.

Today, the Republicans in California have reaped a bitter harvest for their leadership's cowardice on the issue, and as McCain's surreal appearance at the National Council of La Raza demonstrates, the GOP nationally appears determined to make the same fatal mistakes. It does reek a bit of *déjà vu*. The media atmosphere is nearly identical to that of 1994, with editorial boards from the *Wall Street Journal* to the *New York Times* declaring from their oxygen-thin perches that the vast majority of the American people want a comprehensive reform plan on immigration that results in the largest amnesty in history. Not surprisingly, not a single editorial board among the newspapers supporting amnesty has called for a national plebiscite over the issue.

As for the Left, they face their own problems with immigration, especially as the economy continues to sour. The Democrats have nervously, if successfully, avoided discussing the deep support for Prop. 187 among its party members or the continued support among main street Democrats for tough immigration enforcement measures, including deportation. Barack Obama felt comfortable claiming the ICE raids were creating terror in Latino neighborhoods, but he knows that a majority of the party doesn't feel the same way. But unlike the Republicans, whose leadership is essentially rudderless (and spineless) on the issue, the Democrats have allowed their Latino caucus to dictate its plank on immigration, effectively brushing off the concerns of their union and environmental wings. The major media outlets have dutifully followed the script and continue to portray anxiety over illegal immigration as a problem primarily between social conservatives in the GOP and the rest of the nation.

With California now facing its twilight years as a state that once promised opportunity and quality of life to a majority of its citizens, the issue of illegal immigration and mass immigration now spreads deep into the rest of the nation outside of the American Southwest, reflecting much of what happened in the Golden State between 1986 and 1994. Rapid and overwhelming demographic and cultural changes strike home, even as opportunities for working- and middle-class Americans shrink. Among the communities that can least afford it, more people have to compete for and make do with less. The scope of the changes being fueled by immigration was highlighted by U.S. Census Bureau statistics that showed White populations dropping in more than half of all counties in the United States since 2000, a demographic slide fueled almost entirely by immigration and high Latino birthrates—as well as White Americans' propensity to move in the face of radical changes.

In San Diego County, where Obama and McCain addressed La Raza, the population grew by 161,000 new residents between 2000 and 2007, of which 150,000 were Latino. Even being geographically so close to the southern border and a traditional gateway to immigrants coming into the United States, those figures are astounding. But the real scope of the impact can be seen clear across the nation in the heart of America's Yankee past: Hartford County, Connecticut, where the population grew by 19,600 people—all but 1,000 of them Latino.

That kind of ethnic ratio to population growth is being repeated all over the nation from small hamlets and rural towns in the heartland to the suburbs of major metropolitan areas and it's a trend that under the presidency of either Obama or McCain is likely to continue and increase. The same challenges that California faced and failed in the late 1980s and early 1990s—when it was still in a position to act decisively—will now be confronted by a growing number of cities and states all over America.

What the rest of America chooses to do remains to be seen, though the glut of local and statewide ordinances and laws designed to intimidate illegal immigrants that are now being proposed indicate that many areas will try to staunch the influx on their own in the face of federal reluctance to enforce immigration laws. While Latino activists manage to push Obama into parroting their rhetoric that ICE raids are "terrorizing" their communities, they neglect to point out that more illegal immigrants cross the Rio Grande into the United States every month than all of those captured and deported in the ICE raids in the past year.

After almost a year of what the Bush administration pathetically hailed as the most aggressive efforts at immigration law enforcement in the past quarter century, there were more illegal immigrants in America than ever.

If Obama or McCain are successful in pushing through Congress an immigration reform package that results in a mass legalization of illegal immigrants already in the country, there will be two immediate results: the first will be the bitter and irrefutable rebuke of the media-recycled claim that there are 12 million illegal immigrants in the United States. When as many as twice that figure and possibly even more step forward to claim amnesty, it will be a darkly rich moment to savor as the establishment media gasps and sputters in feigned shock. That will undoubtedly be followed by self-righteous proclamations that it's better that 35 million illegal immigrants be brought into the legal system than allowing them to "live in the shadows."

But the second immediate result of any such amnesty is that it will trigger an even larger wave of northward migration from Mexico and Latin America into the United States, both legal immigration through "family reunification" set-asides for those brought into the system and increased work visas that will likely be mandated as part of any legislation, as well as an explosion of illegal crossings that are sure to dwarf the near biblical tide of migrants in recent years. The

1986 amnesty—which was sold to the American people as a one-time-only necessity in order to secure the border and effectively enforce our laws (sound familiar?)—not only legalized the three million illegal immigrants already here but triggered a stampede the resulted in as many as 10 times that number breaking into the nation in search of a better life while waiting it out for the next amnesty. If assurances that this, in fact, will be the last amnesty for illegal immigrants ring hollow among Americans, you can be sure that they are warnings not worth the breath expended to utter them among the impoverished masses that make up the vast majority of Latin America's swelling populations. To them, there is rightly only one lesson to be drawn from the proposed amnesty: that there will be another one after it—and that it can be forced upon the American people by simply breaking into the country and squatting there in enough numbers and with enough perseverance.

As the traditional hallmarks of the United States as a geographically discernable, sovereign nation-state continue to evaporate into the rapturous vision of America as a borderless business model where profit triumphs over patriotism, the beleaguered citizen can expect little notice and certainly no help from its political leaders.

Not long before McCain and Obama took the stage in San Diego to praise the National Council of La Raza, American citizens like teenager Jamiel Shaw Jr. in South Los Angeles and Anthony Bologna, a father in San Francisco, paid the ultimate price for Washington's epic betrayal. An illegal immigrant gang member who had just been released from jail the day before mercilessly executed Shaw on the street, apparently for no other reason than he was Black. San Francisco police say Bologna and his two sons were killed in a hail of gunfire by another illegal immigrant gang member—who had a long rap sheet of violent crimes and had been arrested on multiple felonies before but had never been deported.

Shaw and the Bolognas were but four out of hundreds if not thousands of citizens in California who have been robbed, raped, and murdered by illegal immigrants in recent years, and yet the tragedies that have befallen them and their families haven't even ranked a sympathetic aside from Obama or McCain, who instead reserve their camera-ready tears for the illegal immigrants who die while trying to break into the country. If either candidate were truly courageous, they would have stood in front of the NCLR's annual conference and recited the details of the murders of Shaw and the Bolognas and told the group that the first priority of any president is to provide for the safety of the American people. A true measure of leadership from either of them would have been if Obama or McCain told the NCLR that the group must halt its fanatical efforts to effectively kill any effort to deport illegal immigrants—efforts which have created the environments in "sanctuary cities" like Los Angeles and San Francisco that result in Americans being killed.

But they came to patronize and pander to La Raza; not to confront it.

The canonization of immigrants illegally in the United States continued unabated, with Obama and McCain heralding the "good, hard-working" migrants, even as men like Humberto Higareda Robles continued to wreak havoc on America's streets. Robles isn't a suspected killer like Edwin Ramos—the gunman police say mowed down the Bologna family in a spray of bullets—yet Robles is even more indicative of the chaos that now unfolds daily across California and much of the nation.

It's impossible to know what Robles was thinking as he sat behind the wheel of a 2001 Ford Aerostar van, driving it fast and recklessly over the hardscrabble streets of Pomona in the early afternoon of July 4, less than 10 days before Obama basked in La Raza's glory. It's impossible to know just how much Robles had been drinking, where he was heading, or what he had in mind once he got there.

In fact, it's impossible to know much of anything about Robles at all, because as an illegal immigrant from Mexico, there is little corroborative information about his true identity or a factual accounting of his past. The only information that has been independently established is the facts surrounding his numerous crimes in the United States.

Pomona police do know, for example, that they have repeatedly arrested the man identifying himself as Robles on the streets of this working-class city; and his growing record of domestic violence, drunk driving, and hit-and-runs all point to an ominous day of reckoning for Americans at the hands of Robles—who again was released to prowl the streets of Southern California rather than face deportation back to Mexico.

While it's impossible to tell just what Robles was thinking as the van he was driving careened across the streets of Pomona on Independence Day, even though he was drunk, had a warrant out for his arrest, and was in the country illegally, it's a safe bet he wasn't overly concerned about being caught, arrested, charged, convicted, and then deported.

He knew the system well.

And looking at Robles's case history now, it's easy to understand why he wasn't overly concerned about his fate in the event he was taken into custody.

Shortly after 2:30 p.m. on that holiday afternoon, Pomona police officers responded to the neighborhood south of the intersection at Mission Boulevard and San Antonio Avenue, where witnesses had reported a hit-and-run traffic accident that left two people injured. According to the police investigation, the van Robles was driving slammed into Jesus Acosta's Ford Mustang at the intersection, injuring both Acosta and his passenger Naomi Alvarez.

Witnesses told police that Robles sped away from the scene but lost control of the van a few blocks later, where it jumped the curb and smashed into a utility pole. Robles fled the smoking wreckage on foot and disappeared into the ramshackle neighborhood.

As police and paramedics worked the two accident scenes, Robles emerged in a nearby driveway, having changed into different clothing. Witnesses pointed him out to police, who questioned and then arrested him for felony drunk driving and hit-and-run. Police discovered that Robles had been injured in the successive wrecks and transported him to Pomona Valley Hospital Medical Center, where he was treated before he was booked. At the jail, police discovered Robles also had a warrant for his arrest on a domestic violence charge filed against him back in 2002.

He had been arrested and released in that case, then failed to appear in court.

As Robles was in the country illegally and had been arrested for felony crimes, an ICE hold was placed on him at Pomona's jail this time around, which meant he would be handed over to immigration agents for deportation proceedings once the pending charges were resolved. Yet Robles seemed footloose and fancy free in the face of prison time and a free trip back home to Mexico. According to police, Robles laughed when he was told the couple in the car he struck were injured and were in the hospital. He was belligerent and taunted police and medical staff at the hospital. Asked if he understood his Miranda rights, Robles taunted them with obscenities.

Just over a week later, inside the Los Angeles County Superior Court building in Pomona, Robles was brought in front of Judge Judson W. Morris Jr., a 20-year veteran of the bench who has come out of retirement to again wield a gavel and help clear the county's perpetual backlog of cases. If the docket is any indication, the courtroom here, as it has been for years now across the teeming county that is home to an estimated two million illegal immigrants, resembles more a cattle call or an assembly line than a methodical deliberation of justice. At least half of those appearing in front of Morris need the translator who stands alongside the public defender. The charges read out against this human tide are a litany of transgressions ranging from the petty to the dangerous; from driving without a license to drug possession to assault.

Considering that he nearly killed two people and was wanted on an assault charge against a third, Robles stood out among those facing the judge that day—not that you would have known it from the prosecution or the judge's sentencing. By the time Judge Morris finally dealt with Robles, he was no longer facing felony charges, the ICE hold had been dropped, and he was looking at two misdemeanor counts. The District Attorney's office decided to drop the felony counts in exchange for a guilty plea to the reduced misdemeanors. Morris gave him 51 days in county jail. Counting time served and "good behavior," Robles was released back on the streets just 72 hours after the gavel came down.

The bureaucratic dysfunction that allowed Robles, and tens of thousands more illegal immigrants just like him, to easily walk out of police custody is, in fact, manufactured by groups like La Raza and then served up by politicians like McCain and Obama, who cynically drape their appeals for amnesty around a bizarre promise to fix the very system they've worked so hard to undermine.

As a result of stridently ethnocentric attacks by Latino activists and elected officials in Pomona, the city's police force only contacts ICE when illegal immigrant suspects are arrested on felony charges—but these same officials and activists know that in most cases, an overwhelmed D.A.'s office is eager to plea down the case in order to obtain a conviction. And, as Robles's case demonstrates, they also know that overcrowding in the county jails means that illegal immigrants who plead guilty to a lesser charge will be released back into the community within days if not hours. Virtually every effort to close the loopholes and tighten the system's safeguards to ensure that people who have no legal right to be in the country are handed over to federal immigration authorities are swiftly and mercilessly attacked as a racist conspiracy targeting Latinos. In Pomona, Latino city council members have gone as far as comparing the DUI check points run by its police department—which is headed by a Latino, Chief Joe Romero—to the deadly sweeps carried out by the Nazi's dreaded Gestapo in occupied Europe. Why? Because drivers without their licenses have their cars impounded at the scene; and many illegal immigrant drivers thus lose their vehicles at the checkpoints.

Driving without a license, without registration, and without insurance means the police will seize your vehicle, whether you're an American citizen or not. Yet Latino elected officials are vehement in their demands that illegal immigrants either be issued legal driving licenses and subsidized insurance or be given a free pass by police on the streets. As Pomona police have learned, enforcing the laws they are sworn to uphold subjects them to being called Nazis by ethnocentric radicals elected to the city council. And that radioactive rhetoric, which is in widespread use around the state and nation, is digested and then regurgitated for even wider consumption by the two major presidential candidates. Yet it's funny that Obama, when calling for an end to hateful rhetoric, neglected to call for an end to the vile smear campaigns that La Raza and its allies routinely use against virtually anyone they feel opposes their agenda of mass amnesty and open borders.

While the dog days of summer will give way to a watershed election in the fall, Americans should expect no relief whatsoever from the continuous assault on its borders, its beliefs, and its budget. The racialist Latino groups that seek to effectively evict the United States from at least seven southwestern states and to render its territorial claim invalidated by hard facts on the ground, are larger and better funded than ever before—and they are on the march. The demographic war in America's Southwest has spread like a prairie fire to virtually every corner of the nation and our future will be determined by its outcome in places like Pennsylvania, Ohio, Michigan, and throughout the Old South.

But as the battle for America's future rages, I think about the biting observation by novelist Janet "Taylor" Caldwell that has been widely—but wrongly—attributed to Roman philosopher Marcus Tullius Cicero, and I fear not the enemy at the gate.

I fear the American among us.

For it's the American among us—indeed, often *in front of us*—who sells out his fellow citizens, unlocking the gates, opening the windows, and whistling as he looks the other way while chaos envelopes our home. It's the American among us who smirks at those of us who protest what is happening, sarcastically patronizing and belittling our fears even as they assassinate our character. It's the American among us who cynically waves the flag when the cameras roll, who invokes the best traditions of the republic even as they embrace and ally themselves with those who have made no secret of their desire to dilute and ultimately destroy the very culture that has been the bedrock of the nation. It's the American among us who earnestly professes that the old ways are dead, that the relative tranquility and opportunity that was widespread in our land but a generation ago is now gone forever, and *that's just the way it is*. It's the American among us who tells us forthrightly that we must accept this, since the foreigner who wishes to come here—or who is already here—has rights and considerations that are equal to if not more important than our own. It's the American among us who, with their own future already secure, lectures the rest of us that we must be willing to silently accept the continued erosion and eventual disappearance of the way of life that enriched them. It's the American among us, whose job has never been at risk to someone else who has no legal right be here, who smiles as they insist that migrants in the country illegally are only doing jobs that we are not willing to do.

It's the American among us who is trading away our inheritance, a legacy that could never have been taken from us.

CRAZY, JUST NOT LIKE A FOX

Glenn Beck's personality disorder mirrors our nation's psychosis on immigration

First published in 2010

So, what's wrong with Glenn Beck?

I mean, what's *really* wrong with him beyond the tragically clear symptoms of a pathological personality disorder that have manifested during his live television show in recent weeks?

You know, Beck's outbursts of weeping that stop as suddenly as they start, his sobbing replaced mid-sentence with the glazed-eye, beatific smiling euphoria as his manic mood swings full tilt in the other direction. Or the painfully casual dissolution of all inter-personal boundaries as he tosses the details of his mother's suicide and his own alcoholic binges onto the grill for mass consumption, these confessions invariably followed by his nervous habit of engaging in exaggerated, juvenile mugging in a desperate effort to compensate for the inner terror and turmoil he's experiencing.

I get all of that—or at least I understand that Roger Ailes believes televising a man's nervous breakdown is sadly now "must see TV."

But as I watched my colleague Rick Oltman on Beck's show last week attempting to make an intellectually sound and civilly reasoned case for the enforcement of our nation's immigration laws, I was struck by how Beck found it necessary to go through the motions proclaiming the inherent value, the intrinsic necessity, and the fundamental *goodness* of legal immigration.

Beck's simplistic message was as clear as his psychosis: it doesn't matter how many people are coming to America—just so long as they have the proper paperwork. Introducing Oltman on his show, Beck immediately stumbled over himself suggesting that Californians for Population Stabilization was a sinister name for a think tank.

"That kind of sounds spooky," Beck offered with that wide-eyed zeal of a kid in front of a campfire eagerly awaiting the next ghost story. "Are you just anti-illegal immigrant, or are *you* anti-immigrant?"

Though Oltman was invited on the show to ostensibly talk about President Obama's illegal immigrant aunt from Kenya (she overstayed her visa and has ignored two deportation orders since 2000), Beck just had to make sure that Oltman would confirm that CAPS supported legal immigration.

When Oltman confirmed that CAPS *does* support an established legal pathway for people to migrate to the United States, Beck declared with relief, "You are for legal immigration! Okay, good."

But just why is that "good"?

The United States already has the most permissive immigration policy among the industrial democracies and grants admission to more legal immigrants every year than any other nation on the planet—more than one million annually. As many as three times that number come into the country illegally each year as well.

But according to Beck, if five million immigrants were granted legal admission to the U.S. this year it would be fine, because they did so in accordance with our laws.

I understand why Oltman didn't bother trying to elaborate with any further nuance that CAPS, in fact, does want to see serious reductions in *all* immigration into the United States—including legal immigration—to levels that would effectively bring to a halt our country's surging population growth. Since immigration and births to immigrants account for the vast majority of our population growth, a "cooling off" period where immigration was dramatically slowed would offer a wide array of benefits, not the least of which would be to unemployed Americans seeking jobs and American workers now facing even greater competition in the workplace.

Seriously reduced immigration levels would also allow renewed efforts to better assimilate new arrivals to American culture and values the breathing room to work, which in turn would strengthen the common threads that bind us as a nation. The environment would benefit from reduced immigration levels and population growth and so would immigrants themselves, since they would have a better shot at more opportunities and resources that are spread among fewer people.

Oltman was ready to have this conversation, but it's clearly better suited for Charlie Rose.

Once sufficiently satisfied that Oltman wouldn't be spouting anti-legal immigration heresy on his show, Beck promptly derailed on cue, slipping into a weird charade routine that many of his viewers might recognize from the eighth grade.

Oltman made a valiant effort to answer his questions—which bottomed out with Beck actually asking the guest his producers booked for his show, "So why I am talking about this?" I only wish Oltman would have replied, "Which of the voices in your head are you referring to, Glenn?"

But as the continued televising of Beck's personal train wreck raises ethical questions for cable news outlets, America's schizophrenic framing of immigrants and immigration into simple black and white, good and bad, legal and illegal, needs to be reassessed in a national dialogue that deals with the numbers of new arrivals and the country's population growth.

Beck might call that "scary" and start bawling.

I think it would be a long overdue dose of American common sense.

AMERICA'S THIRD ACT

Like "Bleeding Kansas" before it, Arizona may foreshadow a coming conflict

First published in 2016

The real question surrounding Arizona's attempt to crack down on illegal immigration isn't whether its new law will survive legal challenges or some other bureaucratic end-run to circumvent it, but whether the American nation once again faces fundamental differences that simply cannot be reconciled?

And if so, is America now sliding inexorably toward violent confrontation?

The hurricane of vitriolic hyperbole that erupted in the wake of Gov. Jan Brewer signing what is claimed to be the "toughest" law in the nation against illegal immigration highlights an America that is more starkly divided than perhaps at any time since the social upheaval that rocked the nation during the late 1960s.

Arizonians fed up over out-of-control illegal immigration and the toxic histrionics its new law has sparked from business class elites and their odd bedfellows in the Latino pan-nationalist movement again exposes a dangerous balkanization of America.

The risk today lies not along the fringes, but directly in the middle.

The right-wing militia movements that have ostensibly seen dramatic membership growth since President Obama's election and the radical Left's umbrella movement of virulent racialists and violent anarchists in the nation's major cities have long simmered on the sidelines, stewing in their mutual inability to really matter much in American political outcomes.

For all the romanticizing of the campus upheavals that stretched from 1965 to 1969, the ultimate result was Richard Nixon in the White House. The shootings at Kent State 40 years ago this month were followed by Nixon's 1972 "Law & Order" landslide.

And consider that throughout the 1970s and early '80s, the fabled Weather Underground and revolutionary farm teams like the Black Liberation Army and the Symbionese Liberation Army collectively detonated bombs, robbed banks, and murdered people across the country, only to be rewarded with the counter revolution of the Reagan era.

But the vast sweep of middle America that has long stood as a socioeconomic seawall against the violent chaos that has washed across many other nations is now rapidly eroding in front of our eyes under a tide of economic despair and a growing suspicion that they have been betrayed.

Few issues feed that nagging sense of betrayal like illegal immigration.

The ink of Governor Jan Brewer's signature hadn't even dried on Arizona's SB 1070 before the weeping, wailing, and gnashing of teeth commenced from open border advocates, who echoed the outbursts of hysteria that followed the passage of California's Prop. 187 in 1994.

Then, as now, the airwaves and headlines were filled with recrimination from those who reap the benefits of illegal immigration, whether in hard profits or demographic politics. Wild-eyed shrieks of *"Nazis!"* and *"Racists!"* and *"Hatemongers!"* were commonplace, and it seemed no smear was too fantastically false or ethically out of bounds to level against the proposition's supporters.

Thus the vast majority of Californians who voted for Prop. 187 learned that they weren't just demanding that the rule of law and some common sense be applied to staunch the illegal immigration that was sinking their schools, jamming their hospitals, draining their coffers, and filling their jails; but rather, that they were the political descendants of Adolf Hitler and the modern torchbearers of his genocidal agenda.

Obscene analogies to the Holocaust were casually kicked around as opponents likened Prop. 187's elimination of public benefits for illegal immigrants to the social blueprint that led to death camps like Dachau and Auschwitz and the wanton slaughter of tens of millions of people.

Like Arizona's new law—which is wildly popular among residents of the Grand Canyon State and is supported by 65 percent of Americans in national polls—California's own effort to stop the tidal wave of illegal immigration pouring across its southern border was passed by 60 percent of voters, one of the most sweeping electoral rebukes of government malfeasance in the state's modern history. Despite such a popular mandate, however, the legislation was eventually killed in 1999 by the subterfuge of then newly elected governor Gray Davis, who cynically let it die in "mediation."

And now it's Arizona's turn.

During the past three weeks, America has watched as the overwhelming majority of the Arizona's citizens have been denigrated and smeared in a ferocious onslaught portraying them as cowboy Klansmen looking for Mexican nationals to hang. In San Francisco and Los Angeles—twin cities that have seen American citizens brutally murdered on their streets as a direct result of their so-called "sanctuary" policies—illegal immigrants and their supporters have staged rallies vowing a violent response to Arizona's law and both city councils have vowed to harm Arizona economically.

These reactions merely feed the suspicions of most American citizens that illegal immigrants are glorified squatters who game the system while remaining rabidly loyal to their home countries (and that's mostly Mexico), while the professional political class brazenly panders to business interests addicted to cheap labor and lax employment laws.

For all the heat Arizona has raised, at the root of what's happening is a stone-cold question: what happens when a majority of Americans—many of whom are well armed—determine that the government has become a malignant tumor that facilitates a cancer of lawlessness which enriches their corporate benefactors at the expense of the average citizen?

What happens when the majority of Americans decide they have had enough of being called Nazis and racist child-killers and are no longer willing to either ignore it or talk past it or be shouted down?

What happens when they conclude that it's not America's immigration system—the most generous immigration system of all developed nations—that's broken; but rather, the government is so rotted to the core that it's no longer salvageable?

What happens when it's not 11 states attempting to secede from the Union in a four-year familial bloodbath, but rather 200 million Americans collectively reaching the conclusion that Washington has betrayed its right to govern by auctioning off the sovereignty of the nation, subverting the rule of law and sabotaging the will of the majority?

What happens on the day the majority decides there is nothing left to talk about and no point in voting?

What happens then?

While America will never see another Gettysburg, another Antietam, another Shiloh, if the present divide continues to expand and harden as the economic prospects of average Americans continue to plummet, then the government is closer than it probably cares to think to an explosion of destabilizing violence that could fatally undermine its legitimacy.

This is indeed the fundamental danger, and it's being highlighted in Arizona today.

If the majority of Americans' estrangement from the government continues apace while epic numbers of immigrants persist in crossing the borders not just illegally, but defiantly, then Washington will inevitably face a violent reckoning all over the country.

Cocooned in the cozy gloss of their martini lunch schedule, the bloated Beltway aristocracy still seems inclined to dismiss the growing disenfranchisement from middle America and its vocalizations as "crazy talk."

But if Washington has any sanity left whatsoever, they will be thankful a majority of Americans are still willing to talk, write letters, and vote—for now.

They continue to ignore those voices at their great peril.

REQUIEM FOR THE HILLSIDES

A billionaire developer puts a face to the disease of over-built Southern California

First published in 2016

When I was a teenager back in the late 1970s, I used to marvel at the sublime beauty of the rolling hillsides that rose just north of the 57 and 60 Freeway interchange, usually taking in their gentle swells as I returned home to the Pomona Valley from various adventures in Newport Beach, long before that seaside town was converted into a gated cove for new money millionaires.

It was a time when open space still separated many cities in Southern California, allowing them a sense of distinct identity—and breathing room. Perhaps all those open fields, vineyards, and groves that once marked much of the region were never fully appreciated because we took them for granted, not glimpsing the wave of concrete and asphalt that would wash across them in the tidal wave of development that was to come.

As developers bulldozed and built their way from Irvine to Chino Hills to Rancho Cucamonga, eventually swallowing the region in a sea of stucco cookie-cutter box homes and soulless shopping malls, those hillsides that rose along the 60 Freeway somehow managed to escape their death-by-bulldozer.

Drivers cresting over the 57 Freeway's northbound slope in Diamond Bar would be greeted by these silent giants, surfacing amid a sea of development like breaching whales defying extinction, their hues either a soothing spring green or light winter brown.

But that's all about to end.

Late last year billionaire developer Ed Roski—who wants to build a massive 75,000-seat stadium and entertainment complex on the 600 acres of undisturbed open hillsides and surrounding land—carried out an end run around California's longstanding environmental laws. Roski was able to get the legislature and Gov. Schwarzenegger to drop California's environmental safeguards that would normally apply to such a project, ostensibly for the sake of the jobs it will create in the financially failing state.

In October, Schwarzenegger appeared on the hillsides to sign the environmental waivers in the presence of jubilant corporate executives from Roski's so-called Majestic Reality.

While some environmentalists decried the suspension of the California Environmental Quality Act at the behest of a mega developer, the project to tear the hillsides down wasn't without its community supporters, with one of its most ardent boosters being *Los Angeles Times* columnist Tim Rutten, who promoted the project with such zeal one wonders if he moonlights as a bulldozer operator.

Yet amid the threatened lawsuits, the money-slicked backroom brokering in Sacramento and the *Times*'s trumpeting of jobs the development will create (that on average will pay less than $8 an hour, or less than workers make at In-n-Out Burger), there seemed to be precious little pondering of what will be lost: the hillsides.

In an overbuilt, overcrowded Southern California, those hillsides rolling alongside one of the most perpetually congested freeways in the region offered perhaps one of the few remaining glimpses of the breathing room the region once enjoyed. Once they have been graded into oblivion, Roski's mega stadium will ironically rise a mere stone's throw from the South Coast Air Quality Management District's headquarters—a fitting rebuke to the environmental regulations that Sacramento so quickly jettisoned.

Like the lush cropland and eucalyptus groves in Ventura County that were destroyed in favor of expanses of outlet malls (many that now sit empty) and the garish sprawl of tract housing (many now unsold or in foreclosure), the hillsides' tombstone will be yet another stadium and entertainment venue in Greater Los Angeles—a darkly iconic tribute to our leaders' inability to envision a state that doesn't rely on endless growth.

It's also an ominous portent of things to come.

As the state's economy sinks deeper into perpetual deficits while its population swells, the exemption that Roski was able to grease out of Sacramento is only the beginning. It's a precedent which places virtually every single parcel of open space in California in the crosshairs of developers who can promise jobs.

Considering Roski and his crew don't even have a major sports team committed to the stadium project, whether the thousands of minimum wage jobs he has promised will ever materialize remains to be seen. Or if they do, how long they will last.

One thing is certain though: the hillsides—which were far more majestic in their natural state than anything Ed Roski has ever built—will be gone forever.

Roski even seems to understand the nature of what he's about to kill, telling the *Times*, "We have physically spent time and effort on all the other different opportunities; and you just can't find 600 [open] acres" in Los Angeles County.

No, Ed, you can't. And thanks to guys like you, we probably never will again.

THE CALIFORNICATION OF WASHINGTON

The formerly Golden State's northern sister is still Evergreen but inexorably in transition to an over-developed and congested slice of Southern California

"If we could get to a billion people here, America would be unstoppable. That would be amazing."

— Katherine Mangu-Ward, *Reason Magazine* editor, September 2017

First published in 2018

Surrendering a quality of life is a curious thing.

Outside of America's Great Cities, where the metric these days includes muggings, murders, and the random mayhem of vandalism as well as spent needles and public defecation, the capitulation is most often marked by a molasses-paced retreat by residents—both old and new—that unfolds day by day, week by week, and month by month as the years drip off the calendar and hallmarks like organic open space fade away as the fields disappear, the pastures are paved over, and the hillsides buckle under ever larger housing developments while the air thickens amid the idle of growling traffic slowed to a lava flow.

Such was the fate of Californians as they watched the landscape that once reflected the Golden State's proverbial laid-back lifestyle be supplanted by—incrementally at first and then eventually in a wild orgy of a land rush not witnessed since America's great push west—a development boom and population surge that will persist to its moment of total collapse. Or as comedian Ron White once replied when asked by the guy in the seat next to him how far a single engine would get the plane they were flying on, "All the way to the crash site."

It doesn't take a team of NTSB investigators to discern what happened to California; recovery and analysis of black box data will not be necessary.

Commutes that once took fifteen or twenty minutes have disappeared into hour-and-a-half-long slogs across networks of freeways that are maxed out while an adequate rail system remains in Sacramento's perennial gestation of cynical one-party dysfunction. The evaporation of affordable housing stock, now as rare in Southern California as a monsoon season in the Sahara, spawned building sprees of vast tracks of cheaper housing in locales that put living wage jobs often at near triple-digit mile distances from where workers could afford to own a home.

So-called "master-planned" communities sprouted like mushrooms but there seemed precious little notice given to the fact that the masters' plans called for people to live there but work at an ultimately unsustainable (and unholy) distance away.

And the deep seas of those already decrepit two-story, no-yard shit-boxes is still not enough.

California's Department of Housing and Community Development released a report late last year that projected the state needs to add approximately two million new homes over the next seven years to meet the anticipated population growth. And consider that California's official projection anticipates the bare necessity of accommodating what is effectively between six million to eight million more people poured into a state in a perpetual freshwater crisis that has resulted in an escalating series of water-use restrictions for its current residents.

The perverse policy long emanating from Sacramento holds that Californians, and particularly in the state's parched south which teems like an anthill that is constantly being kicked, must be in a permanent state of resource crisis for the pleasure of having an uninterrupted stream of more people coming in to join the collective huddle.

Of course, there were protestations to this long retreat from a reasonably comfortable quality of life, but far too little and way too late and ultimately of no relevant long-term political consequence to preserve any significant spread of the state's halcyon days of yore, though incidental relics of that era still remain and can occasionally be glimpsed amid the sweeping sprawl of Southern California.

And now it's the turn of Northern Washington.

I have been repeatedly reminded of this in Issaquah through the past five years as I find myself pondering the town's transformation from another vantage point that is reminiscent of my native Southern California amid stopped-dead, bumper-to-bumper traffic on what were once residential streets as well as the highways and freeways. The roll of Washington State's Route 900 is of particular note as it slides down the northerly descent between Cougar and Squak Mountains and funnels into the gridlock that begins to coagulate as the mountain town's artery of 17th Avenue hardens and clots with every manner of vehicle the closer it draws to Interstate 90.

At Northwest Maple Street and 17th Avenue, the arterial has long been frequently clogged to the point of risking a civic cardiac event, with motorists watching the series of traffic lights which ostensibly manage the intersections that converge on the approach to I-90 change repeatedly in front of them with little more than one or two car lengths of movement through each cycle. Just a little farther east, where the westbound I-90 unloads at Front Street, motorists hooking a left to head south into old downtown Issaquah routinely find themselves in a steel floe as the traffic that's jammed at Gilman Boulevard by the XXX Root Beer Drive-in (featuring Buddy Holly's last tour bus that really isn't his tour bus, though it is a bus...) brings creaks, cracks, and occasionally breaks into an all too brief nudge forward before freezing again. Once past Gilman, drivers can drift past the Darigold dairy (known by a generation of Americans for their ice cream cups) at a brisk 20 mph before the stop n' go starts again right around Fins, a cozy little higher-end joint next to the Village Theatre. From there it's gray skies and red lights for the hundred-plus-yard-run up to Sunset Way.

A small town meets big traffic. And it's only going to get worse.

With hundreds of new housing "units" under construction in Issaquah that will bring thousands of more residents and their vehicles to the once sleepy mountain town just outside of Seattle, it's clear that whatever proposed stent that's offered to buy time along with developer-funded doses of civic morphine to keep the patients calm if not comfortable, the lard of growth will continue to take its toll.

This is what happens in a culture that's dominated by the cultish mantra of "Growth Is Good." Or more aptly: "Growth Is God."

Whatever caveats, qualifiers, and euphemisms like "managed growth" or "smart growth" or "planned growth" and "mitigating measures" are attached to that transparently false campaign soundbite turned political truism peddled by developers and their perversely-dubbed "public servant" lackeys, when the sole prism through which progress is viewed is *growth*—be it economic, consumption, development, or population—the end result will ultimately be less of a quality of life for pretty much everyone, whether they are third-generation natives or new arrivals fresh out of the cab stand at SeaTac, whether they are tech-rich players with investment homes to boot or two-plus jobber grunts scrambling every month to cover the rising rent on a room in a shrinking universe of what passes as affordable housing in Greater Seattle these days.

It's a peculiar moment because most everyone in Northern Washington seems to know what's happening; they possess some grasp of the danger that's sprouting in front of their very eyes a little more each day, and yet most seem at a loss as to what to do about it or perhaps even suspicious at the prospect that something, in fact, can be done about it. In this era that's now rather replete with fantastical analogies to *Star Wars*, complete with an evil emperor and an oh-so-noble Rebellion (er, *Resistance*), when the average resident just east of Puget Sound today considers the rabid growth unfurling around them, they probably feel something like Luke Skywalker as he first jelly-fished to Obi-Wan Kenobi about how he couldn't get tangled up in the fight against The Empire: "I can't get involved. I've got work to do. It's not that I like The Empire; I hate it, but there's nothing I can do about it right now."

And yet in Northern Washington if there is any flickering hope of preserving what's left of the quality of life that once defined the region as surely as it did in Southern California more than a generation ago, right now is the Last Act of the Last Chance.

Of course, most mornings in places like Issaquah, Sammamish, and Snoqualmie still don't seem to begin with such stark choices requiring absolute decisions. It's still easy to rise and shine amid the gloriously storming skies in this place and time and believe—or at least not difficult to convince oneself—that the moment of reckoning has not only not quite yet arrived but is still lingering somewhere over the horizon of brake lights that bathe the interstates and many of the roads that feed them.

The growth and its immediate consequences are unavoidable and an increasingly constant irritant, but it can still feel like a relatively low boil. The trees are being cut down, the earth is being torn open, and the insta-homes are rising in legion—as surely as the spread of the Zombieland junkies that continue to hive throughout Seattle-Tacoma—but the tipping point remains at least somewhat obscured by the glitter of skylines that tech built and the shimmering tide pools of wealth that continue to unroll along the shoreline.

The development pushers and their growth-addicted acolytes will invariably scoff at the premise that Northern Washington is somehow on track to resemble Southern California, pointing to the vast disparity between the regions in population size and the sheer scope of the Left Coast states' human densities and therefore the degrees of the intractable social ills that accompany more people jammed into a given space. But they are long past disingenuous and have descended to a point of shamelessly occupying the low ground as they work tirelessly to import more and more people into communities all over Northern Washington completely irrespective of the impacts on existing infrastructure and thus the quality of life or the rich character of the rural villages, small towns, and the once small cities they are intent on submerging to the point of drowning for one inescapable reason: pure, unadulterated greed.

So they will offer their own comparisons to refute any suggestion that what's happening in Northern Washington is anything remotely akin to the bulldozer-driven blowout that has irrevocably rolled over Southern California.

The population of Los Angeles County alone is now well past 10 million people, a number that surpasses Washington's entire state population of 7.5 million by nearly a third as much. Washington's signature city, Seattle, with a population hovering under 800,000, isn't even a quarter of the population of Los Angeles proper, which is now well over four million, though LA also has five times the square miles within its city limits. But simply considering the agate of an overall human population with the space that's ostensibly available to accommodate and sustain it in a vacuum devoid of honest measurements of quality-of-life indexes is, most charitably, deceiving. The argument that there is still plenty of *terra firma* to go around in Southern California and Northern Washington can well be made by developers and the public officials they own amid a blizzard of charts, maps, data from commissioned studies, satellite imagery, and the forecasts of the most expensive experts that developers, City Hall, and the Statehouse can buy.

But it all disintegrates on impact with reality and common sense. Or as the experts like to sniff, "Anecdotal experiences that provoke emotional responses from residents."

In January 2011, *National Geographic* published a nifty little graphic that depicted the fact that every man, woman, and child on the planet could fit—were they to stand shoulder-to-shoulder—within a 500-square-mile area, or as they phrased it, "How about the City of Los Angeles?"

NatGeo apparently missed or chose to paste over the underlying point that Angelenos now live everyday with the sinking feeling that much of the world is indeed already living there.

A magazine with a rich and storied history defined by uniquely capturing not only the human experience on planet Earth but, more importantly, the cost and consequences of humankind's spread across the globe for every other species and the habitats that support them was bizarrely reduced to playing what essentially was a developer's game: using a colorful if meaningless chart to make a bullshit point, one that simply begged the question: "So what?" It was useless trivia employed apparently as some sort of soothing reassurance that there is still plenty of space left for lots more people all over this blue orb we all call home.

It was *National Geographic Does Disney.*

But a few flips of the pages into *National Geographic*'s theme issue entitled "Population 7 Billion: How Your World Will Change" finds veteran scientific journalist Robert

Kunzig observing confidently, "People packed into slums need help, but the problem that needs solving is poverty and lack of infrastructure, not overpopulation."

It's such a stunningly simplistic conclusion that it sounds somewhere past a Trump Twitter burp and well into a zealous Maoist slogan of certainty tinged with a threat.

Kunzig goes on to expand a tad on the formula which holds that every human can be, geometrically speaking, jammed into Los Angeles, noting that he attended the 2010 annual conference of the Population Association of America in Dallas, where one of his demographic takeaways was that if we wanted to give the entire population of the planet a little more breathing room—say something along the lines of New York City's density—they would still fit comfortably into Texas. As such, Kunzig figures that by mid-century and with six continents to work with, a population of nine billion-plus would amount to a no more human density level than that of present-day France, a European country which he duly notes "is not usually considered a hellish place to live."

See, for the jet-setting journos who enjoy six-figure salaries (and the always helpful town car service to and from the airport) in compensation for going on safari into the jungle of humankind's smoldering sprawl to file reassuring dispatches that are crafted well within the bright lines of a politically pre-approved narrative, it really is just that simple. Worried about the vanishing habitat that thousands of species rely upon for mere existence as the human cycle of migrate-swarm-devour-migrate-swarm-devour continues unabated? Let your heart rest easy, for *National Geographic* has reported the entire population of the planet can fit rather snuggly into Los Angeles, a little more comfortably into Texas, and rather lavishly into France, no *problemo*. If it seems that planet Earth is now literally swimming with people, *it only seems that way*, and our best minds have determined all will work out in the end, with a little elbow grease and a whole bunch of new apps and tech-bang-whiz stuff they are cooking up even as you read this from the Silicon Valley in California to Bellevue in Washington.

And that's worth noting because it's that very breezy estimation from Kunzig—a casual calculus of a journalist who has walked amid the teeming human swarms of Calcutta for a ripe paycheck but who, of course, would eat a .357 before he had to actually live there—which percolates at the core of what has happened in Southern California and what is now happening in Northern Washington.

It's that same casually dismissive attitude—which would never be tolerated professionally or privately in Kunzig's circle were he to apply it to arguments over climate change—which permeates the official position that governs growth and development in the United States today and particularly on its West Coast. There is indeed a direct correlation between the axis of overpopulation deniers and growth junkies and the degradation of quality of life, whether it's in the far reaches of the Third World or on the northwestern seaboard of the United States. It's all interconnected.

For those Washingtonians who feel they can find adequate shelter in the so-called "progressive" genetics of the state's coastal plain, that somehow the best of intentions will fix it, once more they need look no further than Sacramento, which today is dominated to near exclusivity by what amounts to a politburo of lefty Californians as headed by the Golden State's version of its own Kingfish: Governor Jerry Brown. As California's longest-serving governor, Brown was in office when California was at its zenith, when its quality of life standard still shone like a beacon that burned perhaps a little too bright. No matter the medicinal grade of legal THC these days, there's not enough *High Times* cover-worthy, epic sinsemilla growing in Humboldt to erase from Brown's coconut the fact that he ruled the roost back in the day, and he surely knows just what a development-driven train wreck he now lords over today.

The days of lighting one up with his chick Linda over a fine Napa bottle are long gone, as is the very landscape that made that wonderland possible. To paraphrase ABC's Jim McKay in 1972: "It's all gone."

But if Brown harbors any regrets, let alone recoiling in horror at what's happened to his beloved California, one would be hard pressed to find it reflecting in any manner or fashion from him publicly. Just this week he issued a statement that was subsequently published in the *New York Times*, bragging that Californians were, "Citizens of the fifth largest economy in the world."

And there it is: *citizens of an economy.*

Not citizens of a unique and once beautiful state that had so long been the cutting edge of a nation and its truly golden cultural epoch; not citizens of a resplendent coastal tribe in love with their way of life on the shoreline of the Western world; no, but rather, *citizens of an economy.* Digits on a ledger, beads on an abacus, or numbers on a tote board, if Californians these days feel like a number that's been fed into a machine it's because they are and the only thing coming out the other end are obscene profits for a precious few.

The Koch brothers got to Jerry too. Or did they?

Maybe Moonbeam was really on their ideological team all along, just running a different playbook to reach the same end zone. And consider this: the Koch brothers are rather madly in love with the reality of everyday life for most Californians today—their boilerplate, furrowed-brow, supposed distaste for the tax structure and industry regulations aside. They love the deep and desperate labor pool, the taxpayer-supported benefits that continue to act as a massive tractor-beam that reaches deep into the favelas across Latin America, and the state's refusal to comply with federal laws the Koch brothers detest as well.

And Brown's tummy certainly seems aflutter over the Koch brothers' priapism for the End Stage of the Golden State.

The superficial bifurcation of the two-party system, particularly as it relates to growth and the human population surges that fuel it, are now as equally meaningless for everyday people in Washington as they've long been for the working folk in California. The Left by and large, with some notable exceptions among the Green Party and the more serious eco-players still lingering amid the smoldering remnants of Earth First! and ELF, has by any objective account simply given up on trying to preserve a sustainable human habitat, let alone a comfortable quality of life for anyone beyond the donor class that feeds their management. The Republicans' Ghost Dance in either state can be reduced to the stock syrup of selling off public assets—particularly the state parks—and brokering corporate sponsorships for every element of crumbling infrastructure, schools, and culturally historic heirlooms. The GOP's death hallucinations in California and Washington conjure euphoric visions of the Netflix Hollywood Bowl, light rail by Wells Fargo (which charges you for passes you never bought), and the Amazon Gorge Amphitheatre.

It's an epic cluster F-bomb.

And that's even more apparent in Northern Washington today than it was in Southern California a generation ago. The self-immolation of Southern California didn't really have any precedent in America, not on the scale or scope of the sprawl and corruption that it ultimately involved. In Northern Washington today, the template of Southern California is undeniably clear and its resulting impacts on residents are inescapable, and yet the clear-cutting, density-jacking, political-packing continues apace.

On December 29, 2016, the *Issaquah Press* published editor Scott Stoddard's final broadside against the orgy of growth, entitled "Enough Is Enough," in which he opened with an impassioned reactionary's shout of, "It's time to draw a line in the sand." His few-hundred-word editorial blast against the City Hall-sanctioned bulldozers was printed above a storm gray sky fading into a panoramic photo of another hillside massacre, a life-quality killing yet bloodlessly dubbed "Westridge development." Stoddard was taking a last aim at the 1,800 homes that Shelter Holdings was preparing to build in Issaquah, along with another 316,000 square feet of commercial space, should the compact known as the Issaquah Highlands Development Agreement that had called for a vast commercial tract of 1.2 million square feet of commercial space and *three residences* expire in 2017. Shelter Holdings' intentions were to exchange nearly a million square feet of commercial and retail space for those 1,800 homes—and consequently something on the order of between 7,000 to 8,000 more people and certainly another 3,500 or more vehicles at the least.

Stoddard signed off with a fateful demand: "Sorry, Shelter Holdings. Three residences, not 1,800. If you can't abide by the rules, sell the land. See, City Council? It's that simple. Draw a line in the sand. The future of our traffic-strangled city depends on it."

It may well be that uncomplicated, at least to a City Hall ethically bound to the best interests of its residents and the quality of life they have been charged with preserving, but unfortunately for Stoddard and his newspaper of note in the mountain town, reminding the city's elders of their obligation doesn't carry quite the weight that it should. Less than two months after Stoddard's column was published, *The Issaquah Press* was scuttled and sent to the bottom by its corporate parent The Seattle Times Company, ending the small daily paper's 117-year run.

But Stoddard's missive may not have been entirely in vain, at least for the moment. As Keith Niven, Issaquah's Economic Development Director put it to me last month, "Shelter Holdings never gained community support for that proposal for 1,800 residences. Their post-development agreement zoning allows for them to build commercial and retail on their property. They have moved forward with a number of land use applications."

Shelter Holdings may not have got its 1,800 homes, but it's still on course to build, across three separate "collections" on the jigsaw puzzle-like pieces of property that it owns in the Highlands, the more than 300,000 square feet of commercial and retail development. And that massive commercial development will be flanked to the west with 73 single-family homes in something called Westridge North Single Family and another 111 townhomes dubbed Westridge Townhomes North (albeit under the auspices of another developer) that will add another nearly 200 residential units to the Highlands in that area alone, which translated through the basic formula of reality means another 1,000 or more people and another 400 or more vehicles, non-inclusive of whatever the commercial development brings in between 5th Place NE and 9th Avenue NE on a daily basis.

Stoddard's stand was valiant, but it evokes King Canute and the tide of development continues. Niven's cool observation that Shelter Holdings' grand plans for a cauliflower of homes in Issaquah's Highlands never gained "community support" may well be true enough but still begs the question, just how much of the mountain town supported the debacle of Atlas, the vast cubist residential tumor that sprouted irrevocably on Gilman Boulevard and 7th Avenue NW a few years back, or how much of the town wanted to see the stacked Anthology Gateway Apartments now emerge on what but four years ago was a fine field alongside the I-90 marked notably by a small shack resplendent with a moss-covered roof?

How many popular votes did jamming another couple thousand people in that once green field garner?

Just across from the melanoma of Anthology on the southside of Newport Way NW is the entrance to Cougar

Mountain Regional Wildland Park, a lush 28,000-acre sprawl of nature's finest, Mother's own brand of development that stands in a stoic-if-sad defiance of the humanity now swarming around it as developers stand atop their land-movers like H.G. Wells's aliens from the Red Planet, gazing upon it *with envious eyes.*

While there are no publicly known plans to plow into the park itself just yet, there are plans for what's known in military terms as a "beachhead," a landing zone. Fifty-seven single-family homes are on the board for something called the Bergsma Development that's not technically in the park, but in an adjoining 45-acre lot that is part of what's known colloquially as "the Issaquah Alps." Simply put, it's yet another deep slice of the variety now so easily glimpsed gashed into the hillsides from Newcastle to Snoqualmie.

The civic response to this has been something called "Save Cougar Mountain," a movement mostly evident by yard signs adorned with that slogan that have been planted around town on arterials where any vehicle moving more than 30 mph reduces it to a blip of a blur, and a website, SaveCougarMountain.org, which provides a principled if somewhat academic argument against the pending encroachment.

Noble as it may be, the anemia looks all so familiar.

Money talks and passive bullshit walks. By the time well intentioned souls start circulating flyers, posting yard signs, and launching .org websites that begin with the word "Save," you can safely put your money on the horse named after the Carole King song "It's Too Late (Baby)" to win.

If there was any doubt as to where the rubber meets the road from Southern California to Northern Washington when it comes to the greater civic good and the protectionist ideal of preserving a standard quality of life versus the sheer power of not only developers but the corporate teat that feeds them, the Seattle City Council settled the question definitively last month when after unanimously passing in May a "head tax" on major employers of 14 cents per hour for every employee—and let's be clear, this was aimed primarily at the major tech corporations that have strangulated the affordable housing and rental stocks in Washington—to raise a projected $45 million that would be pumped into efforts to ameliorate the city's endemic homeless crisis, Amazon (and its accomplices) immediately spearheaded a full-force corporate bitch-slap across the council's face, quickly chastening them into a humiliating reversal in a seven to two vote that Councilwoman Lisa Herbold blubbered was the result of a fight the city couldn't win "at this particular time."

Herbold's shameless explanation of the council's disgusting and cowardly reversal begs the question, if the homeless crisis that has been exacerbated in no small part by filthy rich companies like Amazon isn't a fight it could win now, when could it? Councilwoman Kshama Sawant at least had the courage to declare before the council's reversal, "This is a cowardly betrayal of the needs of the working people."

And it was. Yet it happened nonetheless, decisively.

From the epicenter of Seattle and its Mini-Me across Lake Washington, Bellevue, the shockwaves from the explosive build-out of Northern Washington roll through towns like Issaquah, Sammamish, and Snoqualmie, with new housing tracts breaking north up Washington State Route 203 and into the verdant farmland and the communities of Carnation and Duvall. Their reverberations reach into the previously quaint hinterlands of places like Anacortes along the upper crust of Fidalgo Island and over the Cascades through the Snoqualmie Pass and into old mining outposts like Cle Elum, altering landscapes as they enlarge economies and increase rents, leases, and mortgages build by build, development by development, project by project, even as they reduce the quality of life in every one of those communities and the state writ large.

In Anacortes, a harbor town that is poured one part working-class hardscrabble of the shipbuilding and oil refinery variety, one part fine reflection of historic accomplishment and yet these days increasingly topped off with an aggressive tilt of the *nouveau riche* development bottle, the consequence of reconfiguring a community in increments, like so much civic plastic surgery, is quickly evident. Like a deep cap of Galliano, legacy housing with all of its space and individual character that ran on either side of Oakes Avenue that carries motorists out of the old downtown and to waiting ferries just a stone's throw west of the Ship Harbor Inn that are bound for the islands of Lopez, Orcas, and San Juan are disappearing and being replaced by collections of shit-box insta-homes and faux Hamptons seaside houses which cater expressly to a sense of cocooned entitlement that stands in stark contrast to the town's long established character.

The development of San Juan Passage, which began to sprout along the shoreline just east of the Ship Harbor Inn in 2016, is Exhibit A of just how quickly and completely a municipal makeover can take root. Billed as *"The retreat you've always dreamed of... styled for year-round living,"* marketing materials for the development promised "water's edge view homes" on stunning lots between a cozy 2,677-square-foot and a more comfortable 3,414-square-foot for prices that opened at $1.2 million. On the early one-sheets promoting the project the wild-bidding that had decades ago become a fixture in Southern California's housing market were on full display at San Juan Passage, with original prices literally covered in Liquid Paper and new prices handwritten in, with $1.35 million suddenly bumped to $1.5 million so fast that a new pressing was out of the question; they had to just start manually altering the price tag. I thought it would have been a nice touch if they just would have X'ed it out and written the new price in, maybe with a smiley face for good measure.

Or perhaps, like Maine lobster on the menu, simply written, "Daily market price, inquire with your waiter."

It's late morning at the Anchor Inn, a proper working-class joint which opened in the 1930s and sits on the main drag of Commercial Avenue that feeds into the old downtown of Anacortes, and I find myself on a familiar barstool and nursing a familiar drink: double Stoli on the rocks with two limes. The local early birds are here, all five of them, all older White cats spaced appropriately apart and along with me looking like a chorus line of Hemingway in various states of disintegration, admiring their glasses as they consider what went wrong after it had all been quite right for so long, old Ships of the Line lingering on the horizon as the bulkheads creak and moan before the final run falls upon them.

The bartender, Kana, who happens to also be the owner, is originally from Ventura and we trade reflections on the California that once was and the great exodus of its middle class that has befallen the state as its implosion has accelerated over the past generation. Her old hometown was once a sleepy little coastal burg surrounded by lush farmland that unspooled around motorists as they made their way along U.S. Route 101 as it winds from Thousand Oaks through the pass and down the westerly slope into Camarillo and then through Oxnard before entering Ventura and holding onto the coastline up to Santa Barbara. More than thirty years earlier I had made that trip often and hit the old Ventura County Fairgrounds throughout the mid-1980s to dance and dig the Grateful Dead's sweeping resurgence on the California shore, but it's all gone now. Well, most of it is anyway, buried under the slow roll of bulldozers that replanted the fertile fields with seas of townhomes and outlet-anchored malls selling china off the rack.

Kana tells me that she and her husband had planned their escape from California carefully, finally choosing the Northern Washington port town of Anacortes only after considering bars for sale—they were looking for a bar to buy wherever it was they landed—all over the country, but the Anchor Inn was the first one they actually walked through and, initially, they took a pass. They placed an offer on another joint somewhere else, but after that fell through they returned to Anacortes and bought this beautifully authentic little watering hole and moved down around Deception Pass.

But the push factor from Southern California wasn't terribly far behind them.

Kana tells me that rents all over town have jumped dramatically, by her estimation fueled in part by the naval air station on Whidbey Island (officers and servicemen looking for off-base housing) but the habitat ecosystem has also been jolted by developers gobbling up land to raze existing homes and replace them with either luxury homes or knock-offs more densely packed together. How long the farmland that straddles much of Washington State Route 20 between the Salish Sea and Interstate 5 will last is uncertain, but its eventual fate isn't and the garish transformation of the farmland that once blanketed the Ventura coastline is a grim augury of what awaits the fields and farmhouses.

Unlike Issaquah now, Anacortes still has a hometown newspaper that's hanging on and the roil of development must play some role in keeping the *Anacortes American* rolling off the presses and into homes around the island as well as the news racks that still dot the old downtown. The newspaper's offices, housed in a charming building on 6th Street where it has operated since 1913, is just a stone's throw from the shipyards and the gemstone of the Majestic Inn that was built in 1890, though not as today's hotel that during the summer months offers a fine rooftop bar with a sweeping view of Guemes Channel, as well as the dozens of shops, cafes, boutiques, vessel charters, and random little retail oddities (such as The Business, a tiny record store that features bins of albums for which the customer names the price) that define the still-beating heart of the town. But if real estate sections and supplements alone were enough of a revenue infusion to sustain a small-town newspaper, then the *Issaquah Press* would surely still be alive today. It's an interesting proposition for newspapers throughout Washington today; to bite the hand of developers who provide at least some of the cash that feeds their already anemic revenue flows and readership bases?

That question was answered years ago in Southern California by the *Los Angeles Times*, which decided to take a position on the waves of development and growth consuming the region that ranged between occasionally agnostic to unabashed advocate, usually purposing its news and editorial pages as an extension of the Chamber of Commerce to advance an agenda of accommodating growth at virtually any cost to the state's quality of life. On May Day, 2015, the newspaper of record in the City of Angels published a front-page feature story headlined "Lawn's End" that declared California suburbanites had to confront the reality that the "arid West is no place for a front yard carpet of green." Reporter John M. Glionna's lede aptly set the stage: "When Gov. Jerry Brown ordered that California rip up 50 million square feet of lawns to conserve water amid the West's deadening drought, the Golden State gasped. Meanwhile, the Silver State yawned."

Using Las Vegas as its water conservation counterpoint, Glionna's piece doesn't waste much time before it gets to its first quoted source: author Michael Pollan from Berkeley, who went on record to declare that lawns were "absolutely absurd" and would one day be looked upon as akin to "littering, smoking in bars, and public urination."

While Glionna's story is a well-written waltz played across a grassy dance floor, it took its familiar rhythmic turns without stepping on the toes of the developers who have filled Greater Los Angeles and Las Vegas with a population surge that has not only remade Southern California and

Southern Nevada but has transformed them into portraits of dysfunction. A photo from Sin City appears in an above-the-fold photograph on A1 that captures what Glionna and his editors determined is the wave of the future: a row of identical new homes jammed together in the Nevada desert *sans* the now deadly greenery of front lawns. In fact, the "homes" are practically built out onto the sidewalk. And though the case for lawns is made, both esthetically and in terms of utility (think oxygen, soil erosion, and heat abatement), Glionna is fastidiously careful to not mention—even in passing—the bacchanal of building that has carpeted the Mojave Desert not so much with water-consuming lawns as a sea of homes that house a never-ending tide of people who not only impact water resources but tax virtually every other natural asset as well.

It's a fascinating omission, and a telling one.

But like the doomed small-town daily *Issaquah Press* in Northern Washington, the rampant growth throughout Southern California is unlikely to save a former behemoth like the *Los Angeles Times.* The once mighty newspaper the Chandler family built continues its end-stage transformation, with its long strangulation at the hands of the Chicago outfit known as Tronc, Inc., which operates effectively as a Murder Incorporated for the newspapers it owns, finally coming to an end this June when South African billionaire Patrick Soon-Shiong bought the paper and promptly announced he was shuttering its fabled downtown LA headquarters and moving its editorial remains to a soulless growth of a corporate office building on Imperial Highway in El Segundo.

Tronc had sold the historic *Los Angeles Times* building back in 2016 to Canadian developer Omni Group, which then leased it back to the newspaper before announcing plans to demolish it and raise residential luxury towers in its place.

Just as a goof, Soon-Shiong should have relocated the "Los Angeles" newspaper to Oceanside and consolidated it with the *San Diego Union Tribune*, which he also bought from Tronc, and then debuted an editorial mutant topped with a nameplate of *Los Diego Union Times* outfitted with a couple dozen reporters to cover the region from Tijuana to Tujunga and made what remains of the growth-at-any-cost cadre formerly of Spring Street either move or drive four hours back and forth to work each day. Now that would have been a hoot; well, in a sad comeuppance-via-karma sort of way, but one that may yet still happen as Soon-Shiong's executive management team considers "new efficiencies" for the not-so-brave new world that is devouring the landscape whole.

A storm rushes across the Rosario Strait and the jukebox suddenly makes like *The Shining* and cues up The Carpenters' "Rainy Days and Mondays," and we sit inside the Anchor Inn in Anacortes talking development, growth, newspapers, and the quality of life as if it's now reduced to scattered game preserves. It's a Monday. Now it's raining. And perhaps what we feel has come and gone before, though I am not so sure, but Kana and I start laughing at the serendipity of it just the same.

It's all mucked up, so let's have another round. And we do.

In the Cascades, the former mining town of Cle Elum has also felt the reverberations of Greater Seattle's growth, a human shockwave that has rolled over the Snoqualmie Pass with repercussions that have killed mom-and-pop storefronts and replaced them with big-box shit dumps that cater to the cold bottom line. I was reminded of this one afternoon as I walked out of The Caboose, a fine joint where the pours are blessedly jigger-free and standing on the back patio for a smoke you can suddenly find yourself listening to Firefall's first album coming off the juke, and made my way east along the north side of 1st Street to discover that the long-standing Cle Elum Drug was no more. Its classic street front sign was gone, its windows no longer adorned with inducements to step inside, its long stretch of narrow aisles empty. Another cadaver left on Main Street, U.S.A.

As I ponder the shell of what once was a cozy bedrock business dedicated to the better health for the working folk in this town a couple who had also been in The Caboose walk up behind me and the dude offers a simple, "Yeah, it's gone."

"What happened?" I ask.

He and his lady don't miss a beat, answering in unison: "Safeway."

Joel and Allison own Erwin's Altered Americana just across 1st Street and they've watched the flow without ebb reach even into the elevation of Cle Elum. As we stand on the one street of this beautiful one-street town, they explain that the big-box drug retailer that rose like a towering inferno on the western stretch of 1st Street spelled a death sentence for Cle Elum Drug and its band of workers, some of whom were promised jobs by the chain brand. After the small local drug store closed down, they tell me a local bought its sign in order to save it.

As for what the store represented up here, its fate remains to be seen.

"Rents here are going up," Joel tells me.

"Retirees?" I ask.

"No, tech commuters," he says.

"How do they reliably get back down the pass from late November to March?" I ask.

"You got me," he says. "But they're coming."

Tech commuters in Cle Elum? Why, that sounds about as possible as, well, states that allow wild building sprees and population pumps without any consideration whatsoever as to what that really means for the existing infrastructure or the architecture required to accommodate it or the impact on life in its entirety.

It's late July and Southern California is burning, as now per usual. And fire season doesn't even really officially start until September. It's a collective blaze that still makes the news in all of its roaring waves of candy orange glory, capturing if only for a brief spell of eventually no consequence the immensity of its devastation that's always followed by grim post-mortems about what can be done to prevent the next inferno—with the exception of even pausing the building.

That's never a possible remedy, let alone the solution.

As I watch my native Southern California's annual "flame on" from a comfortable if precarious perch in Northern Washington, I consider whether or not I really care anymore or if I am just enjoying the light show as I run down the clock on my own earthly tour and maybe sharing some notes along the way.

Some days it's hard to tell.

But I do know this much: from Sacramento to Olympia, the suits don't even pause that long to consider where they have been, what they have done, or where it's all going and what it means for everyone else.

And as Washington watches the California bonfire tonight under a blood moon, well, I wonder how many of them truly grasp what the spectacular glowing rain of its embers actually means for life up here.

Because if they don't already, believe me, they soon will.

EPILOGUE

These are dark days for California—and for our country.

The worst financial crisis since the Great Depression that descended upon America with the collapse of make-believe subprime mortgage markets has been followed hardly a decade later by an economic landscape that has been cratered by the sweeping shutdowns that were ostensibly ordered to combat the pandemic but resulted in a vast scrambling of the American landscape. Real unemployment—that being the actual number of working-aged people not working versus the government's count of unemployment benefit recipients—has spiked well into the double digits. The California that found itself reeling from the bursting of a real estate bubble in the late 2000s which crashed much of the development frenzy it fueled is now witnessing another tidal wave of building as four-story cookie-cutter multi-family housing developments are exploding throughout the state where local municipalities have been stripped of their ability to control zoning or manage growth.

As California's revenue wells have run dry—it faces a $68 billion deficit in 2024-25—its outlays to a surging population that is increasingly made up of people in need have only grown. The Golden State has stepped over the financial precipice and whether it survives the fall in any recognizable form isn't yet known, mainly because we continue to plummet—we haven't hit bottom yet.

But the signs aren't good. One only need gauge the barometer of our future—the schools—to truly grasp the magnitude of the disaster we now face.

The Los Angeles Unified School District, the second largest school district in the United States, stands as a grim testament to how far the state has fallen amid the devastating impact of mass migration and illegal immigration.

The numbers speak for themselves:

The district's nearly 600,000 students in more than 1,000 schools are some of the worst academically performing pupils in the nation, with test scores routinely only half of California's state average—which are horrifically bad in and of themselves. In 2022, only 41 percent of LAUSD's students met or exceeded grade level English and only 28 percent were proficient in math. Only 18 percent of the district's 11th-graders were proficient in math.

Even citing this catastrophic failure evokes howls of protest from an entrenched educational establishment and the so-called progressive Left; and they lay the blame for it squarely at the feet of government, ostensibly for not adequately funding schools in the state and for mandating the very shutdowns they demanded.

But the facts tell a different story.

California has thrown mountains of money at school districts like Los Angeles Unified, even as its performance index rolled into a death spiral. In 2008, the LAUSD's budget was nearly $20 billion, with annual spending per pupil reaching almost $10,000, the vast majority of those dollars spent on instruction and student and staff support services. In 2024, the LAUSD's budget remained almost static, but with fewer overall students and per-pupil spending increased to nearly $13,500 per student yet producing the same disastrous results.

Only a small (though not insignificant) fraction of the money shoveled into the district has gone to its administration, yet the Left continues to weep and wail and gnash their teeth over the false claim that "fat cat bureaucrats" leech off money desperately needed by students sweltering in crumbling classrooms. But that's just a convenient lie the progressives tell themselves over and over again, so they don't have to confront the gravity of the truth that is staring them in the face.

The truth is that California and the federal government could throw $50,000 per pupil into the Los Angeles Unified School District each and every year and it would amount to nothing more than an even bigger waste of money—because money isn't the problem.

Washington's refusal to close the border and enforce immigration law has everything to do with it, as does Sacramento's suicidal facilitation of illegal immigrants moving to California.

Nearly 75 percent of LAUSD's students are Latino and more than 50 percent of them receive taxpayer-subsidized "free" breakfast and lunch on campus. While the state refuses any effort to factually quantify how many illegal immigrants or children of illegal immigrants are currently in the classroom, the state's Department of Education reports that 35 percent of the district's students are categorized under the politically correct euphemism "English language learners"—which simply means they can't speak English. Across California as a whole, one out of every four students in the state's classrooms can't speak English.

This is but one of the ultimate results of the 1986 mass amnesty that triggered a sustained stampede of illegal immigration—overwhelmingly from Mexico—that transformed once ethnically diverse public school districts that served primarily the children of American citizens into effective daycare centers for literally millions of illegal immigrants and the children of illegal immigrants.

As middle-class families pulled their children out of districts like Los Angeles Unified, either to put them in private schools or flee the state altogether, the district's educators buckled under the stress of trying to adequately teach course material to students who don't speak English and are frequently illiterate in Spanish as well, who have little if any educational support from their families and who are the product of a culture that doesn't consider education a priority.

As one veteran middle school teacher from the Pomona Unified School District, which has suffered the same sweeping demographic shifts as LAUSD, spelled it out earlier in this collection of columns and essays: "If I have a class of 24 students and perhaps three or four of them are a class level behind where they should be in their studies, I can handle that. I can successfully instruct the majority of the students in their course work and still help the other students catch up," he said. "But if I have a class of 24 students and 18 of them are not one, not two, not three but actually four grade levels below where they should be, what the hell am I supposed to do with that? Baby-sit, that's what. And that's what a lot of us are doing here, baby-sitting. Providing daycare. We've got eighth-graders walking in here from Mexico that are on a third-grade level, maybe, and we're supposed to meet the test standards? That's a joke."

The waves of illegal border crossings into California have never really ebbed enough to allow for any significant assimilation of the immigrant communities, but instead they only fueled their expansion.

Illegal immigrants aren't "living in the shadows" in California, but rather in parallel communities that are in America, but not of America. With their ethnic nationalism running full tilt in this cloistered environment, the culture of the old country has flourished, a development that is clearly manifested in public school districts from Los Angeles to Pomona to Santa Ana and far beyond. Students have little if any support from parents at home—parents are frequently illiterate themselves and are often working multiple jobs to make ends meet. Since much more value is placed on work—even menial, subsistence-level work—immigrants and the children of immigrants are either actually encouraged to drop out of school in favor of work or face no opposition at home if they decide to stop attending class in favor of simply not going.

The LAUSD's dropout and truancy rates remain abhorrently high and regardless of the precise number, there can be no argument that the consequences of the dropout rate is overwhelming for the surrounding communities, impacting everything from competition for entry-level jobs to rising crime rates, incarceration rates, emergency rooms waits, and a general strain on the dwindling social services offered to American citizens in need.

In an effort to cope with the crisis, Californians have watched as once tranquil public schools have been converted into one-stop social centers for immigrants; with English classes being offered to parents, along with "parenting classes" for the parents and even nurseries for their students who are having babies.

But to take up the issue of the cultural currents at the root of this disaster that has unfolded across districts like Los Angeles Unified is to be met with a violent chorus of accusation, namely that anyone who cites mass immigration and the cultural value system migrants bring with them can only be a heartless racist who hates immigrants and children. This is the tack taken often by the immigrants themselves, but more importantly it is the position of the power structure across the district and among the media elite at newspapers like the *Los Angeles Times*, a dwindling broadsheet which long ago married its news coverage to an editorial narrative that supports illegal immigration in pursuit of a much larger, far more radical agenda.

And thus as every savant and visionary guru steps forward to be sanctioned by City Hall and blessed by the LAUSD's School Board to divine some mystical path out of the tar pit of pathetic, outrageous failure that the district has been mired in for years—be it by means of more and more money, or more teachers, or more classrooms, or more computers, or more armed guards, or more of anything whatsoever—the one thing they must never allow to be spoken and they must never allow to be heard is the suggestion that we acknowledge the obvious: illegal immigration has transformed the Los Angeles Unified School District into effectively a Third World school district with all of its attendant chaos, corruption, malfeasance, and dedication to failure.

No, there will be an artic blizzard in hell before we hear even a single one of the powerbrokers in Los Angeles acknowledge the driving force behind the collapse of the district. It's much easier to blame Proposition 13 and demand even more money from its shrinking base of taxpayers—though more than 70 cents of every dollar of the state's General and Special Funds spent in California today goes to education, health, and welfare.

Los Angeles Unified School District is a microcosm of California and California is now a snapshot of the future America faces if it doesn't act immediately.

Faced with the perfect storm of millions of migrants crowding into the state as more Americans find themselves living on the street amid the squalor of homeless encampments that now appear to be everywhere and an unprecedented explosion of crime, legislators long ago stopped even acknowledging (if only to contest it or justify it) the billions of dollars Sacramento shells out annually to support the millions of migrants now in California, whether illegally or legally.

Like the bureaucrats in Los Angeles, the grandees in Sacramento are too far invested into the status quo to turn back now. They are prepared to oversee the final collapse of the state and then administer its ruins effectively in the same manner that Mexico City bureaucrats dole out patronage to their chaotic, squalid fiefdoms, the immensely rich and powerful political class lording over impoverished masses with huge geographic swaths of the state controlled by cartels.

If that sounds like a Doomsday scenario (and it is one…), just consider this: In 1980, most Americans would have laughed dismissively if told that in less than a generation's time, one of the largest school districts in the nation would be overrun and transformed into a failure that produces as many dropouts as graduates, where hundreds of thousands of students who can't speak English rely on taxpayer-funded handouts to eat, and where a majority of students routinely test virtually illiterate across a wide range of basic academic subjects.

And yet those have been the hard facts on the ground in Los Angeles for years now.

It happened in Los Angeles, it's happening in California and, without a radical reassessment of immigration policy within the next few years in Washington, it will indeed happen to the rest of the nation as well.

Any temptation to dismiss or laugh at the ugly fate of the Golden State should be tempered by what it really means everywhere else.

As the old Chicano saying goes on: "You can laugh now, but you'll cry later."

ACKNOWLEDGEMENTS

I first began to write about the impacts of mass migration and illegal immigration more than 30 years ago, as I began to better understand the life-altering consequences that were unfolding with increasing speed across the state of my birth. But it was through many conversations with many different people about illegal immigration on a scale never before seen by a modern nation-state, let alone tolerated or even encouraged, that the idea for *California Twilight* really started to take shape in the early 2000s and I would like to acknowledge my gratitude here to some of the people who contributed to its creation.

The late Dr. Diana Hull, a brilliant academic who retired from Baylor College of Medicine, where she had been a clinical associate professor in the college's Department of Psychiatry, to become the president of Californians for Population Stabilization (CAPS), which she guided through its most successful years. Diana brought me on as a Senior Writing Fellow at CAPS and through the years proved to be a wonderful mentor of sorts on the subject of mass immigration that's fueling unsustainable population growth and the devastation it tends to wreak across industrialized First World nations.

Warren Johnson, a professor emeritus of geography at San Diego State University and the author of the groundbreaking *Muddling Toward Frugality* in 1978, which was already required reading during my studies at Cal Poly

Pomona just a few years after it was first published, also offered friendly encouragement to this work, as did a diverse array of other writers and academics, including legendary Stanford biologist Paul Ehrlich, whose 1968 bestseller *The Population Bomb* ignited the modern Malthusian movement, and Leftist agitator and author Mike Davis, whose *Planet of Slums* in 2006 painted a grim account of conditions in the growing number of "hyper-cities" that was prescient to what America is facing today.

The late Tom Hayden offered some insightful perspective for me along the way after I had first met him through the *LA Weekly* and later would run into him at various eateries and bars around my neighborhood in Claremont, where Hayden had picked up a plum gig at one of the Claremont Colleges, that beautiful academic enclave of immense wealth and privilege that seeks to obscure its elitism with absurdist peacocking of progressive values, wrapping the campuses with Christo-scale displays celebrating obedience to the politically correct order of the day.

Paul Watson, a co-founder of Greenpeace and later the Sea Shepherd Society, was also supportive and offered his take on where the world was inevitably heading after it passed a global population of two billion people, or just a quarter of its present human footprint.

I would also like to raise a glass to Patrick J. Buchanan, the happy warrior who has dedicated much of his life to a defense of America and its way of life even as he chronicled its long road to this existential moment with bestselling books like *The Death of the West*, *State of Emergency*, and *Suicide of a Superpower*. Every time I either interviewed Buchanan as a working reporter or spoke socially with him at various conferences, he always delivered dead-on estimations of America's condition and the prowess of his pen and the virtue of his values remain undiminished.

Peter Brimelow is another excellent writer whom I had the pleasure of getting to know and write for as well over the years, and his influence on *California Twilight* is notable. Brimelow was a journalist who rose to become a senior editor at *Forbes* and *National Review* and his 1995 masterwork *Alien Nation: Common Sense About America's Immigration Disaster* led to no less than Sen. Eugene McCarthy declaring, "Brimelow provides us with much common sense on declaring our independence from the mounting migration pressures coming to bear on our nation." In the three decades since McCarthy offered such kind words of praise for his work, Brimelow has weathered relentless attacks from mass migration advocates who rightly fear his genius as well as his commitment.

A tip of the hat must be offered to Ann Coulter and her wickedly effective pen and fearless commitment to the actual facts surrounding not only the catastrophic consequences of mass immigration but everything that accompanies it. Coulter was one of the first proponents of consequence to call for an immigration moratorium and an end to birthright citizenship for immigrants, rightly concluding that even if Washington stopped futzing around with border enforcement it would prove meaningless in the face of millions of migrants entering America legally, making insta-citizen babies as well as sending for their extended families in what's known as "chain migration." She has been a true inspiration whom I admire for being the actual writer that she is, researching and composing her own bestselling works over a period of years in stark contrast to the FOX News Channel personalities who affix their names to flash written "books" by ghost writers (and soon to be AI) kept busy in Rupe Murdoch's stable cranking out an assembly line of product for their on-air talent to hawk, pitch, and peddle. Coulter is the real deal and in a career of notable praise, I must say Ann's describing my deconstruction of Karl Rove in *The Notorious P.I.G.* as "beautiful writing" remains a favorite.

Additional thanks to Senators Jeff Sessions and Nathan Deal for their insights, as well as Tom Homan, the acting director of ICE, for his assist.

And a shout out to my sandbox brothers and old friends Mondo Lanier and Glenn Stires, two of the best cops a writer could grow up with, for their years of perspective and hard facts that helped further inform *California Twilight*. To my old buddy Brian Brandt, a California son if there ever was one and one of the best big trial guns to practice in a California courtroom, who also grew up not far from me and over the decades and the drinks shared his own experiences with the disintegration of the state that helped shape this work as well.

A round of shots at the bar for The Long Run lineup of the old ink-slingers crew: David Cogan, Sam Anson, Adrian Maher (whose book *Uninvited: Confessions of a Hollywood Party Crasher* remains a favorite), and John Seeley, whom I will never forget looking over both his shoulders before he offered up in a hushed tone his support for some of Pat Buchanan's positions. We were at a backyard shindig in the Koreatown neighborhood of LA and Johnny, an old liberal warhorse himself (and one heck of a good guy) who cut his teeth during the days of "Cuba, si! Nixon, no!" was worried a passing progressive patrol might overhear him saying something even tangentially nice about Buchanan.

A summer Tom Collins for Tulsa Kinney, an old friend and favorite editor whom I haven't seen in way too long. And a Harvey Wallbanger for Gordy Grundy, last of the international playboys and a vivid writer in his own right who always offered valuable perspective on California's fate, be it from the bar at Traxx in LA's grand Union Station, which we had managed to make entry into after it had closed one night courtesy of the owner (I think) to the shoreline sands at the Moana Surfrider in Honolulu, where the steady stream of drinks ferried over to the table offered a fleeting sense of refuge.

I would like to also thank my mother, Leilani, for bringing me into California with or without an epidural at Park Avenue Hospital in Pomona—the same red brick hospital where singer-song writer Tom Waits was born—and for providing a still ongoing oral history of the town and the times as they were before I became old enough to remember. To my father, Floyd James, for much of the same, and to my brother Michael James, the California firefighter who for 42 years extinguished blazes and saved lives before finally hanging up his helmet.

To my cousin Jenni, for the Flagstaff getaway, the long walks in the woods, and all those years of everything else.

And to Julianne, my lover and muse and another Golden State native and to whom *California Twilight* is dedicated.

For more news about Mark Ray Cromer, subscribe to our newsletter at *wbp.bz/newsletter*.

Word-of-mouth is critical to an author's long-term success. If you appreciated this book, please leave a review on the Amazon sales page at *wbp.bz/CAtwilight*.

ALSO AVAILABLE FROM WILDBLUE PRESS

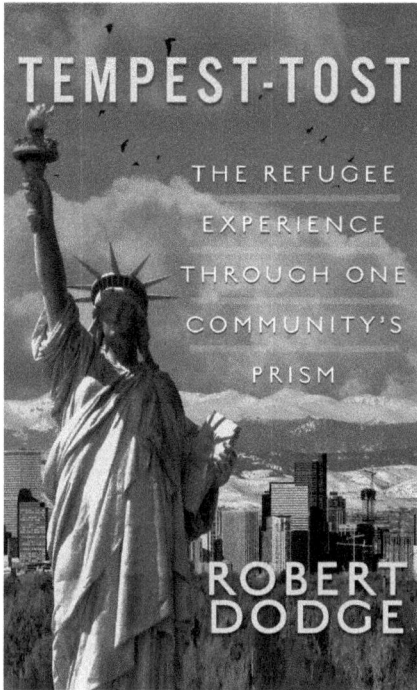

https://wbp.bz/tempest

"Dodge takes us behind the headlines and introduces real people and their very real struggles yearning to breathe free. Page-turning, proactive and highly recommended"
—Craig McGuire, author of Brooklyn's Most Wanted